Municipal Expenditures Revenues and Services

Economic Models and their Use by Planners

Municipal Expenditures Revenues and Services

Economic Models and their Use by Planners

Edited by
W. Patrick Beaton

Assisted by
Lizabeth A. Allewelt

CENTER
FOR URBAN
POLICY   RESEARCH

Published in the United States of America
by the Center for Urban Policy Research
Building 4051—Kilmer Campus
New Brunswick, New Jersey 08903

Library of Congress Cataloging in Publication Data
Main entry under title:

Municipal expenditures, revenues, and services.

     1. Urban economics—Addresses, essays, lectures.
2. Municipal finance—Addresses, essays, lectures.
3. City planning—Addresses, essays, lectures.
I. Beaton, W. Patrick.
HT321.M85   1983   336'.014   82-17786
ISBN 0-88285-087-3

To Marisa, Mary Cristina
and Angela

Contents

Introduction

Intervention in the operation of the "market" has in the past been viewed as an unmitigated public good by many members of the planning profession. The evils of the untrammeled market have been put forth as the cause of much social misery and public blight. However, after many years of railing about smokestacks and fat-rendering plants, their loss or the loss of the jobs they represent is necessitating a reexamination by the urban planner of the what, why, and how of the public and private economies of cities. Similarly, the cornerstone of much planning policy and most master planning—zoning—is being challenged as a precipitator of urban decay and the failed aspirations of the poor. Again, the planning profession has had to reexamine its policy tools.

Economists in turn have used their theoretical and quantitative tools to examine, criticize, and propose new urban-related policy. The decade of the 1970s was a watershed for works of this character. Although no less weighted with subjective content, the integration of theory and empirical analysis for use in policy analysis and fore-casting has to a considerable extent set the research and policy agenda of the prior as well as the current decade. Topics no less broad and encompassing or unique and specific as optimal city size, metropolitan fragmentation and fiscal federalism or property tax capitalization, the so-called tax revolt, and municipal demand and supply functions are treated with equal facility.

Many of the policy-related challenges confronting planners of today are buttressed with what appears to be the puzzling but compelling logic of microeconomic theory. The deductive model of microeconomics utilizing precisely defined terms appears all the more inaccessible to the planner, given what appears to be a focus on individuals or actors—the entrepreneur and consumer, who are not normally integrated into the societal or aggregate thinking of the planning profession.

Clearly there are elements within the planning profession that for many years have integrated economic theory into their policy analyses; equally evident, however, is the degree of resistance, misunderstanding and alienation felt toward this body of scientific thought.

In the sections that follow, I have sought to locate seminal works that use economic theory to explore or explain phenomena of great concern to the urban planner. When used in conjunction with such study aids as the Schaum Outline Series books, *Theory and Problems of Mathematics for Economists* and *Theory and Problems of Microeconomic Theory,* each of the works included herein can be mastered by the planning student.

The articles contained herein can be classified into two sets, the elaboration of theory with reference to the municipal setting and the application of various elements of theory to the municipal revenue structure, municipal goods and service production, and zoning.

The many diverse elements of basic economic theory are initially reviewed in the work by Randall Holcombe. This includes an examination of Samuelson-type public goods, public choice theory, the Tiebout market simulating mechanism, and the Niskanen theory of supply by bureaucracies. This work is followed by an intensive examination by Buchanan of the theory of clubs, where the concept of a public good is merged with the concept of congestion costs.

Using the theoretical methods and tools as a supporting structure, the authors in the second section examine the municipal revenue instruments. Peter Mieszkowski leads off this section with an examination of the incidence of the property tax and its ability under various conditions to be shifted between consumers and holders of reproducible capital. Matthew Edel and Elliott Sclar expanded upon this type of analysis by examining, from the point of view of theory, the conditions under which capitalization of a jurisdiction's property tax will or will not take place. Bruce Hamilton follows these earlier works by looking at the intrajurisdictional impact of property tax capitalization by different income groups. This work leads directly to a reconsideration of the use of zoning in conjunction with the property tax system of revenue generation. Given the current attractiveness of local tax or expenditure limitations, the property tax section concludes with an examination of the various types of fiscal controls currently under legislative consideration.

The second half of the analysis of the revenue structure examines the economic impact of intergovernmental aid. James Wilde's analysis focuses on the categorical grant, whereas Ronald Fisher studies the block grant concept in the form of the federal revenue-sharing program.

Moving to the output side of local government, I review the theoretical underpinnings of expenditure determinants analysis, and Paul Courant, Edward Gramlich and Daniel Rubinfeld expand the theoretical analysis of the demand for municipal goods by considering the role that public employees have in altering the equilibrium level of municipal goods.

This volume concludes with three views of zoning. Bruce Hamilton's contribution is to show zoning to be one possible pricing system driving the Tiebout mechanism toward an efficient equilibrium position. William Fischel expands the theoretical analysis of zoning by linking elements of the theory of clubs with the various formal mechanisms the public can use in assuring an efficient solution to the land use development issue. Werner Hirsch's article examines in detail the problems encountered in obtaining an efficient land use pattern given municipal dependence on the property tax.

In conclusion, each of the primary articles presented in this reader, as well as the work presented in the two review articles, present or expand the use of economic theory into the realm of urban planning. Not only are the theoretical content and conclusions of importance to the planning student, but the method and analytical tools which continue to carry forth this form of scholarly research should be considered an essential part of the planner's preparatory studies.

1

Concepts of Public Sector Equilibrium

Randall G. Holcombe*

ABSTRACT. *This paper relates and describes some of the more common concepts of public sector equilibrium within the same basic framework in order to emphasize the most important similarities and differences. Some concepts, such as Samuelson equilibrium and Lindahl equilibrium, are optimality conditions rather than equilibrium conditions. Other concpets are equilibrium models of institutional processes that make no optimality claims. Still others fall into both classes. Characteristics of the concepts are identified and it is shown, for example, that the Samuelson optimality conditions generally apply to any good – "public" or "private" – where individual quantity adjustments cannot be made.*

I N THE PAST thirty years, there has been an increased awareness in the English language economics literature concerning the way in which resources are allocated through the public sector.[1] Along with this awareness has come the development and use of a large number of concepts of public sector equilibrium. The purpose of this paper is two-fold. First, the paper develops a theoretical comparison among several models of public sector equilibrium in order to show the theoretical relationship of one model to another. Second, the applicability of the various models to real-world institutional structures will be described.

In order to clearly compare the various concepts of public sector equilibrium, each will be examined within the same basic framework, using the simplest form of each model. While such a framework may obscure some of the elegance of the concepts and will make the description differ in some details from that of the original author,[2] hopefully these shortcomings will be outweighed by the advantage of being able to show clearly the relationships among the various equilibria.

In most cases, the origins of the particular concepts of public sector equilibrium can be traced to specific writers. This paper will use that

* Auburn University. Copyright © 1980, *National Tax Journal* 34 (1): 77-80. Reprinted by permission.

1

fact by referring to each concept by the name of its originator. This method of appellation should eliminate one potential source of confusion. For example, both of the familiar concepts of Samuelson equilibrium and of Lindahl equilibrium could be thought of as "public goods equilibria"; and while the reader may be more familiar with the term "median voter equilibrium" than Bowen equilibrium, the Niskanen equilibrium is also a type of median voter equilibrium.

The concepts to be described in this taxonomy are Samuelson equilibrium, Bowen equilibrium, Lindahl equilibrium and Wicksellian unanimity, Tiebout equilibrium, and Niskanen equilibrium. Probably the most widely referenced, and the first to be discussed here, is the Samuelson equilibrium.

Samuelson Equilibrium

In his pioneering articles on public goods, Paul Samuelson (1954, 1955) defined a collective consumption good as one in which an individual's consumption of the good does not substract from any other individual's consumption; so that if the total amount of the good is represented by X, and individual i's consumption by X_i, then $X = X_i$ for all i. Representing individual i's marginal valuation for the good by V_i, and the marginal cost of producing the good by MC, Samuelson demonstrated that the optimal level of output in a community of n persons will satisfy the condition

$$\sum_{i=1}^{n} V_i = MC \tag{1}$$

The satisfaction of equation (1) produces Samuelson equilibrium. As described in the Samuelson articles, equation (1) represents only the conditions for optimality in the production of public goods and not a true equilibrium in the sense that there is a equilibrating force moving the economy toward the satisfaction of that condition.[3] Samuelson (1954, pp. 388-389) suggested the difficulties that would be involved in designing a set of institutions that would produce optimality in public goods.[4]

Although the Samuelsonian optimality conditions were first formally developed to apply to Samuelson's polar definition of a public good, the conditions also describe optimality under any conditions when all consumers must consume the same amount of a good.[5] If the good were purely private by Samuelson's definition, but with the restriction that $X_i = \frac{1}{n} X$ for all i, then X amount of the good would have to

be produced in order for individual i to receive X_i. Using again V_i to represent individual i's marginal valuation of the total amount of the good that is produced, equation (1) describes the optimality condition, even though $\sum_{i=1}^{n} X_i = X$, meaning that the good is a Samuelsonian private good.

The Samuelsonian optimality condition is even more general than the above example and applies any time the amount of the good produced for one consumer implies a unique amount provided for all other consumers. In other words, the Samuelson equilibrium condition applies whenever a given level of total production of the good implies a unique level of consumption for each individual, so that

$$X_i = f_i(X). \tag{2}$$

Since X_i is a function of X and V_i is a function of X_i, then $V_i = g_i(X_i)$, so $V_i = g_i(f_i(X))$, or $V_i = h_i(X)$. Since the individual's marginal valuation of his consumption is a function of the total amount produced, the optimality condition is that stated in equation (1). This is true any time the restriction in equation (2) is present, and the original application to Samuelsonian public goods is merely a special case where $f_i(X) = X$ for all i at all levels of output. The optimality conditions would remain unchanged if X were

a Samuelsonian private good, and $\sum_{i=1}^{n} f_i(X) = X$.

This means that the Samuelsonian optimality conditions are fully applicable to any situation in which the institutional structure (or any other constraint) implies that the proportion of the total output of a good consumed by each consumer is uniquely implied by the level of output, so that equation (2) is satisfied. If a community is served by public schools, each family consumes that output in proportion to the number of children enrolled in the system.[6] Given the public school system, the choice in the quantity dimension is whether to increase the output of the total system so that each individual can enjoy a proportional increase in output. This could be viewed as the choice that voters make when they decide in millage referenda whether to increase the school budget. Incidentally, a graphical analysis of the problem appears the same as in the Samuelsonian public goods case as well. The quantity axis simply measures some standard unit of output (e.g., per pupil expenditures on education).

The Samuelsonian optimality conditions apply far more generally than was suggested in Samuelson's original articles. Whenever an individual is not excluded from consuming a homogeneous good, the units of a good can be defined in such a way that equation (2) is satisfied. For examples, per pupil educational expenditures, the number of lanes (or miles) on a highway, the national defense budget, the broadcast wattage of a television station, or the size of a municipal swimming pool could each be considered within this framework. The Samuelson equilibrium will be an optimum any time individuals cannot quantity-adjust independently of the group, and the good need not have any of the characteristics of Samuelsonian publicness. The unique characteristic that makes equation (1) imply an optimum is that the total amount produced automatically implies the amount supplied to each consumer, and whether a good is Samuelsonian public or private or anywhere in between is irrelevant.

The analytical concept of Samuelson equilibrium is very straightforward, but two empirical issues related to the concept make its application to real-world institutions more difficult. The first issue is the optimal size of the consuming group. The optimal group size for a purely Samuelsonian public good is the largest possible group, but when the shared good is not purely public in the Samuelsonian sense, the optimal group size will be smaller. Thus, the solution to a complete optimization problem would have to consider not only the optimal amount of output, but also the optimal size of the sharing group.[7] Another problem is simply estimating the Samuelson equilibrium level of output. While his has been attempted,[8] the data and techniques at present do not provide the ability to yield reliable estimates.

Bowen Equilibrium

The tendency for a majority rule system of government, under certain circumstances, to select the outcome most preferred by the median voter was first explicitly noted by Hotelling (1929), and the idea was developed in detail by Howard Bowen (1943).[9] The so-called median voter model, which produces Bowen equilibrium, is not a single model. Rather, there are several models that all produce the same result. The variants of the median voter model can be quickly sketched with the aid of Figure 1, where a community of five individuals has demand schedules D1 through D5, and the cost of production is divided evenly among them. Thus, each voter has a tax price equal to MC/5.

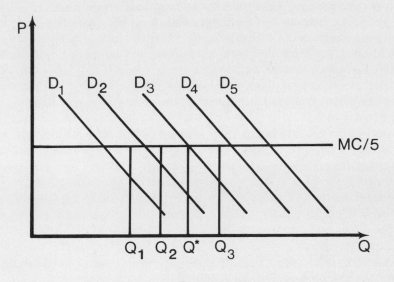

FIGURE 1

One variant of the model describes a committee process in which one quantity of output, e.g., Q2, is proposed against another, Q1, as motions in a majority rule election. The winning quantity Q2 is then considered against another motion, such as Q*. In this type of process, there is only one motion that can defeat every other motion: that motion is the one most preferred by the median voter.[10] The production of the outcome most preferred by the median voter is Bowen equilibrium. In another variant of the model, voters vote for or against marginal increases of the good in a referendum process. A majority of the voters would approve of an increase in output from Q2 to Q*, but a referendum considering whether to increase output from Q* to Q3 would be defeated by a majority. This referendum process also results in Bowen equilibrium. In another variant of the model, voters elect representatives, and the elected representatives select the output to produce. The candidates select platforms containing a proposal for the output to be produced, and the winning candidate will tend toward Q*. If one candidate selects Q1 as his platform, the other can select Q3, which is closer to the median, to win the votes of D3, D4, and D5, and therefore win the election. The first candidate can defeat a platform of Q3 with a platform of Q*, and candidates will tend to converge upon the median.[11] These various models lead to the general conclusion that a system of majority rule will result in Bowen equilibrium.[12]

Since the median voter will be in marginal equilibrium when his tax price, T_m, equals his marginal valuation, V_m, for the good, the Bowen equilibrium condition is[13]

$$V_m = T_m.$$ (3)

Since the cost of a good produced in the public sector is paid for by the taxes of the individuals in the society, $MC = \sum_{i=1}^{n} T_i$. Thus, the Samuelsonian efficiency condition in equation (1) can be rewritten as

$$\sum_{i=1}^{n} V_i = \sum_{i=1}^{n} T_i$$ (4)

In order for Bowen equilibrium to be efficient, equations (3) and (4) would have to be simultaneously satisfied, which implies[14]

$$V_m \bigg/ \sum_{i=1}^{n} V_i = T_m \bigg/ \sum_{i=1}^{n} T_i.$$ (5)

Equation (5) simply states that if the median voter's marginal tax share is the same proportion of the sum of the marginal tax shares as his marginal valuation is of the sum of the marginal valuations, then a Bowen equilibrium will simultaneously produce a Samuelson equilibrium. Although there may be good reason to suspect that the condition in equation (5) is not always fulfilled, the condition is substantially more general than the frequently employed assumption of symmetrically distributed demand curves.

Also worthy of note is the fact that Bowen equilibrium by itself makes no claim for economic efficiency. It is simply the result of an institutional process that is used for making social choices. This stands in contrast to the Samuelson equilibrium, which is economically efficient, although devoid of institutional content.[15]

Analytically calculating Bowen equilibrium is more straightforward than estimating Samuelson equilibrium because only the preferences of one individual must be estimated, and the results of elections can provide data to identify Bowen equilibrium.[16] However, many other factors could influence the outcomes of elections, from the personalities of candidates to voter turnout. In a referendum, for instance, voters may never be offered the median voter's most preferred option.

The agenda setter could then have the power to control the options offered the voters and thus the outcome of the referendum.[17] Holding a majority rule election does not by itself guarantee a Bowen equilibrium, although the empirical evidence to date seems to suggest that majority rule elections in general do produce an outcome close to Bowen equilibrium.

Lindahl Equilibrium and Wicksellian Unanimity

The familiar concept of Lindahl equilibrium exists when each individual finds that his marginal tax price equals his marginal value for a good, or where

$$V_i = T_i, \quad i = 1, n. \tag{6}$$

This conception of Lindahl equilibrium is in the spirit of Lindahl's analysis,[18] although Lindahl considered the mechanism of adjustment to be the altering of the percentage of the total cost paid by each individual. If an individual pays a lower percentage of the total cost, he will demand a larger quantity of output, and there will be one cost-sharing arrangement for which all individuals agree on the quantity of output to be produced. In Lindahl's framework, the individual considers his total tax bill—TC_i for individual i—and selects his most preferred level of output based upon the changes in TC_i for different levels of output. For the individual to be in equilibrium, $dTC_i/dX = V_i$ must be satisfied, and since $dTC_i/dX = T_i$, equation (6) is the Lindahl equilibrium condition.

There is a tendency to treat the T_i's as analogous to market prices, with the average price per unit also equal to T_i,[19] and to draw an analogy between Lindahl equilibrium in the public sector and competitive equilibrium in the private sector, since it appears that the same marginal conditions are satisfied. Under close examination, the analogy between the two concepts disappears. For one thing, in order to set every voter's marginal tax price equal to his average tax price at all possible levels of output, the marginal cost of the good must everywhere equal the average cost. Even with a constant marginal cost, though, there are more substantial weaknesses in the analogy.

Given the standard convexity assumptions, the competitive market equilibrium is the benchmark for economic efficiency, and competitive equilibrium prices provide the incentives that produce economic efficiency. The same is not true of Lindahl prices. The optimal allocation of resources occurs in the public sector (when individual consumers cannot quantity-adjust) when the Samuelson equilibrium is produced and Lindahl equilibrium is just one special case of Samuelson equilibrium. Any number of other cost-sharing arrangements could produce Samuelson equilibrium.

Lindahl prices do not necessarily result in what would be considered an equitable distribution of cost shares either. Denzau and Mackay (1976) have shown, for instance, that the individual who receives the greatest total benefit from a good could have the lowest Lindahl price. In their example, an individual who lives next to the fire station could receive a high total value of protection, and thus the marginal value of additional protection would be low. The individual living far from the station receives little total protection, but has a high marginal value for additional protection, and thus has a high Lindahl price. While equity criteria would suggest that the individual living next to the fire station pay the most in taxes, Lindahl pricing would charge him the least.

Lindahl equilibrium does not necessarily produce an equitable distribution of cost shares and is not necessary for economic efficiency. The reason why each individual need not have his marginal tax price equal to his marginal valuation in order to produce efficiency is that the individual cannot quantity-adjust. He must accept the quantity of output which is produced for the whole group. Thus, for purposes of economic efficiency, as well as for equity, the individual's marginal tax price is irrelevant.

This can be illustrated in Figure 2, where the demands of three individuals are shown. All individuals could be charged the same tax price T2, and a majority rule political system that produced Bowen equilibrium would also produce Samuelson equilibrium. Lindahl pricing, charging D1 price T3, D2 price price T2, and D3 price T1, would be another cost-sharing arrangement that would produce Samuelson equilibrium under the same institutional setting. Another set of prices which would satisfy the Lindahl condition in equation (6) would be T1', T2, T3', or if all paid T2, and since the amount of the good produced would be the same in either case, all individuals would be indifferent between those two taxation schemes.[20] However, individual 1 would prefer tax shares T1, T2, T3, and individual 3 would be against changing to those tax shares. With production of Q*, the individuals see no difference between equal tax shares or Lindahl tax shares T1, T2, T3; although they are not indifferent between the alternative Lindahl tax scheme T1, T2, T3.

On purely economic grounds, Lindahl pricing has nothing in particular to recommend it. Other tax schemes could be just as efficient

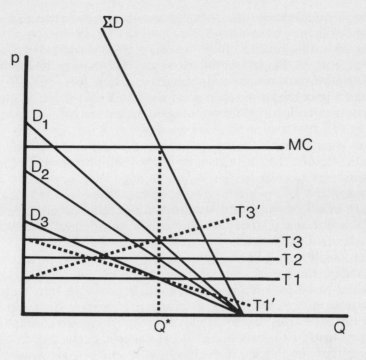

FIGURE 2

and may be more equitable. The reason is that the individual cannot choose the quantity that he will consume. Still, Lindahl prices have an important characteristic: all individuals are in agreement as to how much of the good should be produced.

Despite the fact that with output Q^* in Figure 2 individuals would be indifferent between Lindahl prices T1', T2, and T3', and identical tax prices where all pay T2, with the identical tax prices, individual 1 will want more output while individual 3 will want less. With any tax sharing arrangement, individuals would always prefer lower taxes; but Lindahl pricing is the only taxation method that produces a unanimous agreement on the amount of output to be produced. The characteristic of unanimous agreement on the amount of output, given tax shares, will by itself produce a Samuelson equilibrium.

The significance of Lindahl equilibrium may be as much political as economic. If Lindahl tax shares can be designed, then all individuals will be in agreement as to the amount of output to be produced, which makes it more likely that production will take place efficiently. If, in Figure 2, all individuals have tax price T2, individual 3 would prefer substantially less than Q^*. If he is politically powerful, he may be able to work through the political system to reduce the amount of output below the efficient level.

Viewed in this context, there is a great deal of similarity between the concepts of Lindahl equilibrium and Wicksellian unanimity.[21] Wicksell suggested that if a public expenditure was cost effective, then tax shares could be set in such a manner that there would be a unanimous agreement in favor of the expenditure. Wicksell then recommended that voters consider various financing proposals, along with proposals for public expenditures, and that a unanimous agreement be required for the expenditures to be undertaken.[22] Lindahl prices are the tax shares that would be needed to produce Wicksellian unanimity. In a political setting characterized by Lindahl equilibrium/Wicksellian unanimity, efficient decisions would be more likely to be made, and a majority of individuals would have less power to exploit a minority.[23]

In summary, Lindahl equilibrium is a special case of Samuelson equilibrium, since if $V_i = T_i$ for all i, then $\Sigma V_i = \Sigma T_i$. It is also a special case of Bowen equilibrium, since $V_m = T_m$. But while Lindahl equilibrium does provide an efficient allocation of resources, it is not unique in this respect. Lindahl equilibrium also has no special equity properties to recommend it. The special characteristic of Lindahl equilibrium is that it produces a unanimous agreement with respect to the amount of output to be produced.

Tiebout Equilibrium

The Tiebout model is a model of local government activity and has as its mechanism of adjustement the movement of individuals from less preferred to more preferred political jurisdictions. City managers, according to Tiebout (1956, p. 422), perform the function of minimizing the cost of city output to the residents, with each resident being free to move to the locality that best satisfies his demands. Tiebout's paper describes the general mechanism of adjustment to optimality,[24] and the adjustment process can be considered within the same general framework as has been used for the other concepts of public sector equilibrium in this paper.

Consider the community of three individuals shown in Figure 3, which is much like the community in Figure 2. The marginal cost of producing the local government output is MC, and all individuals must agree on an amount to be produced. The Samuelson equilibrium level of output is Q_2, which is also Bowen equilibrium because of the construction of Figure 3.

The adjustment mechanism toward optimality in the Tiebout model is initiated by the ability of the residents of a community to move to another of the large number of possible communities. For the purpose of this paper, three communities will be a sufficiently large number, and all communities will be assumed to have individuals identical to those in the community represented by Figure 2.

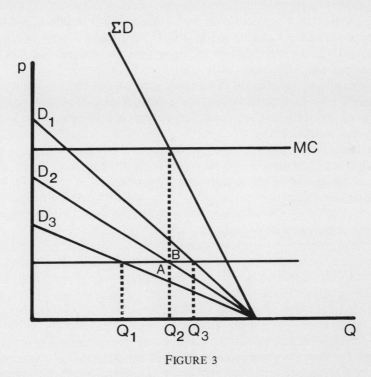

FIGURE 3

Without mobility among the communities, the most efficient level of output in each community would be Samuelson equilibrium quantity Q_2. As was earlier mentioned, the original Samuelson (1954, 1955) articles described no adjustment process that would lead toward optimality, and Tiebout's article was written in part as a response to Samuelson, showing that an adjustment process could exist if the individuals could move from one governmental jurisdiction to another.[25]

With three communities like those in Figure 3, Tiebout equilibrium allocates resources more efficiently than producing Q_2 in each community. If there were a continuous array of communities available with outputs along the Q axis of Figure 3, then the individuals with demand like D_3 would live in the city producing Q_1, individuals with

demand like D_2 would settle in the city producing Q_2, and individuals
with demands like D_1 would reside in the city producing Q_3. In this
simple example, there would be no demand for cities of other sizes.
The resulting efficiency gain would be three times the areas of tri-
angles A and B, which would yield some surplus that could be divided
in such a way as to provide an entrepreneurial incentive.

It should be noted that this is a very stylized version of the Tiebout
model, and the real world may not conform to this model for several
reasons. The literature has done little to examine entrepreneurial incentives in this model. There is a competitive market for city managers, and they do have an incentive to look good, especially since
they can be easily compared to managers of nearby or similar cities.
But since cities are not profit-making institutions, there may be severe
limits on both the ability and the incentives of people to evaluate
their city manager. Perhaps for this reason the literature on the Tiebout model has examined the capitalization of taxes into land values
rather than the entrepreneurial role of city managers.[26] Another possible problem with the model is that people choose where to live
based upon things other than the local government. Thus, the operation of the model depends upon a large enough margin of people
being mobile and responsive to local governments. This condition
may exist in a country as mobile as the United States.[27]

The Tiebout equilibrium allows adjustment in another dimension
not available in the earlier discussed equilibrium concepts, but several
notable characteristics exist in Tiebout equilibrium. For one thing,
every individual is charged a Lindahl price in equilibrium. Also, the
per unit prices charged to each individual will tend to be the same
across individuals. In order to charge different per unit prices to different individuals, some individuals will be charged an above average
price. In a model of intergovernmental competition, those individuals
would be valuable residents, and communities would try to bid for
them by offering slightly lower prices. The competitive process would
end only when uniform per unit prices were charged. The competitive process would also result in efficiency gains as different communities offer different levels of output to entice potential residents.

While some of the fine points of the theoretical model may have
limitations, the basic model suggests strong efficiency reasons for
intergovernmental competition on two grounds. First, the problem
of demand revelation for public goods is better overcome than without intergovernmental competition. Second, a Tiebout equilibrium
will tend to be more efficient with mobility than a Samuelson equilibrium when there is not a mechanism to group similar consumers
together. A third reason might also be mentioned: If political agree-

ment is important, as was noted in the previous section, then there will be more of a consensus of opinion in Tiebout equilibrium than in a general Lindahl equilibrium in which tax shares will be more open to debate. In Tiebout equilibrium, competitive forces will tend to equalize tax prices. In this respect, Tiebout equilibrium is a special case of Lindahl equilibrium. Individuals with similar demands are grouped together, so that the Lindahl condition $T_i = V_i$ for all i is satisfied, and the adjustment process $T_i = T_j$ for all i and j.

In closing this section, it might be worthwhile to note that while Tiebout developed his model for individuals who move from one community to another, the model applies more generally to any type of intergovernmental competition.[28] Thus, on these grounds alone, a voucher system of education[29] would be more efficient than a single school system, and a gain in efficiency would result from allowing individuals to choose their pension system, rather than being forced to take Social Security. This would be true even if the uniform system produced Samuelson equilibrium for the population as a whole.

Niskanen Equilibrium

The final concept of public sector equilibrium to be discussed, Niskanen equilibrium, is mentioned not because of the significance of the specific nature of the equilibrium, nor because there might be some situation in the real world which resembles Niskanen equilibrium.[30] Rather, it will be analyzed because it is the most rigorous attempt at conceptualizing the institutional structure of public sector supply. This factor alone makes the concept a significant step in the development of an economic theory of the public sector.[31] The earlier concepts discussed in this paper have been primarily concerned with the aggregation of individual demands for public sector output. Calling those concepts equilibria has tacitly assumed that the government produces the output determined through the demand aggregation process.

By contrast, Niskanen assumes that government output is produced by self-interested bureaucrats in the same way that micro theory assumes self-interest.[32] Since bureaucrats cannot (legally) keep profits, Niskanen suggests that they are after other things, such as a high salary, power, prestige, ease of running the bureau, etc. All of these things are furthered by increases in the bureau's budget; thus, Niskanen assumes that bureaucrats are budget maximizers.

The budget maximizing bureaucrats do not make marginal sales as do market enterprisers. Instead, each year they exchange a total budget for a total output, which makes the resulting equilibrium an outcome of a bargaining process. The bureau's superior knowledge and expertise allows them to place the purchaser of the output on the all-or-nothing demand curve,[33] so that X units of output of the good will be produced, where

$$\int_{Q=0}^{x} T_m = \int_{Q=0}^{x} V_m \tag{7}$$

Implied in this representation of Niskanen equilibrium is that demand for public sector output is aggregated through the median voter model. This Niskanen equilibrium is a kind of median voter model, but instead of satisfying equation (3), the equilibrium condition in equation (7) implies

$$T_m > V_m \tag{8}$$

in Niskanen equilibrium.[34]

If the median voter's demand curve is assumed linear, then in the limiting case Niskanen equilibrium will produce twice the output that would be produced in the Bowen equilibrium. Because the conditions in equations (3) and (7) can never be simultaneously satisfied, a Bowen equilibrium can never be a Niskanen equilibrium. Niskanen equilibrium is the only concept of public sector equilibrium discussed in this article which cannot coexist with any other concept. By contrast, it would be possible to simultaneously satisfy the equilibrium conditions of all the other concepts discussed.

Perhaps the largest contribution of Niskanen's work is the development of a rigorous model of public sector supply. Niskanen equilibrium differs from the other concepts discussed in that the individuals who produce public sector output are considered as utility-maximizing counterparts to entrepreneurs in the private sector. Since its appearance, Niskanen's book has stimulated a large amount of research on bureaucratic institutions, and hopefully the theory of public sector supply will advance to a level equivalent to the literature on public sector demand.

Conclusion

The purpose of this paper is to describe and relate some of the more common concepts of public sector equilibrium. By analyzing the concepts in their simplest forms, and all within the same basic framework, hopefully the most important similarities and differences among the concepts have been emphasized. Some of the concepts, such as Samuelson equilibrium and Lindahl equilibrium, describe optimality conditions rather than equilibrating mechanisms. Others, such as Bowen equilibrium and Niskanen equilibrium are models of institutional processes which make no claims for optimality. Wicksellian unanimity and Tiebout equilibrium are models of institutional processes which produce efficient outcomes. The distinction between models that descibes optimality conditions and models that describe institutional processes leading to equilibrium is fundamental to understanding the concepts.

Although these concepts are frequently applied to Samuelsonian public goods, the Samuelsonian definition of a public good is not central to any one of the concepts. The characteristic that makes Samuelsonian equilibrium efficient is that each individual's consumption of the good is a function of the total amount produced, and a Samuelsonian public good is only one instance where this characteristic may be present. Also worthy of note is the fact that Lindahl equilibrium has no special claim as the public sector analog to competitive equilibrium in the private sector. When the consumption of one individual implies the consumption levels of all other individuals, prices for everyone except the decision makers are irrelevant to economic efficiency. The advantage of Lindahl equilibrium is more political than economic in that it implies unanimous agreement with respect to the amount of the good to be produced.

This paper has presented a taxonomy of public sector equilibrium models, all within the same framework, so that all characteristics of the basic models can be easily compared. In so doing, many of the finer theoretical points have been glossed over, and many theoretical and empirical difficulties have not been addressed. Instead, each model was simply developed so that it could be easily compared with the others. The variety of concepts vividly illustrates that a simple statement that the public sector is in equilibrium would convey far less information than a similar statement about the private sector. Hopefully, this taxonomy has made some contribution toward making the similarities and differences among the models more apparent.

NOTES

1. For an elaboration of this point, see Buchanan (1975).
2. The framework in this paper will be a partial equilibrium with emphasis on the marginal conditions of each public sector equilibrium concept. Thus, there

will be obvious differences between this framework and Samuelson's (1954, 1955), which is general equilibrium; and Lindahl's (1919), which emphasizes average rather than marginal tax rates.

3. The satisfaction of this condition has been called a Samuelson equilibrium before the writing of this article, however. See, for example, Tideman and Tullock (1976), p. 1156.

4. These difficulties, at least in theory, are not insurmountable. For solutions, see Tideman and Tullock (1976) and the papers cited therein.

5. This point is made by Buchanan (1968, Chapter 4:1970) and by Barlow (1973).

6. Or looked at from the standpoint of an individual, each person consumes or does not consume depending upon whether he is enrolled. A person who has no family members enrolled could still have a positive marginal valuation, if he values the education of others.

7. See Buchanan (1965) on this problem. The problem of the optimal size group is discussed further in the section on the Tiebout equilibrium below.

8. See, for example, Barlow (1970).

9. Other prominent developments of the median voters model appeared in Downs (1957) and Black (1958). Bowen's formulation of the model is significant in that it is most closely integrated into standard microeconomic theory.

10. This variant of the model is described by Bowen (1943) and is considered in far more detail by Black (1958).

11. This model explains the lament of some voters that all the candidates look alike. This variant was briefly described by Bowen and is elaborately detailed by Downs (1957). The description of the median voter model is brief in this paper since much description exists elsewhere. The interested reader is referred to the above-mentioned works.

12. The results of the model is commonly used as an assumption in empirical work. Some examples are Barlow (1970), Bergstrom and Goodman (1973), and Borcherding and Deacon (1972). An example of another voting system that will produce Bowen equilibrium appears in Holcombe (1977).

13. In the specific example graphed in Figure 1, the median voter's tax price equals MC/5.

14. The simple derivation of equation (5) from (3) and (4) appears in Holcombe (1977), along with some additional explanation on the simultaneous satisfaction of the Bowen and Samuelson conditions.

15. See, however, Tideman and Tullock (1976) for a theoretical description of a possible institutional structure for producing a Samuelson equilibrium.

16. See Holcombe (1980) and McEachern (1978) for examples. An early empirical test of the Bowen hypothesis appears in Barr and Davis (1966). Another article along the same lines is Inman (1978).

17. See Romer and Rosenthal (1978) and Holcombe (1980) for a more detailed discussion of the possibility.

18. For an English translation, see Lindahl (1919).

19. Musgrave (1959, p. 76) calls the T_js "unit prices."

20. The reader might object that the tax functions T1' and T3' are not in the spirit of Lindahl's analysis. Despite the problems noted above to have the marginal tax price always equal to the average tax price, it would still be possible to have the average tax prices alway be a constant percentage of the total tax bill. As will be argued later, however, tax prices T1' and T3' retain the essential characteristics (those specified in equation (6) of Lindahl prices.

21. This concept is described in Wicksell's "A New Principle of Just Taxation" (1896).

22. As a practical matter, Wicksell recommended an approximate unanimity of less than 100 percent approval, while recognizing the desirability in principle of the unanimous rule. Buchanan and Tullock (1962, Chapter 6) suggest that a less than unanimous decision rule could win a unanimous approval of a group.

23. The characteristics of Wicksellian unanimity have been estensively analyzed by James Buchanan. See, for example, Buchanan (1962a, 1962b).

24. This adjustment mechanism has sometimes been described as "voting with your feet." For a discussion of the limitations of the Tiebout adjustment process, see Buchanan and Goetz (1972).

25. Tideman and Tullock (1976) recently described another mechanism for producing Samuelson equilibrium but without requiring mobility of individuals. The system is a complex voting process that has nice theoretical properties but could be complicated to implement. The fact that this article appeared over twenty years after Samuelson's paper suggests the magnitude of the theoretical problem of demand revelation for public goods that Samuelson noted.

26. Oates (1969) began this line of inquiry. King (1977) criticizes the results of some of this literature, and provides a list of other studies along the same line.

27. HUD reported that 20 percent of U.S. families moved between October 1972 and October 1973.

28. A similar theme is developed in Buchanan (1970).

29. See Friedman (1962).

30. The concept was originally presented in Niskanen (1968), and additional implications of the idea appear in Niskanen (1971).

31. For conflicting views on the value of Niskanen's contribution, see Thompson (1973) and Tullock (1972).

32. Such an assumption seems very appropriate to the economics literature, since the standard justification for government activity is that self-interested behavior sometimes leads to market failure. If individuals in the market act in their own self-interest when it is against the best interest of society as a whole, there is no reason to believe that they would behave differently just because they are employed by the government. Stated more bluntly, without the assumption of self-interested behavior, the economic rationale for governmental activity disappears.

33. Niskanen (1968) provides a more complete summary of the process.

34. For an argument that the opposite condition holds, see Downs (1960).

REFERENCES

Barlow, Robin, "Efficiency Aspects of Local School Finance: Reply," *Journal of Political Economy* 81 (Jan/Feb 1973), pp. 199-202.
——, "Efficiency Aspects of Local School Finance," *Journal of Political Economy* 78 (Sept/Oct 1970), pp. 1028-1040.
Barr, James L., and Otto A. Davis, "An Elementary Political and Economic Theory of the Expenditures of State and Local Governments," *Southern Economic Journal* 33 (Oct. 1966), pp. 149-165.
Bergstrom, Theodore C., and Robert Goodman, "Private Demand for Public Goods," *American Economic Review* 63 (June 1973), pp. 280-296.

Black, Duncan, *The Theory of Committee and Elections* (Cambridge: Cambridge University Press, 1958).

Borcherding, Thomas E., and Robert T. Deacon, "The Demand for Services of Non-Federal Governments," *American Economic Review* 62 (Dec. 1972), pp. 891-901.

Bowen, Howard R., "The Interpretation of Voting in the Allocation of Economic Resources," *Quarterly Journal of Economics* 58 (Nov. 1943), pp. 27-48.

Buchanan, James M., "Politics, Policy, and the Pigouvian Margins," *Economica* n.s. 29, (Feb. 1962a), pp. 17-28.

————, "The Relevance of Pareto Optimality," *Journal of Conflict Resolution* (Nov. 1962b), pp. 341-354.

————, "An Economic Theory of Clubs," *Economica* n.s. 32 (Feb. 1965), pp. 1-14.

————, *The Demand and Supply of Public Goods* (Chicago: Rand McNally & Co. 1968).

————, "Notes for an Economic Theory of Socialism," *Public Choice* 8 (Spring 1970), pp. 29-43.

————, "Public Finance and Public Choice," *National Tax Journal* 28 (December 1975), pp. 383-394.

Buchanan, James M., and Charles J. Goetz, "Efficiency Limits of Fiscal Mobility: An Assessment of the Tiebout Model," *Journal of Public Economics* 1 (1972), pp. 25-43.

Buchanan, James M., and Gordon Tullock, *The Calculus of Consent* (Ann Arbor: The University of Michigan Press, 1962).

Denzau, Arthur T., and Robert J. Mackay, "Benefit Shares and Majority Voting," *American Economic Review* 66 (March 1976), pp. 69-76.

Downs, Anthony, *An Economic Theory of Democracy* (New York: Harper and Row, 1957).

————, "Why the Government Budget is too Small in a Democracy," *World Politics* 12 (July 1960), pp. 541-564.

Friedman, Milton, "The Role of Government in Education," in *Capitalism and Freedom* (Chicago: University of Chicago Press, 1962).

Holcombe, Randall G., "The Florida System: A Bowen Equilibrium Referendum Process," *National Tax Journal* 30 (March 1977), pp. 77-84.

————, "An Empirical Test of the Median Voter Model," *Economic Inquiry* (forthcoming, 1980).

Hotelling, Harold, "Stability in Competition," *Economic Journal* 39 (March 1929), pp. 41-57;

Inman, Robert P., "Testing Political Economy's 'as if' Proposition: Is the Median Income Voter Really Decisive?" *Public Choice* 33 (1978), pp. 45-65.

King, A. Thomas, "Estimating Property Tax Capitalization: A Critical Comment," *Journal of Political Economy* 85 (April 1977), pp. 425-431.

Lindahl, Erik, "Just Taxation—A Positive Solution," (1919) in Musgrave and Peacock, eds., *Classics in the Theory of Public Finance* (New York: St. Martin's Press, 1967), pp. 168-176.

Musgrave, Richard A., *The Theory of Public Finance* (New York: McGraw-Hill, 1959).

Niskanen, William A., "The Peculiar Economics of Bureaucracy," *American Economic Review* 58 (May 1968), pp. 293-305.

————, *Bureaucracy and Representative Government* (Chicago and New York: Aldine-Atherton, 1971).

Oates, Wallace, "The Effects of Property Taxes and Local Public Spending on Property Values: An Empirical Study of Tax Capitalization and the Tiebout Hypothesis," *Journal of Political Economy* 77 (Nov/Dec 1969), pp. 957-971.

Romer, Thomas, and Howard Rosenthal, "Political Resource Allocation Controlled Agendas, and the Status Quo," *Public Choice* 33 (1978), pp. 27-43.

Samuelson, Paul A., "The Pure Theory of Public Expenditure," *Review of Economics and Statistics* 36 (Nov. 1955), pp. 387-389.

—————, "A Diagrammatic Exposition of a Theory of Public Expenditure," *Review of Economics and Statistics* 38 (Nov. 1954), pp. 350-356.

Thompson, Earl A., "Review of Niskanen's *Bureaucracy and Representative Government*," *Journal of Economic Literature* 11 (Sept. 1973), pp. 950-953.

Tideman, T. Nicolaus, and Gordon Tullock, "A New and Superior Process for Making Social Choices," *Journal of Political Economy* 84 (Dec. 1976), pp. 1145-1160.

Tiebout, Charles M., "A Pure Theory of Local Expenditures," *Journal of Political Economy* 64 (Oct. 1956), pp. 416-424.

Tullock, Gordon, "Review of Niskanen's *Bureaucracy and Representative Government*," *Public Choice* 12 (Spring 1972), pp. 119-124.

Wicksell, Knut, "A New Principle of Just Taxation," (1896), in Musgrave and Peacock, eds., *Classics in the Theory of Public Finance* (New York: St. Martin's Press, 1967), pp. 72-118.

2

An Economic Theory of Clubs

James M. Buchanan*

THE IMPLIED institutional setting for neo-classical economic theory, including theoretical welfare economics, is a régime of private property, in which all goods and services are privately (individually) utilized or consumed. Only within the last two decades have serious attempts been made to extend the formal theoretical structure to include communal or collective ownership-consumption arrangements.[2] The "pure theory of public goods" remains in its infancy, and the few models that have been most rigorously developed apply only to polar or extreme cases. For example, in the fundamental papers by Paul A. Samuelson, a sharp conceptual distinction is made between those goods and services that are "purely private" and those that are "purely public."[3] No general theory has been developed which covers the whole spectrum of ownership-consumption possibilities, ranging from the purely private or individualized activity on the one hand to purely public or collectivized activity on the other. One of the missing links here is "a theory of clubs," a theory of co-operative membership, a theory that will include as a variable to be determined the extension of ownership—consumption rights over differing numbers of persons.

Everyday experience reveals that there exists some most preferred or "optimal" membership for almost any activity in which we engage, and that this membership varies in some relation to economic factors. European hotels have more communally shared bathrooms than their American counterparts. Middle and low income communities organize swimming-bathing facilities; high income communities are observed to enjoy privately owned swimming pools.

In this paper I shall develop a general theory of clubs, or consumption ownership-membership arrangements. This construction

* University of Virginia, Charlottesville. © 1965. *Economica 32:* 1-14, 1965. Reprinted by permission.

allows us to move one step forward in closing the awesome Samuelson gap between the purely private and the purely public good. For the former, the optimal sharing arrangement, the preferred club membership, is clearly one person (or one family unit), whereas the optimal sharing group for the purely public good, as defined in the polar sense, includes an infinitely large number of members. That is to say, for any genuinely collective good defined in the Samuelson way, a club that has an infinitely large membership is preferred to all arrangements of finite size. While it is evident that some goods and services may be reasonably classified as purely private, even in the extreme sense, it is clear that few, if any, goods satisfy the conditions of extreme collectiveness. The interesting cases are those goods and services, the consumption of which involves some "publicness," where the optimal sharing group is more than one person or family but smaller than an infinitely large number. The range of "publicness" is finite. The central question in a theory of clubs is that of determining the membership margin, so to speak, the size of the most desirable cost and consumption sharing arrangement.[4]

I

In traditional neo-classical models that assume the existence of purely private goods and services only, the utility function of an individual is written,

$$(1) \qquad U^i = U^i (X_1^i, \ X_2^i, \dots, X_n^i),$$

where each of the X's represents the amount of a purely private good available during a specified time period, to the reference individual designated by the superscript.

Samuelson extended this function to include purely collective or public goods, which he denoted by the subscripts, $n + 1, \dots,$ $n + m$, so that (1) is changed to read,

$$(2) \quad U_i = U^i (X_1^i, X_2^i, \dots, X_n^i; X_{n+1}^i, X_{n+2}^i, \dots X_{n+m}^i).$$

This approach requires that all goods be initially classified into the two sets, private and public. Private goods, defined to be wholly divisible among the persons, $i = 1, 2, \dots, s$, satisfy the relation

$$X_j = \sum_{i=1}^{s} X_j^i,$$

while public goods, defined to be wholly indivisible as among persons, satisfy the relation,

$$X_{n+j} = X_{n+j}^i \ .$$

I propose to drop any attempt at an initial classification or differentiation of goods into fully divisible and fully indivisible sets, and to incorporate in the utility function goods falling between these two extremes. What the theory of clubs provides is, in one sense, a "theory of classification," but this emerges as an output of the analysis. The first step is that of modifying the utility function.

Note that, in neither (1) nor (2) is it necessary to make a distinction between "goods available to the ownership unit of which the reference individual is a member" and "goods finally available to the individual for consumption." With purely private goods, consumption by one individual automatically reduces potential consumption of other individuals by an equal amount. With purely public goods, consumption by any one individual implies equal consumption by all others. For goods falling between such extremes, such a distinction must be made. This is because for such goods there is no unique translation possible between the "goods available to the membership unit" and "goods finally consumed." In the construction which follows, therefore, the "goods" entering the individual's utility function, the X_j' s, should be interpreted as "goods available for consumption to the whole membership unit of which the reference individual is a member."

Arguments that represent the size of the sharing group must be included in the utility function along with arguments representing goods and services. For any good or service, regardless of its ultimate place along the conceptual public-private spectrum, the utility that an individual receives from its consumption depends upon *the number of other persons with whom he must share its benefits.* This is obvious, but its acceptance does require breaking out of the private property straitjacket within which most of economic theory has developed. As an extreme example, take a good normally considered to be purely private, say, a pair of shoes. Clearly your own utility from a single pair of shoes, per unit of time, depends on the number of other persons who share them with you. Simultaneous physical sharing may not, of course, be possible; only one person can wear the shoes at each particular moment. However, for any finite period of time, sharing is possible, even for such evidently private goods. For pure services that are consumed in the moment of acquisition the extension is somewhat more difficult, but it can be made none the less. Sharing here simply means that the individual receives a smaller quantity of the service. Sharing a "haircut per month" with a second person is the same as consuming "one-half haircut per month." Given any quantity of final good, as defined in terms of the physical units of some standard quality, the utility that the individual receives from this quantity will be related functionally to the number of others with whom he shares.[5]

Variables for club size are not normally included in the utility function of an individual since, in the private-goods world, the optimal club size is unity. However, for our purposes, these variables must be explicitly included, and, for completeness, a club-size variable should be included for each and every good. Alongside each X_j there must be placed an N_j, which we define as the number of persons who are to participate as "members" in the sharing of good, X_j, including the ith person whose utility function is examined. That is to say, the club-size variable, N_j, measures the number of persons who are to join in the consumption-utilization arrangements for good, X_j, over the relevant time period. The sharing arrangements may or may not call for equal consumption on the part of each member, and the peculiar manner of sharing will clearly affect the way in which the variable enters the utility function. For simplicity we may assume equal sharing, although this is not necessary for the analysis. The rewritten utility function now becomes,

$$(3) \quad U^i = U^i [(X_1^i, N_1^i), (X_2^i, N_2^i), \ldots, (X_{n+m}^i, N_{n+m}^i)] .^6$$

We may designate a numeraire good, X_r, which can simply be thought of as money, possessing value only as a medium of exchange. By employing the convention whereby the lower case u's represent the partial derivatives, we get u_j^i / u_r^i, defined as the marginal rate of substitution in consumption between X_j and X_r for the ith individual. Since, in our construction, the size of the group is also a variable, we must also examine, $u_{N_j}^i / u_r^i$, defined as the marginal rate of substitution "in consumption" between the size of the sharing group and the numeraire. That is to say, this ratio represents the rate (which may be negative) at which the individual is willing to give up (accept) money in exchange for additional members in the sharing group.

We now define a cost or production function as this confronts the individual, and this will include the same set of variables,

(4) $F = F^i [(X_1^i, N_1^i), (X_2^i, N_2^i), \ldots, (X_{n+m}^i, N_{n+m}^i)]$.

Why do the club-size variables, the N_j's, appear in this cost function? The addition of members to a sharing group may, and normally will, affect the cost of the good to any one member. The larger is the membership of the golf club the lower the dues to any single member, given a specific quantity of club facilities available per unit time.

It now becomes possible to derive, from the utility and cost functions, statements for the necessary marginal conditions for Pareto optimality in respect to consumption of each good. In the usual manner we get,

(5) $u_j^i / u_r^i = f_j^i / f_r^i$.

Condition (5) states that, for the ith individual, the marginal rate of substitution between goods X_j and X_r, in consumption, must be equal to the marginal rate of substitution between these same two goods in "production" or exchange. To this acknowledged necessary condition, we now add,

(6) $u_{Nj}^i / u_r^i = f_{Nj}^i / f_r^i$.

Condition (6) is not normally stated, since the variables relating to club size are not normally included in utility functions. Implicitly, the size for sharing arrangements is assumed to be determined exogenously to individual choices. Club size is presumed to be a part of the environment. Condition (6) states that the marginal rate of substitution "in consumption" between the size of the group sharing in the use of good X_j, and the numeraire good, X_r, must be equal to the marginal rate of substitution "in production." In other words, the individual attains full equilibrium in club size only when the marginal benefits that he secures from having an additional member (which may, and probably will normally be, negative) are just equal to the marginal costs that he incurs from adding a member (which will also normally be negative).

Combining (5) and (6) we get,

(7) $u_j^i / f_j^i = u_r^i / f_r^i = u_{Nj}^i / f_{Nj}^i$.

Only when (7) is satisfied will the necessary marginal conditions with respect to the consumption-utilization of X_j be met. The individual will have available to his membership unit an optimal quantity of X_j, measured in physical units and, also, he will be sharing this quantity "optimally" over a group of determined size.

The necessary condition for club size may not, of course, be met. Since for many goods there is a major change in utility between the one-person and the two-person club, and since discrete changes in membership may be all that is possible, we may get,

$$(7A) \quad \frac{u_j^i}{f_j^i} = \frac{u_r^i}{f_r^i} > \frac{u_{Nj}^i}{f_{Nj}^i} \bigg|_{Nj=1} \quad ; \quad \frac{u_j^i}{f_j^i} = \frac{u_r^i}{f^r} < \frac{u_{Nj}^i}{f_{Nj}^i} \bigg|_{Nj=2}$$

which incorporates the recognition that, with a club size of unity, the right-hand term may be relatively too small, whereas, with a club size of two, it may be too large. If partial sharing arrangements can be worked out, this qualification need not, of course, be made.

If, on the other hand, the size of a co-operative or collective sharing group is exogenously determined, we may get,

$$(7B) \quad \frac{u_j^i}{f_j^i} = \frac{u_r^i}{f_r^i} > \frac{u_{Nj}^i}{f_{Nj}^i} \bigg|_{Nj=k}$$

Note that (7B) actually characterizes the situation of an individual with respect to the consumption of any purely public good of the type defined in the Samuelson polar model. Any group of finite size, k, is smaller than optimal here, and the full set of necessary marginal conditions cannot possibly be met. Since additional persons can, by definition, be added to the group without in any way reducing the availability of the good to other members, and since additional members could they be found, would presumably place some positive value on the good and hence be willing to share in its costs, the group always remains below optimal size. The all-inclusive club remains too small.

Consider, now, the relation between the set of necessary marginal conditions defined in (7) and those presented by Samuelson in application to goods that were exogenously defined to be purely public. In the latter case, these conditions are,

$$(8) \quad \sum_{i=1}^{s} (u_{n+j}^i / u_r^i) = f_{n+j}/f_r ,$$

where the marginal rates of substitution in consumption between the purely public good, X_{n+j}, and the numeraire good, X_r, summed over all individuals in the group of determined size, s, equals the marginal cost of X_{n+j} also defined in terms of units of X_r. Note that when (7) is satisfied, (8) is necessarily satisfied, provided only that the collectivity is making neither profit nor loss on providing the marginal unit of the public good. That is to say, provided that,

$$(9) \quad f_{n+j}/f_r = \sum_{i=1}^{s} (f_{n+j}^i/f_r^i).$$

The reverse does not necessarily hold, however, since the satisfaction of (8) does not require that each and every individual in the group be in a position where his own marginal benefits are equal to his marginal costs (taxes).[7] And, of course, (8) says nothing at all about group size.

The necessary marginal conditions in (7) allow us to classify all goods only after the solution is attained. Whether or not a particular good is purely private, purely public, or somewhere between these extremes is determined only after the equilibrium values for the N_j's are known. A good for which the equilibrium value for N_j is large can be classified as containing much "publicness." By contrast, a good for which the equilibrium value of N_j is small can be classified as largely private.

II

The formal statement of the theory of clubs presented in Section I can be supplemented and clarified by geometrical analysis, although the nature of the construction implies somewhat more restrictive models.

Consider a good that is known to contain, under some conditions, a degree of "publicness." For simplicity, think of a swimming pool. We want to examine the choice calculus of a single person, and we shall asume that other persons about him, with whom he may or may not choose to join in some club-like arrangement, are identical in all respects with him. As a first step, take a facility of one-unit size, which we define in terms of physical output supplied.

On the ordinate of Fig. 1, we measure total cost and total benefit per person, the latter derived from the individual's own evaluation of the facility in terms of the numeraire, dollars. On the abscissa, we measure the number of persons in possible sharing arrangements. Define the full cost of the one-unit facility to by Y_1, and the

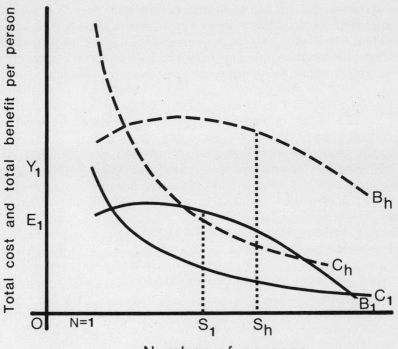

FIGURE 1

reference individual's evaluation of this facility as a purely private consumption good to be E_1. As is clear from the construction as drawn, he will not choose to purchase the good. If the single person is required to meet the full cost, he will not be able to enjoy the benefits of the good. Any enjoyment of the facility requires the organization of some co-operative-collective sharing arrangement.[8]

Two functions may now be traced in Fig. 1, remaining within the one-unit restriction on the size of the facility. A total benefit function and a total cost function confronting the single individual may be derived. As more persons are allowed to share in the enjoyment of the facility, of given size, the benefit evaluation that the individual places on the good will, after some point, decline. There may, of course, be both an increasing and a constant range of the total benefit function, but at some point congestion will set in, and his evaluation of the good will fall. There seems little doubt that the total benefit curve, shown as B_1, will exhibit the concavity property as drawn for goods that involve some commonality in consumption.[9]

The bringing of additional members into the club also serves to reduce the cost that the single person will face. Since, by our initial simplifying assumption, all persons here are identical, symmetrical cost sharing is suggested. In any case, the total cost per person will fall as additional persons join the group, under any cost-sharing scheme. As drawn in Fig. 1, symmetrical sharing is assumed and the curve, C_1, traces the total cost function, given the one-unit restriction on the size of the facility.[10]

For the given size of the facility, there will exist some optimal size of club. This is determined at the point where the derivatives of the total cost and total benefit functions are equal, shown as S_1 in Fig. 1, for the one-unit facility. Consider now an increase in the size of the facility. As before, a total cost curve and a total benefit curve may be derived, and an optimal club size determined. One other such optimum is shown at S_h, for a quantity of goods upon which the curves C_h and B_h are based. Similar constructions can be carried out for every possible size of facility; that is, for each possible quantity of good.

A similar construction may be used to determine optimal goods quantity for each possible size of club; this is illustrated in Fig. 2. On the ordinate, we measure here total costs and total benefits confronting the individual, as in Fig. 1. On the abscissa, we measure physical size of the facility, quantity of good, and for each assumed size of club membership we may trace total cost and total benefit functions. If we first examine the single-member club, we may well find that the optimal goods quantity is zero; the total cost function may increase more rapidly than the total benefit function from the outset. However, as more persons are added, the total costs to the single person fall; under our symmetrical sharing assumption, they will fall proportionately. The total benefit functions here will slope upward to the right but after some initial range they will be concave downward and at some point will reach a maximum. As club size is increased, benefit functions will shift generally downward beyond the initial non-congestion range, and the point of maximum benefit will move to the right. The construction of Fig. 2 allows us to derive an optimal goods quantity for each size of club; Q_k is one such quantity for club size $N = K$.

The results derived from Figs. 1 and 2 are combined in Fig. 3. Here the two variables to be chosen, goods quantity and club size,

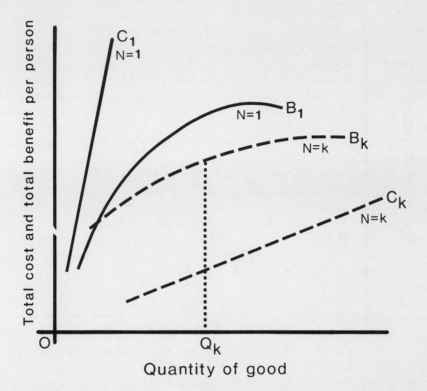

FIGURE 2

are measured on the ordinate and the abscissa respectively. The values for optimal club size for each goods quantity, derived from Fig. 1, allow us to plot the curve, N_{opt}, in Fig. 3. Similarly, the values for optimal goods quantity, for each club size, derived from Fig. 2, allow us to plot the curve, Q_{opt}.

The intersection of these two curves, N_{opt} and Q_{opt}, determines the position of full equilibrium, G. The individual is in equilibrium both with respect to goods quantity and to group size, for the good under consideration. Suppose, for example, that the sharing group is limited to size, N_k. The attainment of equilibrium with respect to goods quantity, shown by Q_k, would still leave the individual desirous of shifting the size of the membership so as to attain position L. However, once the group increases to this size, the individual prefers a larger quantity of the good, and so on, until G is attained.

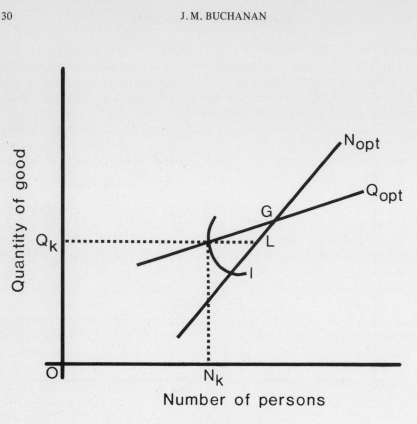

FIGURE 3

Fig. 3 may be interpreted as a standard preference map depicting the tastes of the individual for the two components, goods quantity and club size for the sharing of that good. The curves, N_{opt} and Q_{opt}, are lines of optima, and G is the highest attainable level for the individual, the top of his ordinal utility mountain. Since these curves are lines of optima within an individual preference system, successive choices must converge in G.

It should be noted that income-price constraints have already been incorporated in the preference map through the specific sharing assumptions that are made. The tastes of the individual depicted in Fig. 3 reflect the post-payment or net relative evaluations of the two components of consumption at all levels. Unless additional constraints are imposed on the model, he must move to the satiety point in this construction.

It seems clear that under normal conditions both of the curves in Fig. 3 will slope upward to the right, and that they will lie in approximately the relation to each other as therein depicted. This reflects the fact that, normally for the type of good considered in this example, there will exist a complementary rather than a substitute relationship between increasing the quantity of the good and increasing the size of the sharing group.

This geometrical model can be extended to cover goods falling at any point along the private-public spectrum. Take the purely public good as the first extreme case. Since, by definition, congestion does not occur, each total benefit curve, in Fig. 1, becomes horizontal. Thus, optimal club size, regardless of goods quantity is infinite. Hence, full equilibrium is possible of attainment; equilibrium only with respect to goods quantity can be reached, defined with respect to the all-inclusive finite group. In the construction of Fig. 3, the N curve cannot be drawn. A more realistic model may be that in which, at goods quantity equilibrium, the limitations on group size impose an inequality. For example, in Fig. 3, suppose that the all-inclusive group is of size, N_k. Congestion is indicated as being possible over small sizes of facility, but, if an equilibrium quantity is provided, there is no congestion, and, in fact, there remain economies to scale in club size. The situation at the most favorable attainable position is, therefore, in all respects equivalent to that confronted in the case of the good that is purely under the most restricted definition.

Consider now the purely private good. The appropriate curves here may be shown in Fig. 4. The individual, with his income-price constraints is able to attain the peak of his ordinal preference mountain without the necessity of calling upon his fellows to join him in sharing arrangements. Also, the benefits that he receives from the good may be so exclusively his own that these would largely disappear if others were brought in to share them. Hence, the full equilibrium position, G, lies along the vertical from the N = 1 member point. Any attempt to expand the club beyond this point will reduce the utility of the individual.[11]

III

The geometrical construction implies that the necessary marginal conditions are satisfied at unique equilibrium values for both goods quantity and club size. This involves an oversimplification that is made possible only through the assumptions of specific cost-sharing schemes and identity among individuals. In order to generalize the results, these restrictions must be dropped. We know that, given any group of individuals who are able to evaluate both consumption

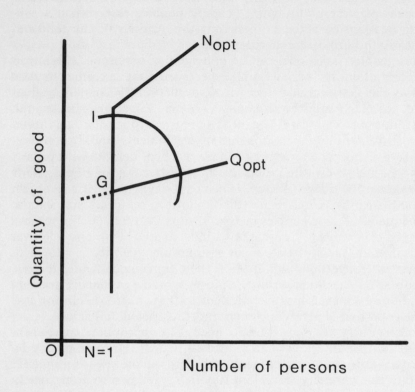

shares and the costs of congestion, there exists some set of marginal prices, goods quantity, and club size that will satisfy (7) above.
However, the quantity of the good, the size of the club sharing
in its consumption, and the cost-sharing arrangements must be
determined simultaneously. And, since there are always "gains from
trade" to be realized in moving from non-optimal to optimal
positions, distributional considerations must be introduced. Once
these are allowed to be present, the final "solution" can be located
at any one of a sub-infinity of points on the Pareto welfare surface.
Only through some quite arbitrarily chosen conventions can standard
geometrical constructions be made to apply.

   The approach used above has been to impose at the outset a set
of marginal prices (tax-prices, if the good is supplied publicly),
translated here into shares or potential shares in the costs of providing

separate quantities of a specific good for groups of varying sizes. Hence, the individual confronts a predictable set of marginal prices for each quantity of the good at every possible club size, independently of his own choices on these variables. With this convention, and the world-of-equals assumption, the geometrical solution becomes one that is relevant for any individual in the group. If we drop the world-of-equals assumption, the construction continues to hold without change for the choice calculus of any particular individual in the group. The results cannot, of course, be generalized for the group in this case, since different individuals will evaluate any given result differently. The model remains helpful even here, however, in that it suggests the process through which individual decisions may be made, and it tends to clarify some of the implicit content in the more formal statements of the necessary marginal conditions for optimality.[12]

IV

The theory of clubs developed in this paper applies in the strict sense only to the organization of membership or sharing arrangements where "exclusion" is possible. In so far as non-exclusion is a characteristic of public goods supply, as Musgrave has suggested,[13] the theory of clubs is of limited relevance. Nevertheless, some implications of the theory for the whole excludability question may be indicated. If the structure of property rights is variable, there would seem to be few goods the services of which are non-excludable, solely due to some physical attributes. Hence, the theory of clubs is, in one sense, a theory of optimal exclusion, as well as one of inclusion. Consider the classic lighthouse case. Variations in property rights, broadly conceived, could prohibit boat operators without "light licenses" from approaching the channel guarded by the light. Physical exclusion is possible, given sufficient flexibility in property law, in almost all imaginable cases, including those in which the interdependence lies in the act of consuming itself. Take the single person who gets an inoculation, providing immunization against a communicable disease. In so far as this action exerts external benefits on his fellows, the person taking the action could be authorized to collect charges from all beneficiaries under sanction of the collectivity.

This is not, of course, to suggest that property rights will, in practice, always be adjusted to allow for optimal exclusion. If they are not, the "free rider" problem arises. This prospect suggests one

issue of major importance that the analysis of this paper has neglected, the question of costs that may be involved in securing
agreements among members of sharing groups. If individuals think
that exclusion will not be fully possible, that they can expect to
secure benefits as free riders without really becoming full-fledged
contributing members of the club, they may be reluctant to enter
voluntarily into cost-sharing arrangements. This suggests that one
important means of reducing the costs of securing voluntary co-
operative agreements is that of allowing for more flexible property
arrangements and for introducing excluding devices. If the owner
of a hunting preserve is allowed to prosecute poachers, then prospective poachers are much more likely to be willing to pay for the
hunting permits in advance.

NOTES

[1] I am indebted to graduate students and colleagues for many helpful
suggestions. Specific acknowledgement should be made for the critical assistance of Emilio Giardina of the University of Cantania and W. Craig Stubblebine
of the University of Delaware.

[2] It is interesting that none of the theories of Socialist economic organization seems to be based on explicit co-operation among individuals. These
theories have conceived the economy either in the Lange-Lerner sense as an
analogue to a purely private, individually oriented social order or, alternatively,
as one that is centrally directed.

[3] See Paul A. Samuelson, "The Pure Theory of Public Expenditure," *Review
of Economics and Statistics,* vol. xxxvi (1954), pp. 387-89; "Diagrammatic
Exposition of a Theory of Public Expenditure," *Review of Economics and
Statistics,* vol. xxxvii (1955), pp. 350-55.

[4] Note that an economic theory of clubs can strictly apply only to the
extent that the motivation for joining in sharing arrangements is itself economic;
that is, only if choices are made on the basis of costs and benefits of particular
goods and services as these are confronted by the individual. In so far as individuals join clubs for camaraderie, as such, the theory does not apply.

[5] Physical attributes of a good or service may, of course, affect the structure
of the sharing arrangements that are preferred. Although the analysis below
assumes symmetrical sharing, this assumption is not necessary, and the analysis
in its general form can be extended to cover all possible schemes.

[6] Note that this construction of the individual's utility function differs
from that introduced in an earlier paper, where "activities" rather than "goods"
were included as the basic arguments. (See James M. Buchanan and Wm. Craig
Stubblebine, "Externality," *Economica,* vol. xxxi (1962), pp. 371-84). In the
alternative construction, the "activities" of other persons enter directly into
the utility function of the reference individual with respect to the consumption
of all other than purely private goods. The construction here incorporates the
same interdependence through the inclusion of the N_j's although in a more
general manner.

[7] In Samuelson's diagrammatic presentation, these individual marginal conditions are satisfied, but the diagrammatic construction is more restricted than that contained in his earlier more general model.

[8] The sharing arrangement need not be either co-operative or governmental in form. Since profit opportunities exist in all such situations, the emergence of profit-seeking firms can be predicted in those settings where legal structures permit, and where this organizational form possesses relative advantages. (Cf. R. H. Coase, "The Nature of the Firm," *Economica,* vol iv (1937), pp. 386-405.) For purposes of this paper, such firms are one form of club organization, with co-operatives and public arrangements representing other forms. Generally speaking, of course, the choice among these forms should be largely determined by efficiency considerations.

[9] The geometrical model here applies only to such goods. Essentially the same analysis may, however, be extended to apply to cases where "congestion," as such, does not appear. For example, goods that are produced at decreasing costs, even if their consumption is purely private, may be shown to require some sharing arrangements in an equilibrium or optimal organization.

[10] For simplicity, we assume that an additional "membership" in the club involves the addition of one separate person. The model applies equally well, however, for those cases where cost shares are allocated proportionately with predicted usage. In this extension, an additional "membership" would really amount to an additional consumption unit. Membership in the swimming club could, for example, be defined as the right to visit the pool one time each week. Hence, the person who plans to make two visits per week would, in this modification, hold two memberships. This qualification is not, of course, relevant under the strict world-of-equals assumption, but it indicates that the theory need not be so restrictive as it might appear.

[11] The construction suggests clearly that the optimal club size, for any quantity of good, will tend to become smaller as the real income of an individual is increased. Goods that exhibit some "publicness" at low income levels will, therefore, tend to become "private" as income levels advance. This suggests that the number of activities that are organized optimally under co-operative collective sharing arrangements will tend to be somewhat larger in low-income communities than in high-income communities, other things equal. There is, of course, ample empirical support for this rather obvious conclusion drawn from the model. For example, in American agricultural communities thirty years ago heavy equipment was communally shared among many farms, normally on some single owner-lease-rental arrangement. Today, substantially the same equipment will be found on each farm, even though it remains idle for much of its potential working time.

The implication of the analysis for the size of governmental units is perhaps less evident. In so far as governments are organized to provide communal facilities, the size of such units measured by the number of citizens, should decline as income increases. Thus, in the affluent society, the local school district may, optimally, be smaller than in the poor society.

[12] A note concerning one implicit assumption of the whole analysis is in order at this point. The possibility for the individual to choose among the various scales of consumption sharing arrangements has been incorporated into an orthodox model of individual behavior. The procedure implies that the individual remains indifferent as to which of his neighbors or fellow citizens join him in such arrangements. In other words, no attempt has been made to

allow for personal selectivity or discimination in the models. To incorporate
this element, which is no doubt important in many instances, would introduce a
wholly new dimension into the analysis, and additional tools to those employed
here would be required.

[13]   See R. A. Musgrave, *The Theory of Public Finance,* New York, 1959.

3

The Property Tax

An Excise Tax or a Profits Tax?

Peter Mieszkowski*

A WIDELY accepted proposition of incidence theory is that the burden of a local property tax on reproducible capital is shifted to consumers and is equivalent to an excise tax. This result dates back to the work of Marshall (1897), Pierson (1902), Edgeworth (1925), more recently to the work of Simon (1943), and is used repeatedly in empirical work, Musgrave et al. (1951), Gillespie (1965), and in the literature on housing and urban problems, Netzer (1966, 1968). Netzer has expressed property taxes on the housing stock in the nation as a whole as an excise tax on housing services. Also in the national accounts prepared by the U.S. Department of Commerce, property taxes are lumped together with sales and manufacturers' excise taxes in the category, indirect taxes.

While the proposition that the property tax is an excise tax represents conventional wisdom there are two opposing points of view. One is that the property tax is very similar, if not fully equivalent, in its distributive effects to taxes on profits. This view of the effects of the property tax was first developed by Brown (1924) in a well-known, though neglected section of his book, *The economics of taxation,* and has been restated by Thompson (1965). The second, somewhat different proposition is that a property tax on improvements (reproducible capital) is shifted through a reduction of site rents onto owners of land. This argument, first found in Marshall (1890), has also been recently presented by Richman (1967, 1968).[2] The essence of Richman's argument is that a property tax in a particular city will lead to a less intense use of land there and will

* Dept. of Economics, Queen's University, Kingston, Ont., Canada. First version received May 1971, revised version received September 1971. *Journal of Public Economics* 1 (1972) 73-96. © North-Holland Publishing Company. Reprinted by permission.

decrease land values. It is possible to argue that land rents are determined as a residual, and when a property tax is imposed on capital, developers will bid less for land, as their normal costs are increased by the amount of the tax. Also there is the related, more general, argument made by Rolph (1954) and Rolph and Break (1961) that partial taxes, excise and property, will be borne in large part by imperfectly mobile factors of production.

The main aim of this paper is to attempt to reconcile these opposing views on the effects of the property tax and to demonstrate that there is some truth to each of the three general arguments presented above. Although I attempted to be as eclectic as possible the paper is based on a number of stylized assumptions and certain effects are emphasized at the exclusion of other considerations.

In particular I attempt to demonstrate that excise tax effects will result from taxes imposed at varying rates on different types of property, or at varying rates in different regions or cities. Also there is relatively little conflict between the view that property taxes are excises and the proposition that the basic effect on the property tax is to decrease the yield from real capital *if it is properly recognized that the global (nation wide) effects of the tax are quite different than the partial effects for a single city, or groups of cities.*

From a national perspective the basic effect of the imposition of property taxes by thousands of local governments is to decrease the yield on reproducible capital. Relatively high tax rates in certain cities increase the prices of goods and services produced in these localities. However these price increases will be tempered, even swamped, by decreases in the value of land and decreases in the returns to other imperfectly mobile factors of production. Nevertheless, the discentive effects of property taxes, often stressed by the critics of property taxes, are very real. Unless increases in the property tax rates in a particular city are accompanied by improvements in the quality of public services, residents will have an incentive to move, the size and quality of the housing stock will deteriorate, and the location of industrial activities in high tax jurisdictions will be discouraged.

Throughout the paper we limit ourselves to the consideration of taxes on reproducible, shiftable, capital. Thus we exclude from consideration the question of whether taxes on site rents are borne by the owners of land. As Simon has shown in his famous review of the classical literature this issue hinges on the formation of urban land values and whether rent differentials, arising from locational advantages, are constant in *absolute* magnitude or whether rent differentials observed under various tax regimes will be a constant *proportion* of a base value. Despite the insights gained by the classical writers, Pierson and Edgeworth, the incidence of taxes on urban land rents remains an unsettled question. It seems to me that the key issue is whether the supply of land, which is subject to tax, is variable in supply. For the case of a developed city it is unlikely that a land tax will have much of an impact on the supply of land in urban use, and a land tax will be borne by the owners of land. On the other hand if the price of urban land at the outskirts of a city is closely related to its opportunity cost in agriculture and the demand for urban land is price elastic, taxes on urban land will change the quantity and before-tax price of land.[3]

In addition to assuming that the supply of land is fixed and/or limiting the discussion to taxes on improvements we make the following assumptions and simplifications: The *total* supplies of capital and labor are assumed to be fixed; product and factor markets are perfectly competitve, and factors receive the value of their marginal products. Capital is assumed to be perfectly mobile (shiftable) between industries and different regions, so in the absence of differential risk the after-tax rate of return on all capital in the economy are equalized. Also the value of capital in any use will be equal to its reproduction costs. Property taxes are not capitalized.

Throughout most of the analysis we shall abstract from the effects of the expenditure side of the budget. The only justification of this simplification is convenience, as the level and quality of public expenditures influence housing values and locational decisions. However, if we were to consider the expenditure side we would have to specify the value placed on a particular bundle of services by different groups for varying rates of tax and to recognize that varying tax bases between communities lead to different levels of public services for the same tax rate. To avoid these complications we make the conventional simplification of taking the budget as given, essentially ignore it, and attempt to determine the change in factor and commodity prices that rest from a particular method of finance and compare these distributive effects with those derived for alternative tax regimes.

Given the above assumptions it follows that when all cities in the nation impose the same rate of property tax on all types of reproducible capital the burden of the tax falls on the owners of capital. Under marginal productivity factor pricing any attempt to shift the tax will be frustrated. For example a rise in commodity prices relative to wages results in a decrease in real wage below the value of the marginal product of labor and this will result in an increase in the demand for labor that will restore the real wage to its original level. Also as capital accumulation is assumed to be independent of tax changes the before-tax rentals on capital goods and the reproduction cost of capital goods are unaffected by the imposition of the tax. Asset prices will remain unchanged and the rate of return (rate of interest) will fall in proportion to the size of the property tax.

Contrary to the conventional wisdom the imposition of a general property tax does *not* increase the price of housing services. Although owner occupants have to pay a property tax the price of rental housing is not increased. The cost of housing for the owner-occupant also remains unchanged, as the opportunity cost of capital falls by the amount of the tax, leaving total housing costs unchanged. Changes in the relative income positions of different groups are due solely to the different amounts of wealth that they own. A renter who does not own any wealth will not bear any of the burden of the property tax. An individual who owns a $20,000 house and another individual who owns $20,000 worth of manufacturing equipment will both bear the same tax burden.

Furthermore for the special case under consideration the property tax is *not* a benefit tax. Households pay taxes only in their role of owners of capital. When an initial equilibrium is distrubed by a change in preferences and all communities increase public expenditures, and finance these expenditures by increasing the property tax rate by the same amount, the additional tax burden will fall on the owners of capital. The overall marginal productivity of capital is not changed by an equal increase in tax rates in all communities. In the extreme case where all capital is owned by a single individual and all towns are composed of renters the benefits of the higher public expenditures will be enjoyed at the expense of the capitalist.

The Excise Tax Effects of Property Taxes

The above results are highly stylized by the assumption that all towns tax all capital at the same rate. In fact, thousands of local governments and special districts impose property taxes at different rates with different coverage, and with varying assessment practices.[4]

Tax rate differentials between communities result in excise tax effects. These effects are the result of the perfect mobility of capital which equalizes the after-tax rate of return in all communities. A town, which because of a higher than average propensity, or need, to spend on public goods and services, imposes a relatively high rate of property tax on housing will pay more for the services of housing capital. If certain communities impose a relatively high property tax rate on industrial capital, the cost of capital to these industries will rise and, depending on the competitive position of the industries in the high tax communities vis-a-vis firms in other areas, the price of the products of the heavily taxed industries will rise, and/or wages and the returns on land will have to fall so that the industries in the high tax town can remain competitive.

In order to highlight the excise tax effects of property tax differentials I shall (in this section of the paper) make a number of further simplifying assumptions. First that there are no 'economies of scale' associated with high density industrial and residential development, and transportation costs are negligible. Capital and workers are perfectly mobile between communities so that after-tax rates of return on capital and wage rates are equal in all communities.

Although there is little relation between place of work and place of residence, different households prefer, for a given set of housing prices, different residential locations (cities). If relative housing prices change some of the households will change their place of residence. I also assume that each town is surrounded by farm land and that the supply of land from agriculture to urban use is perfectly elastic at the opportunity cost of the land in agriculture. This last assumption helps to insure that tax induced changes in residential locations will not affect land rents and land values. Adjustments in the relative size of various cities will take place through changes in the amount of land taken out of agriculture. Finally it is assumed that industries are specific to particular towns. This assumption allows us to ignore the possibility of wholesale relocation of industries between towns and to concentrate on the excise tax effects of property taxes imposed on industrial commodities which each town exports to the national market.[5]

In addition to industrial, or export goods, we distinguish 'home goods' such as residential real-estate, trade and services which are produced and *consumed* locally. We begin with the case where different cities levy a varying rate of tax on capital used in the production of 'home goods', i.e. residential capital, trade and services, but each city taxes industrial capital used in the production of export goods at the same rate and the common rate of tax on industrial capital is equal to the *average* rate of tax on residential capital (home goods) in the economy as a whole.

The average rate of tax on residential capital for the nation as a whole is the tax in each community weighted by the amount of capital subject to tax. For example in the symmetrical situation, there are three towns, A, B, C, and town A taxes 1,000 units of residential capital at a rate of 2%, B has a 3% rate of tax and 10,000 units of capital and C, the high tax town has a tax rate of 4% and 1,000 units of capital. The simple, and weighted mean of the tax rate is 3%, and by assumption this is the common rate of tax imposed on industrial capital. Suppose that before the imposition of the property tax system the before-tax rate of return on all capital was 10%.

After the imposition of taxes residents of high tax communities will decrease their demand for residential capital and some households will shift their residential capital to low tax areas. The tax-induced change in the allocation of residential capital may take place at an unchanged rate of return on capital. This will depend on whether the tax induced decrease in the demand for capital in high-tax towns is just offset by an increase in the demand for capital in low-tax towns. When the before-tax rate of return on capital remains unchanged after-tax rates of return on capital fall by the average rate of tax, i.e. from 10% to 7%. On the other hand, if the capital which shifts out of high tax communities cannot be absorbed in low-tax areas at an unchanged before-tax rate of return, the overall tax rate will fall. Suppose this occurred and the before-tax rate of return on capital fell from 10% to 9.5%. The burden on owners of capital will be larger than the average tax rate of 3%. Consumers of industrial commodities and housing services will benefit from the decrease in real profits that does not accrue to government.

Regardless of whether the overall before-tax of return is decreased, increased, or unchanged by the tax, and we shall assume for simplicity that it remains unchanged, there are two basic effects of a system of property taxes imposed at varying rates in different communities. The first is to decrease the after-tax return on capital by an amount that approximates the average rate of property tax in the economy. The second effect is to increase the cost of the services of capital in high areas and to decrease its cost in low-tax communities, for capital markets will not be in equilibrium unless the after-tax rate of return on capital is the same in all communities.

In our example community C, the high tax town, imposes a tax rate of 4%, while the national average is 3%, and while the global effect of the property tax system is to decrease the after-tax return on capital from 10% to 7%, the required rate in community C increases from 10% to 11%. The eleven percent is made up of an interest rate of 7% plus a property tax of 4%. Consequently, relative to the situation where *no* community imposes property taxes the cost of capital has increased by a percentage point in community C. If capital is the only input in the production of housing services, the price of these services (rents) in C will go up by 10%. In community A, whose tax rate is 1 percentage point below the national average of 3%, the cost of housing will go down by 10% relative to the zero tax situation.

The existence of negative as well as positive excise tax effects resulting from property taxes is important for empirical work which allocates tax burdens to groups classified by income level. Ideally, one should work with income distributions for each separate taxing jurisdiction. But if this is not feasible and when the correlation between the level and distribution of income in various communities and the level of property tax is weak it will not be inaccurate to ignore the excise tax effects and to treat the property tax as a profits tax. For if the shape of the income distribution and mean income levels are the same in low tax towns as in high tax towns excise tax effects at the global level will cancel for each group at a particular level of income.

To this point we have abstracted from changes in relative prices in the industrial sector by assumption that all cities tax industrial capital at the same rate, which is equal to the average tax on residential capital.

As in the case of home goods an above-average rate of tax on a particular export commodity, which by assumption is specific to a given town, will increase the cost of capital to that industry. When there is little or no correlation between the production parameters of specific industries (the relative factor intensities and the relative sizes of the elasticities of substitution) and the tax rates imposed on different industries, the capital released from the industries located in high tax towns will be absorbed in industries subject to low rates of tax without an appreciable change in the *average* before-tax rate of return on capital. On the other hand if high tax areas produce predominately capital (labor) intensive commodities and the elasticities of substitution are relatively high (low) in these industries the average rate of return on industrial capital will fall (increase).

As in the analysis of taxes on home goods it is important to measure the excise tax effects of property taxes on industrial capital relative to the mean rate of tax on this type of capital. If the average property tax rate on industrial capital is 3% and the shoe industry is taxed at a rate of 4%, the price of capital to the shoe industry will be 1 percentage point higher. If the average before-tax rate of return is 10% and the share of capital is 0.25, the price of shoes will increase by 2.5%. The relative prices of commodities produced by industries, subject to tax rates below the mean rate for industrial sector, will fall and as in the taxation of residential capital excises tend to cancel, with some commodities increasing in price and others decreasing in price. In empirical work these excise tax effects are important when commodities taxed at below average rates are disproportionately important in the consumption patterns of specific income groups.

We have discussed separately the excise tax effects of property taxes on residential real estate and on industrial property. Assumptions were made to minimize the possible changes in overall rates of return on capital within each of the two broad sectors. In fact, capital is mobile between industry and residential real estate and the possibility of tax differentials between broad industry groups must be accounted for. Housing services, in the aggregate, may be taxed more heavily than industrial capital or vice-versa. If this is true the price of housing in general will rise relative to the price of industrial goods; there will be a reallocation of resources; and since housing is very capital-intensive the price of capital will fall relative to the price of labor. Consumers of housing services and owners of capital suffer a loss in real income while consumers of other goods experience an increase in real income as a result of a decrease in the price of commodities other than housing services.[6]

The Immobility of Labor, the Capitalization of Property Taxes and their Effects on Land Values

The major qualification to the result that local tax differentials increase or decrease the price of locally produced goods and services by the changes in the cost of capital services is the possible decrease in the returns to imperfectly mobile factors of production.

In this section we retain the assumption of perfect mobility of capital, allow for the imperfect mobility of labor and assume that the supply of land in each taxing jurisdiction is fixed. Also our analysis is partial in that we concentrate on the effects of a tax imposition on the prices of commodities, land and labor—in *one* particular town. Thus we ignore general equilibrium adjustments and price changes which occur in the no-tax (low-tax) communities.

While a formal treatment of these effects would considerably complicate the analysis the general effects are fairly straightforward.

To this point we have, through appropriate assumptions, ruled out changes in factor prices. Changes in land rents and wages which result from tax differentials mean that changes in relative commodity prices will be moderated. In high-tax towns factor prices will fall and the increases in the cost of capital will lead to more moderate increases in commodity prices. On the other hand, increases in factor prices in low-tax towns will temper the negative excise tax effects in these communities.

The partial analysis which deals with factor price effects not only allows us to gain some insight on the overall (global) impact of the tax but also enables us to focus on what happens in a community when it increases its rate of property tax relative to the rate prevailing in other cities. However what needs to be emphasized is that the introduction of changes in factor prices is principally a qualification of the previous result that tax-rate differentials lead to excise tax effects (changes in commodity prices). The result that the global effect of a property tax system is to depress the earnings on capital by the average rate of tax in the economy remains unaffected by the consideration of changes in the returns to immobile factors of production.

The simplest view of the effects of tax rate differentials on the returns to immobile factors of production is that they will be fully capitalized in the value of land which is an immobile factor of production. Even if capital is perfectly shiftable the property tax may be fully capitalized in the value of land. For example if the present value of property tax in town A on a house which cost $20,000 to produce is $1,000 larger than in town B it is expected that a lot in A will sell for $1,000 less than an identical lot in B.[7] Similarly a potential developer of an apartment house or some other activity will consider property taxes as costs and will substract them in bidding for prospective development sites.

This simple line of reasoning leaves out two interrelated considerations. First the ratio of improvements to land can be varied in both residential and industrial activities. As is well known from the work on urban structure, (Mills, 1967; Muth, 1969) high land rents close to the central business district resulting from low transportation costs to work places will lead to high density apartment developments and the rental of these units by households who derive little utility from the consumption of land space. On the other hand families with children will incur higher transporation costs to 'consume' large lots in the suburbs where land is cheaper. If a central city increases its property tax rate relative to suburban tax rates there will be a shift in residential and industrial capital to the suburbs. However the fall in land rents will be buffered by increases in the amount of land used by household who chose to remain in the central city and by industry that will substitute cheaper land for higher-cost capital. Although the price of land will fall the decrease in before-tax rents may significantly smaller than the additional tax on improvements.

Second, a good part of tax burden on improvements may fall on labor which may be imperfectly mobile. Taxes on industrial capital by decreasing output decrease the demand for labor and workers may have to take a cut in wages to remain fully employed.

In order to deal simultaneously with changes in land prices and wages we present a conventional production function approach to the determination of factor prices where land is treated as an ordinary factor of production. In this formulation all sites within a city are identical, a central business district (CBD) does not exist, and in equilibrium the rent on land in all activities, high-rise residential, single-family residential, commercial and industrial will be the same. The size of buildings, per unit of land space, will depend on whether marginal cost of floor space increases with the size of the building, and on the return to the complementary services of land, such as parking space, recreational uses of land in apartment house developments and so on. The marginal revenue product of capital on a given plot of land is expected to fall as the size of the building is increased.

To make things as simple as possible all activities of a city are aggregated into a single output, X, which is produced with inputs of labor, L, capital, K, and land, R.[8]

The model is a system of six equations in six unknowns, L, K, X, P_X, w, and r, and an exogenous tax expressed as a per-unit tax on capital, T. The supply of land, R, is taken as fixed. The six equations are as follows:

$$X = f_1 (L, K, R) \qquad \text{, supply of X} \qquad (1)$$
$$X = f_2 (P_X) \qquad \text{, demand for X} \qquad (2)$$
$$K = f_3 (w, r, T, X) \qquad \text{, demand for K} \qquad (3)$$
$$L = f_4 (w, r, T, X) \qquad \text{, demand for L} \qquad (4)$$
$$L = f_5 (w) \qquad \text{, supply of L} \qquad (5)$$
$$P_X X = wL + rR + (P_K + T) K \qquad \text{, price relation.} \qquad (6)$$

Equation 1 is a linear homogeneous production function which relates the output of X to the three factors inputs. Relation 2 is the demand relation which makes the demand for locally produced commodities a function of the price of local commodities, P_X. With this very simple demand formulation I ignore the income effects arising from changes in the population (labor force). Equations 3 and 4 are two of the three factor demand relations for labor, land and capital. Only two of the three equations are independent. These factor demand equations are based on cost minimizing considerations. For a given set of after-tax factor prices and for tax rate, T, the demand for capital labor, and land depends on level of output. When relative factor price change factor substitutions will occur and at each level of output factor proportions will change. Hence changes in the demand for factors will occur as the result of output effects and factor substitution effects. As the after-tax return on capital P_K is given by national conditions and is taken as the numeraire, it has not been included in the factor demand equations. The cost of capital changes only as a result of changes in the rate of property tax.

Equation 5, is a simple supply of labor equation that makes the supply of labor a function of the local wage rate (the wage rate in other communities is taken as given). For simplicity the effect of changes in the prices of home goods (housing etc.) on the supply of labor is ignored.

Equation 6 is a price relation, or total revenue function, that relates the price of the output to the prices of the factors.

In order to investigate the effects of changes in the tax rate, T, on the returns to labor and land, and on the price of X the system of equations 1–6, is differentiated totally with respect to T and a solution is obtained for dw/dT and dr/dT. As this differentiation is straight-forward it is not presented in any detail.[9] The differentiation of the factor demand equations may be the only unfamiliar part of the exercise.

The differentiation of the demand for capital equation, relation 3, yields after some rearrangement

$$\frac{dK}{K} = a_{KL}\, dw + a_{KR}\, dr + a_{KK}\, dT + \frac{dX}{X}. \qquad (3')$$

The a_{ij}'s are the elasticities of demand for factor i with respect to a change in the price of factor j. As defined by Allen (1950) a_{ij} is the partial elasticity of substitution between factor i and factor j weighted by the proportion of factor j in total cost: i.e. a_{KL} is $f_L e_{KL}$ where e_{KL} is the partial elasticity of substitution between capital and labor. Allen showed that $a_{ii} < O$ and that $a_{iL} + a_{iR} = O$ for $i = L, K, R$. He also demonstrated that *either* all three partial elasticities of substitution a_{ij}, $i = j$, are positive *or* that one of the three partial elasticities is negative and the other two positive. I shall assume, for simplicity, that all three of these partial elasticities are positive.

Upon differentiation the solution for dw/dT and dr/dT are as follows:[10]

$$\frac{dw}{dT} = \frac{(f_K E_X - f_K(a_{KK} - a_{RK}))(a_{LR} - a_{RR}) +}{D}$$

$$\frac{(a_{LK} - a_{RK})(f_K(a_{KR} - a_{RR}) - E_X f_R)}{} \tag{7}$$

$$\frac{dr}{dT} = \frac{(f_K E_X - f_K(a_{KK} - a_{RK}))(a_{LL} - a_{RL} - E_L) +}{D}$$

$$\frac{(a_{RK} - a_{LK})(f_K(a_{KL} - a_{RL}) + f_L E_L - E_X f_L)}{}, \tag{8}$$

where the denominator D is equal to

$$D = (f_K(a_{KL} - a_{RL}) + f_L E_L - E_X f_L)(a_{LR} - a_{RR}) -$$

$$(a_{LL} - a_{RL} - E_L)(f_K(a_{KR} - a_{RR}) - E_X f_R),$$

and where f_K, f_L, f_R are the original shares of capital, labor and land respectively, E_L is the elasticity of supply of labor, E_X is the price elasticity of demand for X. The presumptive signs of E_L and E_X are positive and negative respectively and it is easy to show that the sign of D is unambiguously positive.[11]

The main qualitative result implied by this model is that changes in the tax rate, T, can lead to a very wide range of changes in the returns to the imperfectly mobile factors, labor and land. It is even possible (though not probable) especially for land, that a tax on improvements will increase the returns to labor and land relative to the fixed after-tax return to capital. The imposition of property tax increases the cost of the services of capital and this change in relative factor prices results in a substitution of labor and land for land. While the demand for labor and land will be increased at each level of output, the level of economic activity in the city will be decreased by the property tax. The output effect decreases the demand for land and labor for any set of factor prices. Consequently the effect of the tax on the returns to labor and land is ambiguous in sign and in magnitude. When the output effect dominates the factor substitution effect, i.e. when $f_K E_X$ exceeds $f_K (a_{KK} - a_{RK})$ as it probably will, the returns to labor and land fall relative to the after-tax return on capital. Nevertheless any decrease in the return to these immobile factors will be quite modest if the demand for these factors is sustained by the substitution of labor and land for capital. Of course the more elastic is local demand to price increases the more powerful will be the output effect. The change in the relative changes in the returns to land and labor depend in part on the supply response of labor to changes in the wage rate.

When land and labor are both perfectly immobile the change in the relative prices of labor and land depend on the relative responses in the demands for these two factors to changes in their prices and to the change in the cost of capital. If the factor substitution possibilities are greater for labor than for land, the price of labor will increase relative to the price of land. If as expected $(a_{LK} - a_{RK})$ is positive the second term of the numerator of the expression for dw/dT (equation 7) is unambiguously positive. When in addition $(a_{KL} - a_{RL})$ is positive the second term in the numerator of equation 8 is unambiguously negative.

As factor substitution terms appear in both the numerators and denominators of expressions 7 and 8 it is uncertain what effect the magnitude of these parameters will have on the absolute value of dw/dT and dr/dT. On the other hand the effects of these parameters on relative magnitudes of dw/dT and dr/dT are easier to interpret.

By rewriting equation (4'') in footnote 10 dr/dT can be expressed in terms of dw/dT

$$\frac{dr}{dT} = \left(\frac{a_{LL} - a_{RL} - E_L}{a_{LR} - a_{RR}}\right) \frac{dw}{dT} + \left(\frac{a_{RK} - a_{LK}}{a_{LR} - a_{RR}}\right). \tag{9}$$

Assuming $a_{RK} - a_{LK}$ to be negative it follows from equation (9) that when dw/dT is negative the fall in r relative to w will be less the more responsive is the demand for land to changes in the price of land. When dw is positive it is unclear, because of the constant term, whether it will be to the benefit of landowners (relative to workers) for $(a_{LR} - a_{RR})$ to be as small as possible. Nevertheless it is quite likely that the less elastic the demand for land with respect to its price the larger will be the increase in the return on land relative to the increase in wages. There is a straightforward interpretation to these results. If wages fall as a result of a tax-induced decrease in economic activity, the fall will be cushioned by the possibility of substituting labor for land and capital. If the factor substitution possibilities are smaller for land than for labor, the price of land will fall more. On the other hand when the demand for labor and land both rise, the return to labor will increase relatively less as the demand for this factor is more elastic with respect to changes in it price.

The close connection between the price of land and the wage rate also serves to explain the curious result that the price of land does not necessarily fall more when the supply of labor is more responsive to wage rate changes.

As E_L, the elasticity of supply of labor with respect to wage rate change appears only in the denominator in the expression for dw/dT the wage rate will necessarily fall less when the supply of labor to the city is more elastic. However, it does not follow from (9) than an increase in E_L, which leads to a decrease in dw/dT, will necessarily increase (decrease) the magnitude of dr/dT. It is expected that a smaller decrease in the wage rate due to mobility of labor (assuming dw/dT negative) will depress the demand for X and will decrease land prices. Working counter to this effect is the increased demand for land as a result of the smaller fall in wages. The possibility that land prices will fall less, not more, when labor supply is more elastic should be considered as a curiosum as it depends on a high partial elasticity of substitution between labor and land relative to price elasticity of demand for X. Also the model under consideration leaves out the interaction between the demand of certain components of X (the home goods sector in X) and income and population in X.

A narrowing of the possible range for dw/dT, and dr/dT depends on estimation of the parameters in expressions (7) and (8). However, even without hard estimates reasonable restrictions can be placed on the likely range in the change in wages and land rents. For most cities the share of land rents in the total value of output is unlikely to exceed 5%.[12] The share of labor is around 70% and the share of capital 25%. The small share of land relative to labor and capital means land rents may fall dramatically and still not absorb the full

burden of the tax on capital. The change in the price of X is related
to the tax and changes in factor price by the relation

$$dp_X = f_K \, dT + f_L \, dw + f_R \, dr . \tag{10}$$

Suppose that dT is 10%. For $f_K = 0.25$, the price of X will increase by 2.5% when $dw = dr = 0$. Even if $dr/dT = 2$ so that land
rents fall by 20% for a 10% increase in taxes, commodity prices
will increase by 1.5% as the share of land rents in total costs is only
0.05. When there is no possibility of substituting land for labor or
capital ($a_{LR} = a_{KR} = a_{RR} = 0$), then dw is positive so in order to
remain fully employed land will have to absorb not only the tax
but also the increase in wage costs which results from the substitution of labor for capital.

We have experimented with various values for E_X and E_L and the
production parameters and have found that even for low values of
partial elasticities of substitution of land for labor and land for
capital the value of dr/dT does not exceed 2. For example when
$E_X = -1$, $E_L = 1$ and the partial elasticities involving capital and
labor are taken to be 1 while those involving land are assumed to
be 0.1 the value of $dw/dT = 0.02$ and $dr/dT = -1.5$.

These numerical experiments suggest that when the demand for
land is unresponsive to factor prices changes the wage rate will
change very little, especially for moderate responses in the supply
of labor. This will be true for a wide range of values for the partial
elasticity of substitution between labor and capital. For low elasticities of substitution between land and labor and between land
and capital, say in the range 0.05 to 0.1, the price of land will fall
substantially. For example, a 10% tax on capital earnings may well
decrease land rents by 20% of their original value but because of the
small share of land rents in total costs this decrease in the land rents
will not offset the tax levy and prices will rise. It is highly unlikely
that land will bear more than 40% of the total tax burden and quite
likely that consumers will bear 75% or more of the burden in the
form of higher prices.

A Simple Model of a Central Business District

By treating land supply as another factor of production in a neo-
classicial production process and by making all sites within a city
identical we have not allowed for economies of agglomeration that
result in the formation of a central business district (CBD). In this

section we analyse the effects of property taxes in a model where a fixed amount of land serves as a 'base' for buildings of indefinite height. In this model, unlike the previous formulation, the fall in land rents may exceed the taxes collected on improvements.

The demand for floor space at the CBD is a function of price, i.e. $X = f(p_X)$. The marginal cost of a unit of floor space (building an additional floor) is assumed to rise and average costs at any given level of output lie below marginal costs. If developers operating in the CBD take the price of output as given, equilibrium will be reached when marginal variable cost is equal to price (average revenue). For simplicity we assume that only variable cost to be the cost of capital services. The difference between average revenue (price) and average cost multiplied by the level of output will be quasi rents that accrue to owners of land.[13] The imposition of a property tax in a city shifts the marginal cost schedule upwards, increases the price of CBD services and leads to a decrease in output and land rents.

The demand for floor space at the CBD is equal to

$$X = f(P_X), \tag{11}$$

marginal cost (equal to price) is given by

$$P_X = g(X)p_K, \tag{12}$$

where p_K is the cost of capital.

The marginal cost of output which is equal to price is a function of the level of output and the cost of capital. For a change in p_K the change in the price of X is equal to

$$\frac{dp_X}{p_X} = \frac{dp_K}{p_K} + e_s \frac{dX}{X}, \tag{13}$$

where e_s is the elasticity of the marginal cost curve with respect to changes in output. Differentiating the demand relation we obtain

$$\frac{dX}{X} = E_X \frac{dp_X}{p_X}. \tag{14}$$

From (13) and (14) if follows

$$\frac{dX}{X} = \frac{E_X (dp_K / p_K)}{1 - e_s E_X}. \tag{15}$$

We assume that e_s is small relative to E_X. When $E_X = -1$ and $e_s = 0.1$ the fall in output will be 9% when capital cost are increased by 10%. When E_X is raised to -5, output will fall by 33% when the cost of capital is increased by 10%. In order to simplify the relation between the level of land rents and the level of output we assume that *total* variable costs are given by the quadratic function

$$(cX + mX^2) p_K . \tag{16}$$

Land rents are equal to the difference between price (marginal cost) and average cost multiplied by the level of output. For the quadratic total cost function this difference is equal to $(c + 2mX - (c + mX))$ Xp_K which reduces to

$$R \text{ (land rents)} = mX^2 p_K . \tag{17}$$

Taking the cost of capital to be equal to 1 when the rate of property tax is zero the ratio of land rents with the tax to the level of land rents in the absence of tax is equal to

$$\frac{R_1}{R_0} = (1+t)\left(\frac{X_1}{X_0}\right)^2 . \tag{18}$$

Approximating the ratio of X_1/X_0 by means of equation (15) and taking t equal to 0.1 the ratio R_1/R_0 for $E_X = -5$ is equal to $(1.1) (0.66) = 0.48$. Land rents fall by more than 50% of their original value. For E_X equal to -1 the fall in land rents is about a little less than 10%, i.e. $R_1/R_0 = 0.91$.

The decrease in land rents relative to the level of tax collections on the improvements depends on the value of land relative to the value of improvements. Assume that before the tax was imposed the ratio of capital rentals was $4:1$ – and 100 units of capital were employed in the CBD. Capital is measured so that the after-tax return on capital is equal to 1. For $E_X = -0.5$ the imposition of a 10% tax will reduce the amount of capital to 66 units, tax collection will equal 6.6 units and land rents will fall from 25 units to 12. For a ratio of improvements to land of $10:1$ land rents will fall by 75% of tax collections.

For smaller values of the price elasticity of demand the fall in land rents will be much less dramatic. When E_X is equal to -1 tax collections will be equal to 9 units and land rents will fall by 9% of their original value when the capital to land ratio is $10:1$. When the capital to land ratio is $4:1$ the fall in land rents will be 25% of tax collections.

The simultaneous increase in prices and fall in land rents illustrates the need of dealing with both excise tax effects of local taxes and their effect on factor prices. In this model purchasers of the taxed commodities will pay prices that "include" the property tax and land prices may also fall by substantial amounts. There are two possible interpretations to the fall in land values. One is that it reflects a transfer of income from the owners of CBD land to the owners of suburban land where CBD activities have relocated. However if the CBD has some unique features that favor the concentration of economic activity at this site the imposition of the tax in the central city may lead to an overall fall in land values. The overall fall in land values reflects the dead weight loss associated with the dispersal of the CBD.

There are several reasons for doubting that land rents will fall by amounts which approach the level of tax collections on improvements. First dramatic changes in rents depend on very elastic demand for floor space at the CBD. Second by ignoring complementary labor inputs in the provision of floor space at the CBD we exaggerate the increase in prices that result from an increase in the cost of capital. Finally it is unlikely that the value of land will be greater than 10% of the value of improvements.

The Benefits of Public Expenditures and the Differential Incidence of the Property Tax

On balance the introduction of the benefit side of the budget significantly complicates any analysis of the budgetary policies of local governments. A general way of introducing public expenditures is to write the demand for home goods X_H as a function of their price p_H and the level of public expenditures g. An increase in the property tax rate by increasing the cost of capital will increase the price of home goods. However, if the marginal utility of public goods is high consumers will be willing to pay the additional cost and the overall effect of a budget expansion will be to increase the demand for home goods. The demand for industrial goods, largely external, will fall as a result of the budget expansion unless the public expenditure decreases production costs, to compensate for the tax increase, and/or increase the supply of labor.

If town officials do their job well and choose the level and composition of public expenditures in accordance with the preferences of the electorate and attempt to "maximize the value of the town" the results on budget incidence may be simpler and more straightforward than the separate analysis of taxes. Demand for home goods will be less responsive to budget changes and so will the supply of labor and the cost of producing industrial goods.

The introduction of the benefit-side in no way alters our basic conclusion that the property tax system for the nation as a whole depresses the return on capital and changes the cost of capital to higher-tax communities and decreases the cost of capital to low-tax communities. However, it may be highly misleading in empirical work to classify cities into high-tax cities and low-tax cities and to make empirical judgments on the decrease or increase in land rents and wages on a city by city basis, solely on the basis of tax differentials. Endowments of capital per households vary between cities as do the relative amounts of income redistribution which occur in each jurisdiction. A consideration of the separate effects of taxes independently of expenditures is meaningful only with reference to an alternative source of tax finance.

Concluding Remarks

The principal conclusion of this paper is that the *system* of property taxes imposed by local governments decreases the overall return to capital by the average rate of tax in the nation as a whole, and changes the supply price of capital to different cities according to relationship of the specific rates relative to the mean rate of property tax. Cities with relatively high tax rate will pay for the services of capital, low tax rates result in a lower cost of capital.

Changes in the cost of capital lead to a reallocation of residential and industrial activities which in turn influence site values and the returns to other imperfectly mobile factors of production. The analysis of this paper suggests that changes in wage rates will be small in magnitude as labor is partially mobile and labor can be substituted for capital. Changes in land values are likely to be substantial but because of the low share of land rents in total costs are quite unlikely to approach increase sufficiently to offset the tax. Commodity prices will rise and I venture to guess that at least 75% of the burden of the tax differential falls on consumers, when capital is perfectly shiftable. In cities where the level of new construction is negligible tax increases will lead to a downward re-evaluation of the existing capital stock.[14]

NOTES

[1] The research described in this paper was carried out under grants from the National Science Foundation and from the Ford Foundation to the Cowles Foundation at Yale University.

² Marshall argued that a general property tax imposed in all communities would be shifted to consumers. On the other hand he believed that a partial tax, imposed in a single community, if not accompanied by improvements in public services, would fall on land owners as residents would move to escape the tax.

³ This question is complex and there are a wide range of possible outcomes. For example, if the rent on marginal urban land is equal to a fixed agricultural rent, a land tax on urban land rents will increase the cost of the marginal land by the amount of the tax, and the size of the city will decrease. If urban land rents are determined primarily by access to a central work place it is possible, depending on the nature of the demand for land services, that land rents at points close to the center of the city will fall even when the total cost of land services increases in the outskirts. This is due to the decrease in the total land area of the city, which decreases the relative advantage of the central areas. Of course the effects of the higher density of development may outweigh this effect.

⁴ Beck (1963) analyzed the effective property tax rate for about one hundred communities in Northeastern New Jersey and found effective tax rates varying from less than 1% to over 7%.

⁵ Changes in industrial location of industries are sluggish as industrial capital, especially structures, have long-lives. The immobility of capital raises the possibility that an increase in the property tax, *by a particular city,* on existing industrial capital will be capitalized which is contrary to the argument that the tax-induced increases in the cost of capital services will increase the cost of commodities produced in high tax jurisdictions. If different components of a firm's capital stock come up for replacement at different points in time, it may never pay to move as there will always be a large amount of complementary capital which has a useful economic life. However the choice of technique for the process under replacement will be based on a cost of capital calculation that reflects the higher property tax. Consequently as capital is replaced over time bit by bit the after-tax rate of return on capital will be restored to its previous level. These assumptions about the nature of depreciation and replacement help make the assumption of location specific industries a little more realistic.

⁶ In an earlier paper (Mieszkowski, 1970, p. 1110) I sketched an example which was designed to bring out Brown's major insight on the effects of property tax. Brown took exception to the view that a property (profits) tax on residential real estate is shifted to the consumer and argued that a tax on housing would shift capital out of housing and would be a tax on capital in the economy as a whole. Brown also pointed out that the small size of a taxed sector is not a sufficient reason for ignoring general equilibrium adjustments.

In our example, we assume an economy consisting of three groups, A, B, C. A property tax is imposed on apartment dwellings, a service consumed only by group A. Group C owns all of the capital, and originally 1% of the total capital stock is used as apartment buildings. With appropriate assumptions it is possible to show that the imposition of a tax on apartment buildings will decrease the after-tax rate of return on *all* capital by 1%. This means that total profits have decreased by the amount of the tax. Simultaneously the price of apartment units will increase by the amount of the tax. This means that in addition to the taxes collected by government the consumers of products other than the commodity subject to tax gain at the expense of capitalists. Brown's insistence that a tax on housing falls on the earnings of all capital through the shift of capital out of the capital-intensive housing sector can be at best partially correct when there exist substantial differences in the spending patterns among various income groups.

⁷ One of the unrealistic aspects of the assumption that rent on urban land is determined by the opportunity cost of land in agriculture is that in most communities agriculture is not a viable alternative as undeveloped land consists of a number of small scattered

plots. The value of urban land will be determined strictly by urban uses and taxes will play a role in the determination of the value of undeveloped urban land. In this connection it is important to note the work of Oates (1970) and Heinberg and Oates (1970) on the capitalization of property taxes. For a sample of cities in New Jersey and Massachusetts these studies find that the average values of owner-occupied houses in different towns are sensitive to expenditures on schools and varying tax burdens, and largely offset one another. For a given level of expenditures an increase of future tax payments of S1 (on a present value basis) will decrease the value of housing by exactly that amount. While there is some question whether the authors have "sorted out" various interdependences arising from the need of imposing higher taxes in poorer towns, these results suggest that the owners of capital bear the differential burden of property taxes. The fact that the tax is fully capitalized for owner-occupied housing implies that the implicit rents on these houses are determined independently of taxes (though they depend on the level of expenditures) and suggests that the tax burden of a property on rental housing falls on the landlord. If there is new construction in each town these results support the proposition that landowners bear the tax differential on improvements in addition to the taxes imposed on the value of land.

[8] The aggregation of home goods and industrial activities, into a single output omits an important feature, the possible differential change in the prices of the two broad commodity classes, home goods and exports. However, little is lost through the aggregation in understanding the effect of property taxes on factor prices, and the effects of different technologies on these changes.

[9] In carrying out the differentiation we make use of the convention that commodity and factor prices are originally equal to 1. Also because of the choice of capital as the numeraire, $dp_K = 0$. We make use of marginal productivity conditions and the assumption of constant returns to scale. For example in differentiating equation 1 we have $dX = f_{1L} \, dL + f_{1K} \, dK + f_{1R} \, dR$. Since factors are paid the value of their marginal products we can replace the partial derivatives f_{1L}, f_{1K} and f_{1R} with w, $pK + T$ and r, and divide both sides of the expression by X to obtain $dX/X = f_L \, (dL/L) + f_K \, (dK/K) + f_R \, (dR/R)$ where f_L, f_K, f_R are the original shares of labor, capital and land respectively. In differentiating the commodity demand and supply of labor relations we transform the partial derivatives to elasticities.

[10] The differentiation of equations 1–6 yields,

$$\frac{dX}{X} = f_L \frac{dL}{L} + f_K \frac{dK}{K} + f_R \frac{dR}{R} \, , \tag{1$'$}$$

$$\frac{dX}{X} = E_X \, dP_X \, , \tag{2$'$}$$

$$\frac{dK}{K} = a_{KL} \, dw + a_{KR} \, dr + a_{KK} \, dt + \frac{dX}{X} \, , \tag{3$'$}$$

$$\frac{dL}{L} = a_{LL} \, dw + a_{LK} \, dT + a_{LR} \, dr + \frac{dX}{X} \, , \tag{4$'$}$$

$$\frac{dL}{L} = E_L \, dw \, , \tag{5$'$}$$

$$dP_X = f_L \, dw + f_R \, dr + f_K \, dT \, . \tag{6$'$}$$

In order to eliminate the term dX/X from equation $(3')$ and $(4')$ and to introduce explicitly the partial elasticities of substitution for land we make use of the relation for the demand for land

$$\frac{dR}{R} = a_{RL}\, dw + a_{RR}\, dr + a_{RK}\, dT + \frac{dX}{X} = 0 \,. \tag{7'}$$

Subtracting $(7')$ from $(3')$ and $(4')$ and making the appropriate substitution in $(1')$ we obtain two equations in two unknowns dw/dT and dr/dT.

$$(f_K(a_{KL} - a_{RL}) + f_L E_L - E_X f_L)\frac{dw}{dt} + (f_K(a_{KR} - a_{RR} - E_X f_R)\frac{dr}{dT},$$
$$= (f_K E_X - f_K(a_{KK} - a_{RK}) \tag{1''}$$

and

$$(a_{LL} - a_{RL} - E_L)\frac{dw}{dT} + (a_{LR} - a_{RR})\frac{dr}{dT} = (a_{RK} - a_{LK}) \,. \tag{4''}$$

Solving these two equations for dw/dT and dr/dT we obtain relations (7) and (8) presented in the text above.

[11] Recall that I have assumed that a_{ij}, $i = j > 0$ so $(a_{LR} - a_{RR})$ and $(a_{KR} - a_{RR})$ are unambiguously positive. Also for the special case when land is used in fixed proportions with capital and labor, i.e. $a_{Ri} = 0$ expressions (7) and (8) simplify to $dw/dT = (a_{LK}(-E_X)f_R)/D' > 0$

$$\frac{dr}{dT} = \frac{-(f_K E_X - f_K a_{KK})(a_{LL} - E_L) - a_{LK}(f_K a_{KL} + f_L E_L - E_X f_L)}{D'} \,,$$

where $D' = (a_{LL} - E_L)E_X f_R \,.$

[12]   The overall share of wages in national income is about 70%. This leaves 30% to be divided between real capital and land. The balance sheets in statistics of Income Corporation Income Tax Returns (1966) show that for all corporations the value of land relative to the value of depreciable assets is about 13:1. For corporations in the real estate industry; an industry in which large inventories of land are held for development purposes, this ratio is about 3:1. From Netzer (1966) tables 2–7 we calculate the ratio of residential structures to private residential land to be about 7:1. On the basis of these data it seems safe to conclude that average capital rentals are at least five times the level of land rents.

[13]   A variant to this model is the case where all the owernship of land is very concentrated relative to its supply so that developers recognize the effect the size of their buildings will have on the price of floor space in this location and will set output at the level where marginal revenue) are equal. As long as there exists competitive bidding for the land all of the "monopoly profits" will accrue to land owners. For purposes of determining the effect of taxes on land rents the qualitative result for the "monopoly" model are essentially the same as for the competitive model.

[14]   When rate of capital accumulation is sensitive to the rate return on capital (we have assumed the stock of capital to be fixed throughout the paper) price of capital intensive goods would rise relative to other commodities. The change in the price of housing is equal to $f_K dp_K + f_L dp_L$, where f_K and f_L are the shares of capital and labor respectively in the

production of housing and dp_K, and dp_L are the changes in the cost of capital and labor respectively. Suppose the supply of capital is perfectly elastic with respect to the rate of return so a 2% general property tax will, in the long-run, increase the before-tax rate of return on capital by 25%. If capital is the only input in the provision of housing services, i.e. $dp_L = 0$ the price of housing increases by 25% relative to the "typical" (mean capital intensity) commodity. Of course the other basic effect of a decrease in the stock of capital is to decrease wages relative to what they would be in the case where capital is perfectly inelastic in supply.

REFERENCES

Allen, R.G.D., 1950, Mathematical analysis for economists (MacMillan, London).

Beck, Morris, 1963, Property taxation and urban land use in Northeastern New Jersey (research Monograph 7). (Urban Land Institute, Washington).

Brown, H.G., 1924, The economics of taxation (Holt, New York).

Edgeworth, F.Y., 1925, Papers relating to political economy (B. Franklin, New York).

Gillespie, W.I., 1965, Effects of public expenditures on the distribution of income, in: Essays in fiscal federalism, edited by R.A. Musgrave (Brookings Institution, Washington).

Heinberg, J.D. and W.E. Oates, 1970, The incidence of differential property taxes on urban housing: a Comment and some further evidence, National Tax Journal, 23 (March, 1970), pp. 92-99.

Marshall, A., 1890, Principles of economics, 8th edition, (MacMillan, London), Appendix G.

Marshall, A., 1897, Reply to the questionnaire of the royal commission on local taxation, 1897. Quoted by C.F. Bickerdike, 1902, Taxation of site values, Economic Journal 12, 472-484.

Mieszkowski, Peter, 1969, Tax incidence theory: the effects of taxes on the distribution of income, Journal of Economic Literature 7, 1103-1124.

Mills, E.S., 1967, An aggregative model of resource allocation in a metropolitan area, American Economic Association Papers and Proceedings 57, 197-210.

Musgrave, R.A., et al. 1951, Distribution of tax payments by income groups: a case study for 1948, National Tax Journal, 4, 1-53.

Muth, R.F., 1969, Cities and housing (University of Chicago Press, Chicago).

Netzer, R., 1966, Economics of the property tax (Brookings, Washington).

Netzer, R., 1968a, Impact of the property tax: its economic implications for urban problems, J.E.C. Print., 90th Congress, Washington.

Netzer, R., 1968b, Economic effects of the property tax, Research Report No. 1. Washington: National Commission on Urban Problems.

Oates, W.E., 1969, The effects of property taxes and local public spending on property values: an empirical study of tax capitalization and the Tiebout hypothesis, Journal of Political Economy 77, 957-71.

Pierson, N.G., 1902, Principles of economics, Vol. I (MacMillan, New York).

Richman, R.L., 1967, The incidence of urban real estate taxes under conditions of static and dynamic equilibrium, Land Economics 43, 172-180.

Richman, R.L., 1968, Hearings before the National Commission on urban problems, Vol. I. Washington: Government Printing Office, pp. 277-280.

Rolph, E.R., 1954, The Theory of fiscal economics (Ronald Press, New York).

Rolph, E.R. and G. Break, 1961, Public finance (Ronald Press, New York).

Simon, H.A., 1943, The incidence of a tax on urban real property, Quarterly Journal of Economics 57, 398-420.

Thompson, P., 1965, The property tax and the rate of interest, in: The American Property Tax, Claremont, California: The Lincoln School of Public Finance.

4

Taxes, Spending and Property Values

Supply Adjustment in a Tiebout-Oates Model

Matthew Edel and Elliott Sclar*

SUMMARY. *This paper extends the capitalization apprach of Wallace E. Oates to consider supply adjustment in a local public goods market of the sort hypothesized by Charles M. Tiebout. It is shown that Oates's single-period cross-section analysis-demonstrated demand conditions approximated Tiebout's hypotheses in a situation in which supply was not in long-run equilibrium. Analysis of capitalization of taxes, school expenditures, and road maintenance expenditures over five successive census periods in the Boston area indicates a move toward equilibrium in the market for schooling, but not in all other markets for local public goods.*

I

NEARLY 2 decades ago, Charles M. Tiebout (1956) proposed his well-known hypothesis that provision of local government services "reflects the preferences of the population more adequately than they can be reflected at the national level." In response to the arguments of Samuelson (1954) and Musgrave (1959) that no market test existed for the optimal level of (national) public goods output, Tiebout proposed a model under which a market analogue could lead to optimal expenditure on local public goods. The Tiebout model has since become a source of support for local fiscal autonomy, and is frequently cited in discussions of revenue sharing and in opposition to metropolitan consolidations.

*Queens College and Brandeis University. A preliminary version of this paper was presented at the annual meetings of the Western Economic Association, August 16, 1973. Research was funded by the Economics Division of the National Science Foundation and by the Center for the Study of Metropolitan Problems (Metro Center), National Institute of Mental Health. The comments of Ronald Grieson and the assistance of Eugene Kroch and Herman Thomas are acknowledged with thanks. *Journal of Political Economy*, 1974, vol. 82, no. 5.

This has been particularly the case since Wallace E. Oates's (1969) publication of an "empirical study of tax capitalization and the Tiebout hypothesis," which is often interpreted as confirming the Tiebout model.

This paper extends Oates's capitalization approach to consider supply adjustment in the local public goods market. We argue that Oates restated Tiebout's model into a simpler question of whether households have preferences for a tax-service mix. This formulation does not consider whether the supply of public service combinations approaches the elasticity required for the model to yield Tiebout's analogue to the perfectly competitive solution. Oates verified that consumer demand conforms to Tiebout's hypothesis. However, this result was found only because supply was not in long-run equilibrium. If supply conditions in all markets had attained the competitive equilibrium, no capitalization would have been measured.

To investigate further the dynamics of an Oates-type market, we relate house values to local taxes and service delivery over different time periods for the Boston area. For schooling, there was a movement toward competitive equilibrium between 1950 and 1970. However, both continued tax capitalization despite the declining capitalization of school-expenditure differentials, and the continuing failure of highway-expenditure differentials to be capitalized indicate that supply conditions are not moving toward equilibrium in the markets for all public services. These empirical findings indicate that the Tiebout hypothesis cannot be considered as verified for local public service markets in general but only for some particular local service markets.

II

We begin by considering the manner in which local service benefits might be capitalized into land values, or location rents for sites in different tax-service districts, in a system characterized by the Tiebout model. In particular, we may assume that Tiebout's first five assumptions either are met directly in the system we are considering, or affect land values in a purely additive manner if they are unmet. That is, we assume (1) mobility and (2) knowledge among a population of utility-maximizing residents, (3) sufficient numbers of communities to insure competition among them and the availability of communities for each consumer's taste, (4) absence of restrictions on location due to employment needs (or, at least, differentiation among communities on grounds of accessibility to jobs that will enter into land values as a simple function of distance), and (5) absence of externalities between communities from public services.

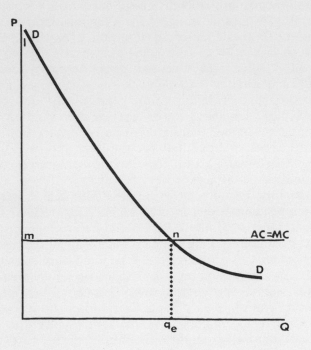

FIGURE 1.—Supply and demand in a market for secular junior high school educations.

Since we are assuming an analogue to a perfect market, point 3 implies that the residents of each town will be homogeneous with respect to their taste for each public service. Thus, for example, if education is provided, families without children, those with few children, and those with many children will be able to find towns fitting their needs and identical in all respects except for the provision of schooling. In addition, we begin with the assumption— which Tiebout approximates in the sixth and seventh conditions[1] — that constant returns to scale prevail in the provision of of service, or that, at least, equilibrium is possible with each town at a minimum-cost scale. For the empirical results presented later to hold it is also necessary to assume that funding is based on a local property tax rather than state or federal subsidies, which would add to benefits in some towns in a nonrandom manner.

In this situation, how will a market be represented in town provision of services? In figure 1, the cost of providing some public service (e.g., secular junior high school educations) is represented as $m/unit (where a unit is, say, a student educated); DD is the demand curve for these junior high school educations. Since the average cost is passed on to consumers as a local tax in towns with these schools, it appears to them as a price. As many people move to towns with schools as are willing to pay a tax of m per average number of children per family. Since average cost, tax per pupil, and marginal cost are all the same, the market result is efficient in that marginal demand (marginal utility) is equated to marginal cost. As long as either there are true constant returns to scale, or the quantity demanded q_e is multiple of the optimal size, minimum cost is also insured.

In this case, the consumers of secular public junior high schools will reap a total consumer surplus of lmn. The schools will cover their costs. But will there be a corresponding producers' surplus to be capitalized into land values? Assuming a sufficient number of towns that anyone can find an otherwise acceptable location either with or without a secular junior high school, no resident would offer an after-tax rent above that attributable to nonschool-oriented attributes of the town. Apart from the additional tax paid for the schools, no resident would pay more than anyone locating in a school-less town to avoid the tax because of a lack of children or a preference for religious junior high schools (which may collect their average costs under the name of tuition fees rather than taxes). As a result, there is neither an increment left to capitalize in land values nor a reduction in ground values caused by the tax.

By contrast, we may see what occurs if the number of towns with schools is strictly limited. In figure 2, the assumption is made that only two towns have junior high schools, when it would require three towns to hold all of the people who would wish to use them, assuming prices were set equal to the average educational cost within those two towns. In this case, the effective supply curve is mnsS' and the market-clearing price is r. Assuming the towns simply try to cover school costs with their taxes rather than making a profit for the public fisc, average taxes will be m, and a consumer's surplus of mrlsn would be available for those lucky enough to reside in those towns. However, the oversupply of would-be residents at price m would be expected to drive the price up to r. In this case, the area mnsr would represent the portion of consumer benefits captured by land rents. There would be, here, net capitalization of a portion of school benefits above real average costs. On the other hand, if a third town were then to open a school—at the same cost

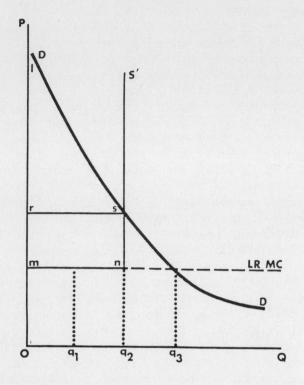

FIGURE 2.—A market for schools with supply restricted to two towns

per pupil m—land value capitalization would disappear. The eventual
situation would be as in figure 1, with the prior capitalization a temporary phenomenon due to the quicker approach to equilibrium by
the first towns to open schools. Thus, if there are long-run constant
returns to scale in service provision, an equilibrium can be approached
as in the Tiebout model, but as that equilibrium is reached differential land values will be removed.

Relaxation of the assumption of constant returns alters the result
only slightly. In figure 3, average and marginal costs rise with the
number of users or the amount of the service provided. Such a
situation may arise if production of the service uses scarce resources
other than land (as in the case of health service provision if the
supply of doctors and nurses is not perfectly elastic). If the service
is sold at its marginal cost, as in a private goods market, the market
will insure optimal resource allocation. There will be a producer's
surplus lrs. This producer's surplus will take the form of land values,

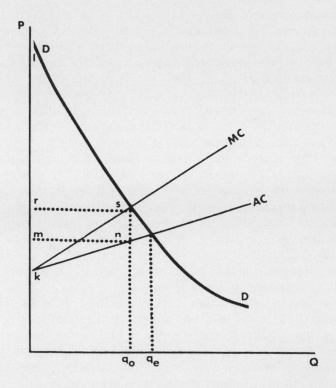

FIGURE 3.—A market for medical facilities with doctors a scarce good

if one has to be a landowner to supply the service, as Grieson (1971) shows is the case for services of buildings. If, however, the service is paid for through taxation, hence sold on an average cost basis, the quantity purchased would be q_e, and while consumer's surplus would be greater producer's surplus would be eliminated. Nor would any of the consumer's surplus be capitalized into land values, for the prospective consumers would all be in equilibrium, paying only a price (the tax) equal to marginal utility (marginal demand).

Capitalization will occur if some nonprice mechanism is used to limit demand to q_0, the optimal quantity at which demand intersects marginal cost. If, for example, zoning is used to limit entry into the school district, but taxes continue to cover average costs alone, then, for those consumers able to enter, marginal benefits will be at the level r while tax costs will equal m. The difference will be left as a pure consumer surplus (mnrs in addition to the original lrs) to families allowed in, if rationing (e.g., racial discrimination) is used to limit entry. However, if land is sold on a market, subject only to a density-zoning constraint, then the price per user must rise to r, and the area mnrs is left capitalized into land values. (This area is equal to the producer's surplus krs in the case of market sale of the service itself.)

In short, if only one service at a time is considered, the first five assumptions of the Tiebout model lead to a situation in which, at equilibrium, there is no capitalization effect. [Taxes cover costs simply, and there is neither a net increment in land values from the presence of the service nor a decrease from the presence of the tax.] Since the tax is a form of average-cost pricing of the service, the equilibrium may or may not be Pareto optimal. In the case of constant returns to scale, presence of capitalization indicates inefficiency. If there are decreasing returns to scale, the presence of positive capitalization is compatible with efficiency (although it does not guarantee that a situation of efficiency exists).[2] In the case of increasing returns to scale, by a similar argument, the provision of efficient service levels financed out of average-cost local taxation would involve negative capitalization.[3] But in these last two cases, efficiency (if it were to exist) would require methods of limiting or attracting entrants to the community through methods not foreseen in the Tiebout model. Zoning might, in this case, make a situation either more or less optimal. To show that there is capitalization in a model with only one public service thus fails to show that a Tiebout mechanism has assured either equilibrium or efficiency.

The situation is more complex if different public services are present within a system of competing towns (see Buchanan and Goetz 1972). In this case, if some services are in equilibrium and some not in equilibrium, different total levels of taxation may be associated with different levels of land values, and presence of services whose provision and financing are in equilibrium may appear to be associated with higher land values. Suppose one service (let us say schooling) is provided by a Tiebout system that is in equilibrium, but there are other services which are not provided in equilibrium. The difference between marginal demand and average cost for these other services will be capitalized. If, however, a comparison of towns, using regression analysis, treats the total tax rate as a single variable, then the net noncapitalization of school taxes and expenditures may appear as offsetting positive capitalization of the expenditures and negative capitalization of the taxes. That is, by comparing the school taxes with other taxes that are unmatched by benefits, the two elements of capitalization are conceptually separable. But if average-cost taxes and marginal benefits are equal in the provision of all services, there will be no way of making this separation by comparison of the towns. If the Tiebout model held perfectly (at least in its first five assumptions) for all services, a regression analysis relating land values to taxes and service levels, holding other background conditions constant, would show no capitalization of any taxes or services.

III

The preceding discussion has indicated that a world in which the conditions of the Tiebout model were met perfectly would see no tax and local expenditure capitalization into property values. Oates sought to demonstrate the "relevance to actual behavior" of the Tiebout model by a demonstration of capitalization using New Jersey data for 1960. His linking of an observable quantity, property value, to the Tiebout model is a fruitful step in public finance theory. However, the version of the Tiebout model which Oates tests is oversimplified.

Tiebout, it will be remembered, presented his theory as a response to the Musgrave-Samuelson agreement that "no 'market type' solution exists to determine the level of expenditures on public goods. Seemingly we are faced with the problem of having a rather large portion of our national income allocated in a 'non-optimal' way when compared with the private sector" (Tiebout 1956). Indeed, his very title was a play on Samuelson's 1954 article. Tiebout's paper sought to show that, at least conceptually (under what he admitted were "extreme assumptions"), a "market type" solution might allow the optimal provision of public services out of local taxes.

Oates, on the other hand, simplifies the Tiebout model into a statement about consumer demand only, with no supply side made explicit, and no optimality issue raised: "Very simply, Tiebout's world is one in which the consumer 'shops' among different communities offering varying packages of local public services and selects as a residence the community which offers the tax-expenditure program best suited to his tastes" (Oates 1969, p. 957). His results, therefore, are never compared with the results predicted from a full Tiebout model. They are, rather, a demonstration that taxes and services have some effect on consumer preferences for town of residence, which is reflected in house prices. The tax and service capitalization which Oates finds would not occur if consumers

were completely indifferent to services and taxes, had no information about their differences among towns, or succeeded in passing
all local taxes on completely to the federal government in reduced
income taxes. Oates eliminates these possibilities, demonstrating
the individual economic rationality of the home buyer.[4] But his
results also would not occur if the pure theory as presented by Tiebout were a complete description for all local service markets.

In the specific case of school expenditures, Oates calculates,
using "typical" values, that the amount of decrease in home values
from capitalization of approximately two-thirds of a 1 percent tax
rate increase would roughly equal the increase in home prices from
the spending of the money raised on an average school. The calculation is presented "as indicating no more than orders of magnitude"
and as a suggestion that, tax and expenditure capitalization being
equal, the market for schooling may be in Tiebout's equilibrium.
However, if the interest rate used for capitalization or the two-
thirds rate of capitalization were different, the lack of net capitalization of schooling would not hold. A Tiebout equilibrium for
education is thus demonstrated only on the basis of strong assumptions, while that at least one sector of town expenditures must be
out of equilibrium is conclusively demonstrated by the finding of any
capitalization. A similar result follows from the similar finding of capitalization by Heinberg and Oates (1970) using 1960 Massachusetts
data.

Oates concludes from his analysis: "These results appear consistent with a model of the Tiebout variety in which rational consumers weight (to some extent at least) the benefits from local
public services against the cost of their tax liability in choosing a
community of residence; people do appear willing to pay more to
live in a community which provides a high-quality of public services (or in a community which provides the same program of public
services with lower tax rates)" (Oates 1969, p. 968). This conclusion
is warranted, but it is incomplete. "A model of the Tiebout variety"
as used by Oates does not consider the elasticity or inelasticity of
supply and hence whether the welfare-economic implications of
Tiebout's original model hold. By introducing the analysis of
capitalization into the discussion of Tiebout's model, Oates has
taken a significant step. However, it is necessary to go beyond his
single-period measure of capitalization to examine changes in
capitalization during supply adjustment in order to determine
whether a Tiebout equilibrium is being approached. In the following
section, Oates's capitalization approach is used to examine such a
historical process.

IV

Examination of data on house values and public finance for a group of towns in the Boston metropolitan area over several decades allows such an examination of the supply-adjustment capitalization process.[5] Boston area data provide an appropriate test because of the extreme dependence of towns in that vicinity on the local property tax for financing services. In Massachusetts, 54 percent of local expenditures were financed from this tax as of 1970, as compared to a 40 percent national average. Highway and educational mainten-ance expenditures, the two funding categories to be considered in detail, have particularly low levels of outside aid. The figure for highway expenditures, it should be noted, does not include con-struction of new roads or highways, for which outside funding is considerable, but only their upkeep, which is a considerable expense in a snow-affected area like New England.

Using a somewhat different sample from the Massachusetts data than Heinberg and Oates, we estimated regressions of a somewhat similar form to theirs, for the 5 census years beginning with 1930. These regressions use six distance variables (latitudinal distance from downtown Boston, longitudinal distance, and their squares and cubes) rather than a single accessibility variable. A variable for per-square-mile highway maintenance expenditures is a second form of public expenditure, along with school expenditures per pupil, whose capitalization into house values is tested. Density and percentage of owner occupiers among residents of a town are used to capture amenity factors not explained by distance. The homeownership term may also capture the shifting of property tax through federal income tax deductions. Tax rates are nominal rates for 1930-60, and both nominal and equalized rates are employed in separate regressions for 1970.

Estimated coefficients appear in table 1 and are superficially similar to Oates's findings for the postwar period. Tax-rate capitali-zation is negative in all years and significant for 1940, 1950, and 1970. School expenditures per pupil are capitalized positively in all 3 postwar census years. However, for 1960 and 1970, the effect is not statistically significant at the .01 level and is quantitatively smaller than for 1950. For 1930 and 1940 the school-expenditure term is not significant, and indeed the sign is negative. The highway-maintenance expenditures are not significantly capitalized in any period.

The regressions appear to show somewhat weaker capitalization than Oates's examples. Assuming a $21,000 house with a tax rate of $50 per $1,000 (a typical figure 5 miles north or south of the city in the 1970 regressions), a $10 reduction in the effective tax rate would amount to a $210 reduction in taxes. Capitalized at an 8 percent interest rate, this would amount to a $2,625 increase in value, about twice the observed increase given by the regression estimate. In other words, tax capitalization in this case would be about 50 percent, rather than the two-thirds found by Oates. Perhaps more important than this difference is the declining payoff in house values from each dollar per pupil spent on schools: the capitalization falls from almost $24 in 1950 to under $9 in 1960 and about $3 in 1970. At first glance, this might appear to show that Bostonians are less concerned with education and taxes than are Oates's New Jersey residents and that they are becoming less concerned with schools over time.

An alternative explanation suggests an approach, over time, to a Tiebout equilibrium in the provision of schooling. According to Hirsch (1968), schooling is a service which can be provided efficiently by relatively small units. Economies of scale exist only up to sizes of perhaps a few hundred pupils for elementary schools and 1,700 for secondary schools. These sizes are within the population range of most Boston area communities; the few that are too small to support high schools can easily form consolidated high school districts. There are also sufficient independent towns in each geographic region of the Standard Metropolitan Statistical Area to allow consumer choice between towns with expensive schools and towns with low school expenditures which attract childless individuals or parents preferring private and parochial schools. (Among the higher-income communities, the comparison between Brookline and Belmont is most obvious.) The conditions cited by Tiebout as assumptions in his model might thus seem to hold for schools. This explanation is consistent with the 1970 regressions: assuming each family, on the average, has three children of school age, $1.00 per pupil spent by the schools would represent a $3.00 benefit to the family (if taxes and other community and housing characteristics are held constant). The $3.00 increase in house values, is thus an approximation to a simple capitalization of the benefits, which would be matched exactly by an offsetting loss of $3.00 *if* families paid average cost through taxes and if taxes were fully capitalized. In practice, the equilibrium is not exactly obtained: tax capitalization appears only partial, the average (although perhaps not the marginally moving) family has less than three children, and some school expenditures are borne by state and federal aid rather than local property taxes.

TABLE 1

Regression Estimates of Effect of Taxes, School and Road Expenditures, and Other Variables on House Prices

Year	Tax Rate ($/$1,000)	Density (Pop./Sq. Mile)	Owner Occupied	School Expenditures ($/Pupil)	Highway Maintenance ($/Sq.Mile)	R^2 (n)
1930....	−503 (1.31)	0.050 (0.73)	n.a.	−2.31 (0.28)	−0.006 (0.44)	.349 (78)
1940....	−651 (2.49)	−0.015 (0.33)	−5.01 (0.40)	−3.55 (0.67)	−5.01 (0.40)	.355 (77)
1950....	−811 (3.03)	−0.017 (0.17)	52.48 (1.99)	23.68 (4.08)	−0.009 (0.49)	.648 (77)
1960....	−126 (0.54)	−0.400 (2.56)	0.001 (0.03)	8.77 (1.59)	0.008 (0.54)	.376 (73)
1970....	−43.3 (2.18)	−0.374 (1.49)	86.67 (1.41)	2.99 (1.48)	0.012 (0.74)	.546 (65)
1970*..	−139.0* (2.06)	−0.211 (0.59)	127.87 (2.10)	3.25 (1.60)	0.023 (1.39)	.551 (64)

Note: These are values of b from regressions in which latitudinal and longitudinal distance and their squares and cubes were also independent variables. House value is measured in dollars from census estimates of town medians. (Values of t are in parentheses.)
* Using equivalent tax rates (other regressions use nominal tax rates).

Nonetheless, comparing the 3 years—1950, 1960, and 1970—it is the low capitalization figure for school expenditures in 1970 that is approximately consistent with a Tiebout equilibrium.

But what, then, of the higher capitalization in benefits for 1950 and 1960? It would appear that these represent higher returns due to a shortage of schools. A situation obtains such as that in figure 2 rather than figure 1; due to limited supply the marginal demand for schooling is far above the average cost. Beginning in the early postwar period, that is to say, there appears to have been a shortage of adequate quantities and qualities of schools, given the baby boom, the rising need for technical skills in the labor force, and the much-noted shortage of teachers and school facilities. In this situation, parents would pay far more than the actual average cost of schooling through increased house prices in order to enter a community with what they considered to be adequate educational facilities. By 1960, the shortage was somewhat reduced from the 1950 level, and capitalization of per-pupil expenditures had declined somewhat. By 1970, there appears to have been very little markup, if any, left. The comparison of the three periods thus seems to be much like the movement from a short-run to a long-run equilibrium in Marshallian economics.[6]

Tiebout's model thus seems to have been a fair representation of the schooling market in the Boston area by 1970. Oates, measuring returns in 1960 both for New Jersey and (with Heinberg) for Massachusetts, would seem to have found greater returns because he took a cross-section view before equilibrium was achieved. His speculation that "it could be . . . the negative association we have observed between property taxes and home values is primarily a short-run phenomenon, which would disappear over a longer period of time" (Oates 1969, p. 967) has thus been borne out. Indeed the logic of the Tiebout model indicates this should occur in an approach to equilibrium.

The figures in table 1 also indicate, however, that while the provision of schooling may have approached a Tiebout equilibrium, the same could not have been true for all other local services. In 1970 tax rates (whether viewed in real or nominal terms) significantly affected house values, even though they were not 100 percent capitalized. What is more, local road-maintenance expenditures were not positively capitalized to a statistically significant extent in any period, although some positive effect is found for 1970. If all expenditures were in a Tiebout equilibrium, taxes should not have been capitalized, while, since taxes were capitalized, road maintenance should have had positive effects on house values if it had positive benefits from a consumer viewpoint. Thus not all markets can be in Tiebout equilibria, and the road-maintenance market appears likely as a candidate to be out of equilibrium.

Road expenditures are as clear an example of violation of Tiebout's conditions as schools are a conforming example. Neither are there clear constant returns to scale, nor is there an absence of spillovers. Indeed, in the Boston area, highway-maintenance expenditures appear mainly related to the flow-through of traffic and population density. Highway expenses in dollars per square mile (HXP) for 1964 are explained by the regression:

$$HXP = 34857 + 31.62 \text{ FLOW} + 11.27 \text{ RES } (R^2 = .784),$$
$$(10.01) \qquad (10.94)$$

where FLOW = commuter flow-through per square-mile area, and RES = residual population density estimated from:

$$DENSITY = 2567 + 4.00 \text{ FLOW } (R^2 = .631).$$
$$(10.29)$$

Addition of a term for median per-family income has no significant effect. Inner-ring communities must maintain roads through which out-of-town commuters pass although their residents get few benefits. Only a few road expenses, such as frequency of snow removal in winter on side streets, are really optional expenses that may rise with income or local preference. Thus, differences in road-maintenance expenditures do not represent a response to demand differences, as in the Tiebout model, and are not capitalized.[7] The same is true for some other road-related services such as traffic-police expenditure and contributions to the Metropolitan District Commission highway system.

Thus, despite the movement toward a Tiebout-type equilibrium for schooling, there appear to be public service markets (including road maintenance, for one) which do not show movement toward such an equilibrium. The Tiebout hypothesis appears to hold for some public service markets. But, since it does not hold for all of them, prudence (reinforced by the general theory of the second best) would caution against acceptance of the notion that a "market-type" mechanism of the Tiebout sort has beneficial efficiency properties if applied to all public services taken together, as compared with any possible alternative systems of public-expenditure determination for metropolitan areas.

NOTES

[1] The actual assumptions used by Tiebout are (6) that for each pattern of consumer wants there is an optimal community size (which yields least costs), and (7) that communities try to attain the optimal size to minimize average costs.

[2] The Pareto optimal situation in this case may involve a more unequal distribution of benefits than a case of "inefficient" oversupply of the service where nobody is excluded by nonmarket means. The problems involved in applying the Tiebout model to cases of income redistributing public services are explored by Rothenberg (1969, 1970) and by Miller and Tabb (1973).

[3] One parallel to this is Goldberg's (1970, 1972) demonstration that a transportation system under certain assumptions is most efficient if it minimizes land values (see also Edel 1971).

[4] Other studies have used analyses of price responsiveness to demonstrate that peasants are "rational" (for discussion see Edel 1970).

[5] This study is part of a longer historical examination of factors influencing Boston-area property values.

[6] The explanation for the negative capitalization of school expenditures for 1930 and 1940 may be that, because of the depression, some communities were left with school average costs above marginal benefits, which they were unable to reduce.

[7] Further discussion of commuter-related expenses is found in Sclar (1971).

REFERENCES

Buchanan, J.M., and Goetz, C.J. "Efficiency Limits of Fiscal Mobility: An Assessment of the Tiebout Model." *J. Public Econ.* 1 (April 1972): 25-43.

Edel, M. "Innovative Supply: A Weak Point in Economic Development Theory." *Soc. Sci. Information* 9 (June 1970): 9-40.

————."Land Values and the Costs of Urban Congestion: Measurement and Distribution." *Soc. Sci. Information* 10 (December 1971): 7-36.

Goldberg, M.A. "Transportation, Urban Land Values, and Rents: A Synthesis." *Land Econ.* 46 (May 1970): 153-63.

————. "An Evaluation of the Interaction between Urban Transport and Land Use Systems," *Land Econ.* 48 (November 1972): 338-46.

Grieson, R. "The Economics of Property Taxes and Land Values." Massachusetts Inst. Tech., Department of Economics Working Paper, 1971.

Heinberg, J.D., and Oates, W.E. "The Incidence of Differential Property Taxes on Urban Housing." *Nat. Tax J.* 23 (March 1970): 92-98.

Hirsch, W.Z. "The Supply of Urban Public Services." In *Issues in Urban Economics,* edited by H.S. Perloff and L. Wingo, Jr. Baltimore: Johns Hopkins Univ. Press, 1968.

Miller, S., and Tabb, W.K. "A New Look at a Pure Theory of Local Expenditures." *Nat. Tax J.* 26 (June 1973): 161-76.

Musgrave, R.A. *The Theory of Public Finance.* New York: McGraw-Hill, 1959.

Oates, W.E. "The Effects of Property Taxes and Local Spending on Property Values: An Empirical Study of Tax Capitalization and the Tiebout Hypothesis." *J.P.E.* 77 (November/December 1969): 957-71.

Rothenberg, J. "Strategic Interaction and Resource Allocation in Metropolitan Intergovernmental Relations." *A.E.R.* 59 (May 1969): 495-503.

————. "Local Decentralization and the Theory of Optimal Government." In *The Analysis of Public Output,* edited by J. Margolis. New York: Columbia Univ. Press (for Nat. Bur. Econ. Res.), 1970.

Samuelson, P.A. "The Pure Theory of Public Expenditures," *Rev. Econ. and Statis.* 36 (November 1954): 387-89.

Sclar, E. "The Public Financing of Transportation in the Greater Boston Area." Ph.D. dissertation, Tufts Univ., 1971.

Tiebout, C.M. "A Pure Theory of Local Expenditures." *J.P.E.* 65 (October 1956): 416-24.

5

Capitalization of Intrajurisdictional Differences in Local Tax Prices

U NTIL the recent work of Peter Mieszkowski, most economists regarded the property tax as simply one more example
of an excise tax which drove a wedge between purchase and
sale price, thus generating a deadweight loss. Problems of unequal
assessment aside, the question of progressivity was to be answered
by measuring the income elasticity of expenditure on housing
(which is of course identical to the income elasticity of demand if
the price elasticity of demand is unity).

But as Mieszkowski (1969, 1972a) pointed out, this analysis
ignored some of the salient features of the property tax. First,
property taxes are levied on a large fraction of the capital stock in
the United States, which suggests that the tax might depress the
rate of return on capital, leaving the value of capital assets unchanged. Second, rates of property taxation vary substantially
across localities and activities. These variations in tax rates, Mieszkowski argued, would be capitalized into the values of the assets.

The Mieszkowski work is widely and deservedly regarded as an
important step forward in the analysis of the property tax. Starting
from this base, I wish to argue that we need to make two additional
steps before the analysis is complete. The first step follows the work
of Charles Tiebout, which suggests that people "shop" among
jurisdictions for their most preferred bundle of public services. If
this is correct, then it is interjurisdictional differences in tax rates
relative to public sector benefits which should be capitalized into
property values, rather than just tax rate differentials as Mieszkowski
suggests.

Second, it is necessary to consider the market adjustment implications of these capitalization effects. If relative asset prices are

* The Urban Institute and The Johns Hopkins University. I wish to thank
Bela Balassa, Gail Cook, Peter Mieszkowski, Jurg Niehans, and especially Herbert
Mohring for helpful comments on earlier drafts. Copyright © 1976, American
Economic Association. *American Economic Review* **66** (No. 5): 743-753, 1976.
Reprinted by permission.

disturbed by tax and benefit capitalization we should expect the asset-price changes to generate subsequent changes in relative supplies, which would in turn generate second-round price changes. In other words, the Mieszkowski capitalization story, even if it properly accounted for the services which are financed out of property taxes, is incomplete in that it does not describe a market equilibrium. This can be seen by noting that a capitalization effect is a shift in the demand curve for an asset. We cannot say how this demand curve shift will influence prices until we know the supply elasticities of the various assets.

In this paper I develop a model in which the excess of local public sector benefits over tax liability (or fiscal surplus) causes shifts in the demand curves for various classes of residential property. The supply-adjustment forces generated by these shifts are examined, and the possibility of nonmarket interference such as zoning is considered. The model is used to generate statements about market distortions or the lack thereof, and the progressivity of the tax/benefit package under a variety of circumstances.

The model does not consider the profits tax effects addressed by Mieszkowski, and to this extent the incidence and progressivity analysis is incomplete. Rather, the discount rate is taken as given, and the possibility that the property tax itself is a determinant of the discount rate is not considered. Also, the model is restricted to a consideration of residential property. Although I have not as yet done so, I believe an extension to taxation of nonresidential property would be straightforward, and some of these effects will be considered briefly here.

It is reasonably self-evident that a property tax in a system of communities which are homogeneous with respect to house value is in fact a system of average-cost prices for public services (assuming every household receives the same amount of public services).[1] Efficient[2] supplies of all housing-public service combinations are achieved when house values vary across communities *only* in accordance with the scarcity value of the inputs into housing. (This position is argued by Matthew Edel and Elliot Sclar, George Peterson, forthcoming, and the author, forthcoming.)

In this paper I will argue that there are important circumstances in which property taxation constitutes average-cost pricing for local public services even if communities are not homogeneous.[3] Occupants of inexpensive houses, with their low tax liabilities, might well be paying as much (or more) for their local fiscal benefits as are occupants of larger more expensive houses in the same community.

This can occur as a result of the capitalization of differential fiscal surpluses into property values. Thus inexpensive houses pay, in addition to their low taxes, a positive capitalization premium on the value of their houses, and conversely high income houses sell at a discount to offset the negative fiscal surplus attached to their property.

I. Capitalization and Horizontal Equity

As there seems to be some confusion in both the popular and professional literature, it is perhaps wise to begin by establishing the following basic proposition: if differential fiscal surpluses are capitalized into demand curves for property, there can be no horizontal inequity in a static world. Horizontal equity and capitalization are essentially two ways of saying the same thing. For they are both statements of the proposition that a given bundle of goods (housing-plus-public service, in this case) must command the same price[4] everywhere. If two otherwise identical bundles carry different tax liabilities, this difference must be made up by an offsetting difference in the capital value of the houses. There is a considerable body of literature on urban public finance which ignores this simple horizontal equity principle; most notably the cumulative-central city-decay work of David Bradford and Harry Kelejian, and discussions of such decay phenomena by James Heilbrun. In various forms, all of these authors argue that central city tax base declines, as distinct from public service declines, have led to increased migration to suburbs.

But if full capitalization occurs, a high tax base is on net no more desirable than a low tax base, since the favorable tax base will be capitalized into the property values. This means that tax base deterioration cannot explain city-suburb migration. (It is rational, however, to migrate from one jurisdiction to another so as to receive the most preferred public service bundle.) Stated most simply, a household can obtain access to a favorable tax base (i.e., a property with a positive fiscal surplus) only at a fair market price. Therefore, it is difficult to see how tax-base decay could induce rational people to move out of a city. It is true that such decay will impose a loss on property owners, but this loss will be realized whether the owner sells (as a capital loss) or stays (as higher taxes).

Among other things this suggests that a portion of the rationale for the famous Serrano Decision of the California Supreme Court is faulty. Contrary to the language of the decision, it would appear that the quality of a child's education is *not* a function of his neigh-bors' wealth.[5] It is important to note that we are discussing only horizontal equity; thus we have not addressed the question of whether *all* members of some economic class are discriminated against.

II. Arbitrage

I begin this section by describing the relationships among property values which are enforced by arbitrage. These conditions will be satisfied, regardless of the supply mix of housing, so long as people are on their demand curves, and so long as fiscal surplus differentials are capitalized into demand curves. Once these relationships are established, we will explore the characteristics of various supply configurations, with particular emphasis on the relationship between the Pareto efficient and the perfect competition outcomes.

The model describes a system of jurisdictions in an urban area, that is, in a single housing-market area. Arbitrage, of course, works within markets but not across markets which are isolated from one another.

Throughout the paper I emphasize the special case where each jurisdiction levies a proportional property tax, but extensions to non-proportional taxes are straightforward.

Consider an urban area containing many communities. There are two types of housing, high income housing (HIH) and low income housing (LIH) (the extension to n types is straightforward). Each community i has some fraction, a_i, of its housing units devoted to LIH, with $(1 - a_i)$ being HIH. There is no nonresidential property. Initially we assume that every community provides, and every household demands, the same level X of the local public service, but this assumption will be relaxed shortly. Further, it is assumed that every jurisdiction levies a proportional property tax which raises just enough revenue to finance X.

Capitalization effects are generated by the deviation of the value of a given property from the tax base per household in the juris-diction. For example, a $30,000 house in a jurisdiction with a $50,000 per household tax base receives a positive fiscal surplus, whereas the same house would receive a negative surplus if it were located in a community with a $20,000 tax base. The tax base, and thus the value of individual houses, will depend upon the mix of HIH and LIH in the framework below.

We assume (for purposes of illustration only) the existence of a homogeneous LIH, and a homogeneous HIH community. In each of these communities, tax liability equals public service provision and there is no fiscal surplus (hence no capitalization effect).

Let us now examine the relationship between the value of LIH and HIH in a mixed community, as compared with values of the two housing types in the homogeneous communities. The value of HIH in the mixed community is given by:

(1) $H_i = H' + (X - H_i t_i) D$

where
$H_i =$ the value of the HIH dwelling unit in community i;
$H' =$ the value of the same structure in a homogeneous HIH community;
$X =$ the per household expenditure on local public service;
$t_i =$ community i's property tax rate;
$D =$ the discount factor which converts a constant annual stream into a present value.

The dwelling unit's tax liability is $H_i t_i$ (with t_i to be determined below). Its tax liability in the homogeneous community is simply X, the per household public-service provision. The difference between these two figures is the fiscal surplus which accures to a house by virtue of its location in a mixed community. The present value of this term is added to the market value of the house in a homogeneous community in order to obtain the value it can command in the mixed community.

A similar equation expresses the value of LIH as a function of the tax rate

(2) $L_i = L' + (X - L_i t_i) D$

where L_i is the value of an LIH house in i, and L' is the value of the same house in a homogeneous LIH community, and other terms are defined above. But in the case of LIH, in a mixed community, $L_i t_i$ is less than X, the per household public service cost, so this term will raise the value of LIH.

Since the property tax must rajse a fixed amount of revenue per household, the tax rate is determined by the tax base which in turn is determined by the mix of house value types in the community:

(3) $t_i = X/(a_i L_i + (1 - a_i) H_i)$

where a_i is the fraction of the housing stock that is LIH. This equation simply states that the tax rate is the ratio of the per household public service expenditure to mean house value.

We can now solve this system to obtain equations expressing each of the endogenous variables (L_i, H_i, t_i) in terms of the other variables of the system.

$$(1')\ H_i = \frac{H' + DX}{1 + [DX/(a_i L' + (1 - a)H')]}$$

$$= \frac{H'(1 + DX/H')}{1 + [DX/(a_i L' + (1 - a_i)H')]}$$

$$(2')\ L_i = \frac{L' + DX}{1 + [DX/(a_i L' + (1 - a_i)H')]}$$

$$= \frac{L'(1 + DX/L')}{1 + [DX/(a_i L' + (1 - a_i)H')]}$$

$$(3')\ t_i = X/(a_i L' + (1 - a_i)H')$$

The tax base per household which I shall call B is equal to tax revenues per household (equal to X given the balanced budget assumption), divided by the tax rate t_i. Solving equation (3) we see that the tax base is equal to $a_i L_i + (1 - a_i) H_i$. Since this is the community mean house value, it is exactly what the tax base ought to be. But we now note that a similar solution of equation (3') tells us that the community's tax base is equal to $a_i L' + (1 - a_i)H'$, which is the mean value of the community's housing stock exclusive of capitalization effects. This implies that capitalization effects must net (or sum) to zero in any community; that any gain in the aggregate value of LIH must be offset by an identical loss in the value of HIH.[6] This fact serves to point up an important characteristic of capitalization effects which are generated by differences in house value mix: They are transfers from the value of one house within a jurisdiction to another, and as such they net to zero. This follows from the fact that, within a community, fiscal surpluses must sum to zero.[7]

We can rewrite equations $(1')$ – $(3')$ as

$$(1'') \qquad H_i \;=\; H'\left(\frac{1 + DX/H'}{1 + DX/B}\right)$$

$$(2'') \qquad L_i \;=\; L'\left(\frac{1 + DX/L'}{1 + DX/B}\right)$$

$$(3'') \qquad t_i \;=\; X/B_i$$

These equations give the relationship among, for example, HIH property values across jurisdictions with different tax bases, and tell us rather obviously that the value of each property type rises as the tax base rises. Although we have emphasized tax base variation due to differences in the mix of housing types across communities, it should be noted in passing that these equations also describe the relationships across communities if tax base variations are due to differences in the amount of nonresidential property.

The arbitrage forces underlying equations $(1'')$ – $(3'')$ enable us to say how the value of each property type changes as the tax base changes, but it yields no information on the level of property values. In other words we know the derivative of the function relating property value to tax base, but not the intercept (H' and L' are arbitrary). We do not know how expensive each type of housing is, but only that it is equally expensive everywhere. The price of (say) HIH plus X can be determined only by an explicit consideration of supply and demand, and this consideration will lead us to our conclusions about efficiency and vertical equity.

III. Capitalization and Efficiency

We stated at the outset that efficiency requires that land value be equal (*ceteris paribus*) in all homogeneous communities. Under these circumstances a contemplated move from LIH to HIH will carry a cost exactly equal to the resource cost difference between the two types of structure (and in both homogeneous communities the tax liability will be just equal to the public service resource cost).

But if people face an efficient set of constraints as between the housing in a homogeneous LIH community and a homogeneous HIH community, they face exactly the same (efficient) constraints

for a contemplated move from *any* LIH unit in the entire system
of communities to any HIH unit. This follows from the assumption
that capitalization will render all LIH (and similarly all HIH) units
in the entire system of communities equally desirable.

Equations $(1'') - (3'')$ now enable us to establish the relationship
between LIH property value and HIH property value in a mixed
community on the assumption that land values are equalized across
homogeneous communities.[8] Equation $(1'')$ reveals that, in a mixed
community, H will fall short of H' since B (the tax base) is less than
H' (which implies that the numerator of the expression in brackets
is smaller than the denominator). By similar reasoning, L exceeds
L'. (The tax base, being a weighted average of H' and L', must fall
between H' and L', and that is sufficient to cause $H < H'$ and
$L > L'$.)

But H' and L' have been set such that land commands the same
price in both activities. If in the mixed community $H < H'$ then land
devoted to HIH in the mixed community must be less valuable than
land in the homogeneous HIH community, and similarly land
devoted to LIH in the mixed community must be more valuable
than land in the homogeneous LIH community.[9] The value of HIH
land in the mixed community must be depressed relative to its
value in the homogeneous HIH community so as to compensate
the owner for the higher tax liability, and the value of LIH land in
the mixed community must be higher than in the homogeneous LIH
community. But if supplies of the two types of housing are efficient,
that is, if land commands the same price in both homogeneous communities, then land devoted to LIH in the mixed community must
command a higher price than otherwise identical land devoted to
HIH in the same community. Efficiency requires this land value
differential because individual tax liabilities do not reflect public
service costs. So the price of the bundle of housing plus public service reflects resource cost if land prices deviate from the opportunity
cost of land in a manner that exactly offsets the deviation of tax
liability from public service cost.

Efficiency, then, calls for land devoted to low income housing
commanding a higher price than land devoted to high income housing in any given community.[10] It is clear, however, that an unre-
strained land market will not allow such a price difference to be
maintained; the supply of LIH will be expanded beyond the efficient
level. So some sort of market interference, such as zoning, is required
to ensure efficiency.

This result is similar to that derived by Martin Bailey. In Bailey's world, one group imposes a cost on another when the groups reside in close proximity to one another, but no costs are imposed when the groups are segregated from one another. Efficiency arises in Bailey's world when land prices are identical in the interiors of the two segregated neighborhoods, which implies that at the boundary of the neighborhoods the value of the "offending" activity must be higher than the value of the "offended" activity. Zoning is required to keep the boundary stationary; that is, to keep the offending activity from expanding at the expense of the other. In my framework the offense is the positive fiscal surplus attached to LIH and financed by the negative fiscal surplus attached to HIH in the same community. The analogue to segregated neighborhoods is the homogeneous communities. Bailey-type boundary effects exist in mixed communities, and in a free market LIH will expand beyond the efficient level in mixed communities. This is essentially an externality problem; LIH imposes costs upon HIH, i.e., a tax burden higher than public service cost, with the result that in equilibrium there will be an oversupply of LIH and an undersupply of HIH. Like any externality this calls for market interference, either in the form of price adjustment (effluent fees, essentially) or direct quantity regulation. The appropriate externality fee, of course, would be simply the negative of the fiscal surplus. This would convert the property tax plus the externality fee to a head tax, with its obvious efficiency properties. In practice, of course, urban land use is regulated almost exclusively through zoning, or direct quantity control on various activities, rather than through price manipulation.[11]

We have now stated the conditions for efficient land allocation in two forms: 1) land must have the same value (*ceteris paribus*) in all homogeneous communities; 2) in mixed communities the value of LIH land must exceed the value of HIH land by the present value of the difference in fiscal surpluses attached to the two types of housing.

There is a third equivalent form of this condition, which follows from the proposition that the fiscal surpluses must sum (or net) to zero in any community: 3) (again correcting for access and amenity attributes of land itself) the mean value of land must be the same in *all* communities. Since mean property value is unaffected by the fiscal transfers involved in the local tax structure, the community mean property value must be determined by the value of services generated by land itself in the various activities. As was described in Section II, mean property value is equal to $a_i L' + (1 - a_i) H'$. But since the land values associated with L' and H' are identical in an efficient allocation, the value of land in the community is independent of the activity mix. If it is not independent, then the activity which would raise mean land value in the community is under-supplied.

A Numerical Example

The efficient land value differentials can be quite substantial, as the following rough calculation demonstrates. We begin by picking "reasonable" values for the variables which appear in equations (1″) and (2″) and measuring the magnitude of the capitalization effect and the associated efficient land price differential:

L′ = $20,000
H′ = $40,000
X = $ 1,000/year
D = 10
a = 0.5

We assume that supplies of LIH and HIH have been adjusted so that L′ reflects only the opportunity cost of the resources (including land), and similarly for HIH. In other words, if there exist homogeneous LIH and HIH communities, land value will be the same in both (correcting for differences in amenities, access, etc.). So our calculations will give us the *efficient* prices for the two housing types in the mixed community.

With a = 0.5, the per household tax base B is $30,000. (Recall that we can calculate the tax base without accounting for capitalization effects, as these net to zero. That is, we can use the L′ and H′ figures.) Substituting this information into equation (1″) yields:

$$H = 40,000 \frac{(1 + 10,000/40,000)}{(1 + 10,000/30,000)} = \$37,500$$

$$L = 20,000 \frac{(1 + 10,000/20,000)}{(1 + 10,000/30,000)} = \$22,500$$

So the capitalization effects, in order to keep these properties in the mixed community exactly as desirable as the properties in the homogeneous communities, have raised the value of LIH by $2500 and depressed the value of HIH by a like amount. (The capitalization effects on HIH and LIH are equal in absolute value only in the special case where a = 0.5.)

If we now assume that the entire capitalization effect is shifted to land, and that land constitutes 20 percent of both L' and H', we can calculate the land value differential which is consistent with efficient allocation of land between LIH and HIH. Capitalization raises the value of the LIH sites from $4000 to $6500, and depresses the value of HIH sites from $8000 to $5500. Since an HIH lot is twice as big as an LIH lot, we must divide the value of the HIH site by two in order to compare the values of like amounts of land. Efficiency dictates that identical units of land sell for $6500 when devoted to HIH in the community under examination. Under these conditions, efficiency requires that LIH land sell for 2.36 times as much as HIH land. Of course this ratio varies according to the values of the variables which are selected. Under plausible parameter assumptions it can range as high as 5 or even 10. So we see that sizeable land value differentials are called for if efficient land use is to be ensured.

Several authors have noted that land values vary according to how the land is zoned, and in at least one case (Mieszkowski, 1972b), such a differential (apartment-zoned land selling for roughly twice as much as single family-zoned land) was cited as evidence of Pareto-inefficient zoning action. The above analysis seriously questions the validity of Mieszkowski's conclusion, and at least raises the possibility that the land use pattern underlying the price structure he observed is fairly efficient.[12]

Variable Supply and Demand for Public Goods

The above analysis can readily be extended to the case of inter-jurisdictional variation in the supply of local public goods. We begin by considering the previous section as an analysis of those communities which supply, and those households which demand, some given level of public service, X_1. An identical framework describes the relationship among property values in that set of jurisdictions which supply a (higher) level, X_2. Efficiency requires that property values be invariant with respect to public service provision, as can most readily be seen by considering two homogeneous (say LIH) jurisdictions, one providing X_1 and the other providing X_2. Taxes

minimize the difficulty of such a task). But in the absence of well-defined theoretical postulates, the results of such a study for one urban area could not readily be assumed to hold for other times and places.

V. Conclusion

This paper has established some of the consequences of perfect capitalization of differential fiscal surpluses into property values, with emphasis on the special case of a proportional property tax in every jurisdiction and equal distribution of local public services. At some points extensions to more general tax and benefit structures were discussed. Among the important results are:

1) With full capitalization there can be no horizontal inequality.

2) Efficient supplies of all possible housing plus public service bundles exist when the following three equivalent conditions are satisfied:

   a) Land value is the same in all homogeneous (with respect to house value) communities, if such communities exist;

   b) In mixed-house value communities, land value differntials exactly reflect the present value of fiscal surplus differentials;

   c) Mean land value (per acre) is identical in all communities, regardless of house value mix or public service provision.

Conditions (a), (b), and (c) hold after correcting for all nonfiscal determinants of land values, such as accessibility and other amenities, and after correcting for the fiscal benefit conferred by nonresidential property and intergovernmental aid.

3) With a proportional property tax, a free market will generate an oversupply of low income housing, and some form of control such as zoning is necessary to restore efficiency.

4) The vertical distribution of net (of benefit) fiscal burdens is determined by the allocation of land among activities, and is independent of the structure of taxes except insofar as the tax structure influences land use.

Most importantly, I believe, this work indicates the necessity of studying the fiscal motivations for, and effectiveness of, such land use controls as zoning. For until we have evidence on this question, we can make no theoretical statement whatsoever about the distributive consequences of different structures of local government finance.

NOTES

[1] In such a world, house value simultaneously represents willingness to pay for housing services and the cost of resources devoted to housing, and tax liability simultaneously represents cost and willingness to pay for public sector services.

[2] Of course, average-cost (cost per household) pricing of public services is only efficient if average cost equals marginal cost; that is, if cost per household does not change with community size. Some authors, such as James Buchanan and Charles Goetz have argued that cost per household does vary with community size and that average-cost pricing is therefore inefficient. Yet is is not clear to me that this is the case. Buchanan and Goetz argue that costs decline with jurisdiction size due to sharing of a public good among a larger population, and that costs eventually rise with population due to congestion. But this is nothing more than the standard U-shaped short-run average cost curve. The publicness is sharing a fixed factor of production (the public facility) and congestion arises as more people use the fixed input (i.e., the law of diminishing returns). But once we allow the size of the facility to change (a long-run consideration) there would appear to be no a priori reason to doubt that the envelope average-cost curve is horizontal, or at least roughly so over a considerable range.

[3] This is perhaps best viewed as an extension of my earlier work (1975) on zoning and property taxation, with the current work relaxing the requirement of homogeneous communities.

[4] The price of such a bundle is house value (including capitalization effect, if any) plus property tax.

[5] I refer not to the issue of whether it requires more expenditure to educate a poor child in a poor children's school, but whether the number of dollars of education expenditure that a household can afford varies according to tax base.

[6] Dropping the subscript i, $aL + (1-a)H = a[L' + (X - Lt)D] + (1-a) [H' + (X - Ht)D]$ from equations (1) and (2). Collecting terms, $aL + (1-a)H = aL' + (1-a)H' + [-aLt - (1-a)Ht + X]D$. It can be seen from equation (3) that the term in the square brackets is equal to zero. Therefore, $aL + (1-a) H = aL' + (1-a)H'$.

[7] Whereas transfers among properties within the jurisdiction will sum to zero, transfers from outside (say intergovernmental aid or nonresidental property) will raise the total value of residental property in a community.

[8] It should be recalled, however, that equations (1'')-(3'') describe the relationship among property values regardless of whether the two types of housing are supplied in efficient quantities.

[9] The assertion that the entire capitalization effect falls on land rests upon the assumption that capital is mobile in the long run. Alternatively, we can assume a small amount of vacant land in the mixed community. The calculus of equations (1'')-(3'') enables us to ascertain the value of a parcel of vacant land in a mixed community, depending upon whether the land is to be devoted to LIH or HIH.

[10] This statement rests on the prior assumption that the fiscal surplus is positive for LIH and negative for HIH. More generally, efficiency requires that land prices vary directly with the fiscal surplus.

[11] I in no way mean to suggest by this remark that local governments are (or are not) in the business of attempting to further the aspects of economic efficiency that are considered in this paper. That question can only be answered by a theoretical and empirical examination of the objectives and constraints faced by local officials.

[12] Of course, in order to answer the efficiency question, one would have to adequately correct for all of the other determinants of land value in order to determine whether the sites are truly comparable to measure the fiscal surplus as a function of the zoning category, and estimate the discount rate.

[13] The only restrictions on the tax structure are that taxes never be high enough to generate negative property values, and that future tax liabilities be known, so that present values are well defined. Even a random assignment of tax burdens will generate capitalization effects which establish total prices dictated by supply and demand.

[14] As an interesting sidelight, a perfect market implies the same mix of housing in every community (assuming every community has a proportional property tax). In each community, LIH land and HIH land must command the same price. But given H' and L' the values H and L vary according to a_1, the housing-stock mix. And for any H' and L' there is only one value of a_1 which will set the values of L and H in such a way that their land values are equal. Hence each community, if its land values are to be equal across activities, must have the same value for a.

[15] This statement does not consider the gains and losses in property values which result from the *change* in tax structure.

REFERENCES

M. Bailey, "Note on the Economics of Residential Zoning and Urban Renewal," *Land Econ.*, Aug. 1959, *35*, 288-92.

D.F. Bradford and H.H. Kelejian, "An Econometric Model of the Flight to the Suburbs," *J. Polit. Econ.*, May/June 1973, *81*, 566-89.

J.M. Buchanan and C.J. Goetz, "Efficiency Limits of Fiscal Mobility," *J. Publ. Econ.*, Feb. 1972, *1*, 25-44.

M. Edel and E. Sclar, "Taxes, Spending, and Property Values: Supply Adjustments in the Tiebout-Oates Model," *J. Polit. Econ.*, Sept./Oct. 1974, *82*, 941-53.

B.W. Hamilton, "Zoning and Property Taxation in a System of Local Governments," *Urban Stud.*, June 1975, *12*, 205-11.

——————, "The Effects of Property Taxes and Local Public Spending on Property Values: A Theoretical Comment," *J. Polit. Econ.*, forthcoming.

J. Heilbrun, "Poverty and Public Finance in the Older Central Cities," in *Urban America: Goals and Problems,* Subcommittee on Urban Affairs, Joint Economic Committee, Aug. 1967, 141-61.

P.M. Mieszkowski, "Tax Incidence Theory: The Effects of Taxes on the Distribution of Income," *J. Econ. Lit.*, Dec. 1969, 7, 1103-24.

——————, (1972a) "The Property Tax: An Excise Tax or a Profits Tax," *J. Publ. Econ.*, Spring 1972, *1*, 73-96.

——————, (1972b) "Notes on the Economic Effects of Land-Use Regulation," prepared for Congress of International Institute of Public Finance, Sept. 1972.

G.E. Peterson, "The Use of Capitalization Effects to 'Test' the Tiebout Hypothesis," *J. Polit. Econ.*, forthcoming.

C. Tiebout, "A Pure Theory of Local Public Expenditure," *J. Polit. Econ.*, Oct. 1956, *64*, 416-24.

Serrano vs. Priest, L.A. 29820, Superior Court No. 93854, cited in *Harv. Educ. Rev.*, Nov. 1971, *41*, 503.

6

The Logic of Tax Limits

Alternative Constitutional Constraints on the Power to Tax

Geoffrey Brennan and James Buchanan *

O N Tuesday June 6th 1978, Californians voted overwhelmingly[1] for the Jarvis-Gann tax limitation proposal, Proposition 13. Several additional proposals were approved in the November 1978 state elections, and attempts to extend constitutional limits to the Federal budget were made in 1979. The "taxpayers revolution" seemed to be genuine and it was interpreted as such by politicians. Regardless of the ultimate outcome, the 1978-1980 period promises to go down as a truly fascinating episode in fiscal history.

For the public finance specialist in particular, tax limitation must be of extreme interest. Strangely enough, however, there is little in the standard analytic repertoire that would enable him to come to terms with what tax limitation is all about. He may indeed be able to analyze the effects of reductions in particular taxes to the extent that the revenue from those particular taxes is made up from other taxes. He may even be able to calculate, by appeal to the relevant benefit-cost analysis for the particular set of expenditure reductions involved, whether the implied "balance budget" reduction is "efficiency increasing." But even this enormously ambitious—and arguably, conceptually impossible—evaluation exercise hardly focuses on the crucial nature of "tax limitation" as an abstract notion. For what is at stake here is a general restriction on the use of particular taxes, or in some cases on the size of government, which is to apply *over the indefinite future*. For this reason, a full cost-benefit (or incidence) analysis requires not only an assessment of any current expenditure cuts, but also of all the future expenditures which

*Virginia Polytechnic Institute and State University.

government might have made if the tax limitation had not been operative.

In this sense, tax limitation has to be understood and interpreted in *constitutional* terms. Tax limits imply a change in the rules of the politico-fiscal game. Their explicit objective is to constrain government from taking actions that the citizenry predicts governments would or might have taken in the absence of tax limitations. If we are to make any sense of the tax limitation exercise at all, therefore, it is obligatory to offer some analysis of the nature of government— of the way in which the political mechanism operates.

Traditional public finance does not supply any such analysis. Implicit in the normative framework extensively used in policy discussion, however, is the notion of the benevolent dictator: government is effectively unconstrained beyond its internally imposed pursuit of ethical excellence, the true perceptions of which are obligingly supplied by the economics profession and other morally astute advisors. In this institutional setting, any constraints such as tax limitation (or electoral processes!) can only be viewed as undesirable restrictions ranging from the mildly irritating to the wildly perverse. Tax limitation cannot be understood within such a political setting without retreat into the assumption of irrational electoral behavior.

Although modern public choice analysis provides explicit models of the political mechanism, it is also of limited value in treatment of tax limitation. The thrust of theoretical public choice analysis implies skepticism about the virtues of majoritarian political processes as a means of making 'social' decisions, but much of the policy application exploits a simple median voter model in which political outcomes are broadly consonant with electoral wishes. In addition, the major focus in the Public Choice analysis of "government failure" is on the comparison of political and market institutions, rather than on ways in which political processes may be made to operate "better." To the extent that such improvements in political process have been sought, attention has been directed almost exclusively toward changes in electoral processes. The role of non-electoral constraints—and of fiscal rules in particular—as a means of moderating government behavior in directions that the citizenry desires has been almost totally neglected.

In this paper, we adopt a "constitutional perspective" in examining fiscal institutions. In this perspective, we introduce a model of political process in which electoral complications are explicitly excluded. This procedure allows us to offer an analytic setting within which the logic of tax limits can be understood, and by means of which alternative types of tax limitation can be evaluated. The structure of our argument is a follows. In section II, we present and attempt to justify the underlying model of government. In section III, we indicate briefly alternative forms that tax limitation might take and the means by which alternative constitutional adjustments might be evaluated. Sections IV, V and VI consider these alternative forms and represent the main analytic input of this paper. Section VII offers a brief summary and conclusion.

Monopoly Government and the Power to Tax

To introduce the model of government that we wish to develop, it may be useful to reflect briefly upon the nature of government in a very abstract and broadbrush way. We may conceive of a world in which there is no government at all—an imaginative technique which in political theory dates back to Hobbes (1943). The Hobbesian insight was that in the absence of any collective enforcement of property rights, including the right to one's own life, life for anyone would be "poor, nasty, brutish and short." This Hobbesian state of nature could be characterized by complete "freedom of entry" in the use of coercive power. Individuals would be in a perpetual state of potential conflict with each other, and opportunities for mutual gains would not be exploited because even the simplest of trades would be too difficult to consumate.

From this setting, we might think of the rise of government as an emergent monopolization of coercive power, with government becoming the institution that is assigned that monopoly right. As Hobbes clearly recognized, however, although the presence of government makes it *possible* to define and enforce property rights to the advantage of all, major problems emerge concerning how government is to be prevented from exploiting its monopoly power for its own ends. In this perspective, government is naturally and inherently monopolistic—and the primary problem of constitutional design is to constrain the actions of government so that the outcomes which emerge are at least tolerable to the citizens who conceptually grant their consent to government in its exercise of monopoly power.[2]

One of the most familiar manifestations of the government's coercive power lies in the government's power to tax. This power to tax is the power which the government has to secure control over resources in which individuals hold nominal property rights.

In itself, the power is held independently of taxpayers' consent and independently of any obligation to use the resources so obtained for purposes of which those taxpayers approve. In this sense, the power to tax is inherently coercive. And it is, of course, necessary that it be so. The ability of collective (as distinct from decentralized) action to circumvent the free rider problem in providing public goods[3] depends on the ability of the assigned authority to collect revenue independently of any current expression of willingness to pay.

In the absence of specific constitutional restrictions to the contrary, the power to tax is simply the *power to take*. If the government seeks to obtain a particular piece of property, it is of no account whether it does so simply by appropriating it directly, or by purchasing it, together with a tax *on the owner* for the full purchase price. In this case, taxing and taking are *identical*. Yet legally, they are not. Most constitutions severely limit government acquisition by direct appropriation, but the essentially equivalent power to tax is not restricted in anything like the same way. This apparent anomaly is explained once we recognize that the power to *tax* is (possibly implicitly) restricted in other ways. Uniformity requirements, for example, might require that others in the same circumstances as the property owner—perhaps with the same aggregate wealth—must pay the same tax. This could imply that whereas taking the property directly would survive electoral scrutiny, the taxing alternative would not do so because more citizens are involved. Other rationalizations for the legal distinction between "taxing" and "taking" could no doubt be conceived, but the example here is instructive in one important sense. It indicates that purely fiscal requirements—restrictions on the generality of taxes in this case—may be necessary to ensure that electoral processes work within tolerable limits.[4] Apparently, *electoral* constraints are not the only form of restriction on government action; apparently, electoral constraints do not work particularly well in constraining government; and apparently, non-electoral constraints can be imposed which in some cases supplement and in others operate in lieu of normal electoral processes.

Tax limitation is, we believe, to be seen in this setting. In this connection, there are two aspects of the current tax limit history that are particularly striking. First, tax limitation proposals did not emerge out of normal poltical processes. Interparty competition and parliamentary procedures apparently failed to secure policies that the electorate desired. Normal electoral constraints were conspicuously inadequate. Second, the apparent objective of tax limit exponents was not to secure a once-and-for-all balanced budget reduction. Constitutional tax limits are explicitly designed to prevent governments from taking actions which, over an indefinite future, it is believed they would have taken, *electoral constraints notwithstanding*. Tax limitation is a *constitutional* affair.

In what follows, we shall adopt a model of monopoly government—of Leviathan—in which we abstract entirely from electoral constraints. In other words, we assume electoral constraints to be utterly ineffective. This is admittedly an extreme assumption. We believe it can be justified on both historical and a priori theoretical grounds. But we will not seek to offer any such justification here. Rather, we will defend the use of this assumption essentially as an analytic device. If one wants to focus on *non*-electoral constraints on government, it is useful to assume electoral constraints away. For those who remain skeptical, we appeal to John Stuart Mill (1977)—

". . . the very principle of constitutional government requires it to be assumed that political power will be abused to promote the particular purpose of the holder; not because it is always so, but because such is the natural tendency of things, to guard against which is the especial use of free institutions."

Accordingly, we assume that government possesses genuine coercive power which it uses—within the limits imposed by the constitution—for its own purposes. These purposes are not assumed to be more than normally benevolent; it is therefore logical to treat government as an income-maximizer in the way we typically treat private citizens. Leviathan's income, thus defined, is the excess of tax revenues over expenditures on public goods, i.e.

$$Y = R - G \qquad (1)$$

where   Y is 'income' to Leviathan (government)
       R is aggregate tax revenue
and   G is expenditure on public goods.

On this basis, "natural" government would supply no public goods at all, unless constrained to do so under the constitution. Maximizing Y involves minimizing G. Thus, we would expect a basic ingredient of all voluntaristic constitutions to be restrictions on the *domain* of public spending. By this, we mean a set of rules concerning those things on which tax revenues may legitimately be spent, supplemented by restrictions on direct misappropriation of funds, "corruption" and such like. Such restrictions are a major part of most constitutions, and are assumed throughout the discussion.

Although such rules exist, we would not expect them to be *entirely* constraining. Some leakage into the pockets of politicans/ bureaucrats, in a variety of forms, can be expected. Thus, only a proportion of R, denoted by α, will be spent on the public goods and services which the citizenry expects to want, and α will be characteristically less than unity. Hence, we can write:

$$G = \alpha R \tag{2}$$

and therefore $Y = (1 - \alpha)R$.

In this simple model, there is a direct relationship between the maximization of Leviathan's income or surplus and the maximization of tax revenues. The central constitutional question for each citizen can now be simply stated: how can each obtain the benefits of public goods supply[5] without exposing himself to gross exploitation by government—exploitation in the form of disastrously excessive tax burdens (and correspondingly excessive levels of public goods). One obvious answer to this question is the possibility of tax limitation, and, of course, our major task here is to examine and evaluate alternative forms that tax limites might take.

Alternative Forms of Tax Limitation

Alternative tax limitation possibilities can be broadly categorized according to the aspect of the tax or tax system which is subject to restriction. Accordingly, we distinguish between limits imposed: first, on tax revenues; second, on tax bases; thirdly, on tax rates.

1. *Revenue limits:*
    In this case, the constraint takes the form of specifying a maximum of the revenue which a government may obtain from a particular tax or tax system. The revenue maximum might involve an absolute magnitude, or perhaps more likely a share of the jurisdiction's total income or total product. The latter type we might refer to as "share limits," and are more commonly applied as restrictions on total budget size (or revenue from a total tax system, broadly defined) than as restrictions on particular taxes.
2. *Base limits:*
    In this case, limits take the form of restriction on the bases to

which government may have access in acquiring revenue. These limits may specify the revenue instruments which government *may* use, or those revenue instruments which government may *not* use. The assignment of the property tax to local governments might be an example of the former; 'balanced budget limitation' is an example of the latter in the sense that it denies government access to debt issue as a revenue-raising device.

3. *Rate limits:*

Rate limits can take a number of forms. Restrictions may be placed on the *level* of rates—usually in the form of a maximum limit above which rates cannot extend. Alternatively, restrictions may be placed on the allowable rate *structure*—that it should be proportional, or that it should be uniform across individuals or across commodities.

In what follows we shall examine these various possibilities in turn, with an eye both to how effective they might be in constraining a revenue-maximizing government and to how efficient they are in achieving a given degree of limitation. The use of these two criteria indicate the normative underpinnings of our evaluation procedure. We believe that that which emerges from consensus at the constitutional level has considerable normative authority, in line with the position we have taken elsewhere.[6] Thus, our predictions about what would emerge from the individual's calculus at the constitutional level become the means not only for understanding the current tax limitation movement but also of evaluating it.

Share and Revenue Limits

Understandably perhaps, share limits seem to hold a peculiar fascination for economists. The idea of specifying a limit to the size of government as a share of some economic aggregate (more or less well-defined), such as gross product or total income for the relevant political jurisdiction, seems to offer a direct way of limiting public activity. But these ratio-type constraints are likely to be much more congenial to the professional economist/consultant than to the practising politician or the average taxpayer. The economic sophistication required on the part of the citizens (and politicians) whose support must be organized to implement any constitutional change can represent a major barrier to the electoral success of this type of constraint. Taxpayers tend to think in terms of specific levies, and of their own treatment under such levies by the taxing authorities. They do not think in terms of such abstractions as total tax revenues or total spending, and surely not in terms of the ratio between two abstract entities, total budgets and total product or income.

But setting these problems of electoral psychology aside, are there any purely technical problems that ratio limits seem likely to pose? There are two that seem to us particularly important—one relating to whether the limits are effective, and the other relating to whether those effective limits are achieved in the most desirable way.

In the simple Leviathan model outlined above, government seeks to maximize its own surplus or income, measured by tax revenues, R, minus the necessary outlay on public goods and services, G. If it is constrained as R, either in absolute or share-of-income terms, it may seek to provide the necessary G indirectly rather than directly, and thereby increase its surplus, Y. One means of accomplishing this result would be to manipulate the structure of taxes while remaining within the overall uneven constraint. Consider, for example, some publicly provided good such as education. Clearly, the government can achieve a required level, either by direct provision of education (i.e. it can tax individuals and provide the service free of direct charge) or by subsidizing private provision. And the subsidy in question may take the form of vouchers (or direct subsidy of some other type) or tax concessions. In principle, each of these alternatives could produce precisely the same outcome, but they clearly involve quite different amounts of nominal tax revenue. The subsidizing of private activity will typically achieve a larger response per dollar of revenue raised than direct provision; obversely, for any given level of activity, subsidy will typically involve less tax revenue than direct provision. Subsidies given as direct payments will likewise involve more nominal tax revenue and a higher nominal government budget than tax concessions which induce an identical private response. At the very least therefore we should require that such "tax expenditures" be incorporated into the relevant measure of total revenue for 'share limit' purposes.

But this in turn raises the question as to whether we ought also distinguish between subsidies and direct provision; for, as we have observed, an identical amount of revenue can involve a different level of government influence depending on the form of government action. Even if the implicit subsidy embodied in "tax expenditures" is made explicit, therefore, the problem associated with translating any given revenue figure into some measure of government "output" remains. And there are important conceptual issues at stake in this. Is it clear, for example, that we do wish to minimize government "output" or influence, independently of its revenue cost? Is there a distinction to be drawn between policies which involve revenues passing through the hands of government agencies, and those which do not? We do not attempt to answer these questions here. But it does seen clear that any share limit which accurately reflected what it is we wish to measure would be extremely complex and itself somewhat open to debate, and the problems of electoral ignorance would be correspondingly aggravated. Equally, the extent to which an aggregate revenue limit would succeed in achieving the objective of placing limits on government activity seems open to some doubt.

Suppose, however, that in the presence of this maximum share (appropriately defined), government is genuinely constrained. Nevertheless, government can achieve its maximum share in a variety of ways between which the citizen-taxpayer behind the veil of ignorance could not be expected to be indifferent. For example, different tax arrangements will induce different excess burdens: in the extreme case government could exploit tax instruments considerably beyond their maximum revenue limits and the excess burden induced by the tax could be many times greater than the revenue raised. There is nothing inherent in the nature of share limits which would give government the incentive to seek out broadly based, minimally distorting taxes. As we have already seen, the government, on the contrary, as the incentive to acquire its revenue limit by the application of very high rates to a base made narrow by strategic concessions.[7] Whether these high rates raise much or indeed any revenue is largely beyond the point: the associated excess burdens seem likely to be very substantial indeed.

Base Limits

The possibility of constraining the activities of government by specifying the *bases* on which taxes may be levied is not one which seems to have attracted much attention in the tax limitation context. Perhaps the reason for this is that it seems to set much of the standard public finance literature on its head. The virtues of broad-based, "comprehensive" taxes are replaced by an explicit preference for the appropriately narrow tax base—'appropriate' in that when the maximum revenue rate is applied, the revenue yield is exactly that required to supply the level of public goods which citizens expect to desire in future periods. Yet it is clear that if the government is constitutionally restricted to particular taxes with well-defined bases, its revenue share is necessarily restricted, and especially so as the activities excluded from taxation are substitutable for those upon which taxes may be levied.

Consider an apparently extreme, but still relevant, example. Suppose that government is allowed to levy personal taxes on money incomes but that it is constitutionally prohibited from taxing income-in-kind. In such a setting, as income tax rates increase, taxpayers will, of course, shift toward income-in-kind. This shift generates an excess burden, familiar from analyses of welfare economics. What economists have overlooked, however, is the constraining influence that such potential shifts can exert on government's fiscal appetites. Faced with the prospect that taxpayers can, and will, shift to nontaxable options, even if at some cost, governments will find that maximal-revenue limits are attained at much lower budgetary levels than would be the case if the tax base should be fully "comprehensive."

The illustrative analytics of figure 1 may be helpful here. Suppose that D_x indicates aggregate demand within the taxable community for some good X, and that X has been assigned to the government

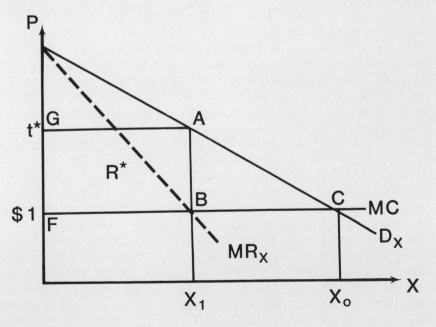

FIGURE 1

as *the* base. For analytic simplicity, we assume that D_x is linear and that X is produced under conditions of constant costs. We define the units of X in terms of a "dollar's worth," so that marginal cost is everywhere one dollar, and X_0 is the total pre-tax expenditure on X.[8] To avoid the possibility of various forms of 'discrimination,' we assume that the government is limited by a requirement that the tax rate structure be uniform both across units of X and between individuals.[9] What uniform proportional tax on X will government choose, given its revenue-maximizing proclivities?

This question is analytically identical to asking what price a profit-maximizing monopolist would charge for X if he were assigned a monopoly franchise in the sale of X: tax revenues in the one case are exactly equivalent to profits in the other. As is well known, we can determine the profit-maximizing output-price combination by constructing a marginal revenue curve, MR_x, which intersects the dollar MC line at X_1: this output is the profit-maximizing output and AX_1 the corresponding profit-maximizing price. Analogously, the tax-revenue maximum involves a gross-of-tax price of AX_1, and a per unit *tax* of $(AX_1 - 1)$ dollars: the tax *rate* involved is t* $\left(\text{given by } \dfrac{AX_1 - 1}{1} \right)$ and the revenue obtained is t X_1, shown as the shaded area R* in fig. 1.

We should note at this point that in this linear case, the MR_x curve necessarily bisects the horizontal distance between the D_x curve and the vertical axis at any price. In particular, X_1 is exactly one half X_0. It follows that the excess burden induced by the maximum revenue tax, the "welfare triangle" ABC, has an area exactly one half of R*.[10]

Two things follow from this observation. First, if we consider assigning to government some broader tax base, it is clear that this same revenue R* could be obtained at a smaller welfare loss. This is the observation on which the traditional 'efficiency' preference for broad-based taxes is found. However, assignment of a broader tax base to government would, under Leviathan assumptions, simply lead to a larger maximum revenue yield. This would not only increase the level of public spending, possibly beyond desired limits, but also would increase correspondingly the excess burden attributable to taxation (to one half of the *new* and *higher* maximum revenue yield). Thus, revenue limits imposed via the assignment of limited tax bases also set limits on the *welfare losses* attributable to taxation.

Second, the use of base limits, as opposed to share limits ensures that the welfare loss attributable to taxation can never exceed one half of revenue raised. As pointed out in the previous section, it is conceivable that in the share limits case tax rates may be pushed above their maximum revenue values, in which case welfare losses will exceed half the revenue obtained, and in the limit will absorb virtually all consumer surplus generated from X. If the practical relevance of this possibility is doubted, it needs to be asked whether one can be sure that the very high marginal rates of tax applying in some Western countries, above ninety percent in some cases, are not already above the maximum revenue limits of the relevant taxes.

The implications of this discussion for conventional tax policy should perhaps be underlined. The overwhelming preference for broad-based taxes which characterizes tax policy orthodoxy is exposed here as extremely dubious. To the extent that government behaves according to the Leviathan assumptions postulated here, or equally, to the extent that constitutional tax limitation is to be interpreted as a widely shared desire on the part of the citizenry to inhibit the growth of government, the familiar policy recommendations of tax economists must be recognized as heading in precisely the wrong direction. Broader-based taxes will ultimately lead to larger revenues being collected than otherwise, with concomitantly larger levels of public goods supply than the citizenry desires at current prices, and larger levels of fiscal exploitation.

There is one possible virtue of base limits which does not seem to be present under direct revenue limits or rate limits. This is the possibility of using appropriately chosen tax-base constraints to establish incentives for governments or governmental agencies to provide the goods and services valued by the taxpayers themselves rather than prerequisites of bureaucratic office. If the constitutionally allowable bases for taxation are chosen so as to be strongly complementary to the public goods to be provided, governments will find it necessary to perform with tolerable efficiency in order to collect tax revenues. A highway agency, for example, charged with producing and maintaining roads will be motivated to fulfill its assigned function if its revenue base is restricted to gasoline and vehicle levies, because the better the roads, the more gasoline will be purchased and the larger and more expensive the cars bought and hence the more revenue the surplus-maximizing agency will provide. Likewise, a government television network will tend to operate in viewers' interests if programs are financed by the sale of television-watching licenses. In the extreme case, this establishes an argument for public provision of services for direct fees and charges. By appropriate choice of tax base, the proportion of revenue expended by government on the goods which citizens want (the parameter α in equation (2)) can be increased, and this is we believe an important feature of base limitation as a means of constraining government.[11]

Although it is not possible to explore 'balanced budget limits' in this setting, it should be clear that these may be interpreted as a form of base limitation. Under a balanced budget restriction, however, government access to allowable revenue sources is constrained not by specifying the tax instruments which government *may* use—but rather those which government may *not*. A balanced budget amendment *denies* government access to debt issue and restricts its access to new money creation as revenue-raising devices. An assessment of the virtues of such an amendment would involve both an evaluation of the peculiar vices of new money creation and debt issue under Leviathan assumptions—peculiar, in the sense that they do not apply to other revenue instruments—and of the influence that the removal of these instruments from Leviathan's armory would have on total revenue capacity of government. We do not attempt to discuss these issues here. We do, however, believe that this is the *setting* in which they should be discussed and understood.

Finally, it should be emphasized that the success of any form of revenue limitation, whether implemented by base limits or direct revenue limits, depends on the existence of additional constraints on governmental regulatory powers. Just as discretionary exercise of tax concessions can achieve government objectives at very low revenue cost, regulations—and the exercise of power by fiat more generally—can be used to substitute for budgetary expenditures. One would expect that the direct exercise of legislative power would be used much more extensively as revenue limits, however imposed, are approached. Constitutional rules which limit government access to regulation could be devised. Some already exist. And it could be that, to the extent that reducing government revenues also reduces the size of the bureaucratic machine in which regulations and their enforcement are born, revenue limits and limits on rule by regulation are over some range complementary. For our purposes here, we simply note the need for such constraints in genuine constitutional reform.

Tax Rate Limits

Rate limits can take two forms: limits on maximum rates that can be imposed; and limits on the rate *structure*. We examine these in turn.

A. Maximum Rate Limits

Maximum rate limits are simple to comprehend and relatively easy to apply. In *conjunction* with base limits, they represent a direct and efficient means of restricting government access to revenue. In the *absence* of base limits, however, they are unlikely to be genuinely constraining. For suppose that a maximum rate limit were imposed in isolation. The immediate result would be that Leviathan would be forced into widening the tax base in order to secure revenues. At first glance, this may seem to be a desirable thing; by setting the rate limit low enough, the citizen-taxpayer could ensure that a genuinely comprehensive tax would raise the revenue required to finance the level of public goods supply he expects to want. And given the widely vaunted virtues of comprehensiveness in the tax system,[12] Leviathan would seem to have the incentive to provide a tax system that is genuinely desirable. Clearly, however, the forces that lead Leviathan to broaden the tax base do not stop when an acceptably broad base[13] is reached: the revenue-maximizing government cannot be expected to stop obligingly when some conceptual 'horizontal equity' norm is achieved. A tax on *gross* rather than net income might, for example, be instituted. And as well as the maximim rate income tax, we would expect the maximum rate sales tax, the maximum rate company income tax, the maximum rate payroll tax, the maximum rate wealth tax, the maximum rate estate duty and so on. In the limit, government would appropriate revenue up to the natural limits set by individuals' preparedness to work, to save, to take risks and so on. In general, one would expect this level of revenue to go well beyond that which the citizen-taxpayer would desire—and, of course, these natural limits would be operative whether maximum rate restrictions were imposed or not. Of themselves, therefore, rate limits do not, in any way, ultimately constrain the *level* of revenues—though they may force governments to collect the available revenue in expensive and inefficient ways.

It is clear, however, that when base limits are also operative, rate limits can be used to ensure revenue collection with minimal excess burden. Recall that with base limits used in isolation, the welfare loss under revenue-maximizing rates will be exactly half the maximum revenue.[14] Suppose we consider two alternative tax bases, X and Y, and Y is the larger; suppose further that X yields a maximum revenue R_x^*, that provides the level of public goods supply citizens want. Under base limitation alone, X will be the preferred tax base since Y will yield too much revenue. But there is a tax rate, t_y, which when imposed on the larger base Y will yield the

same revenue, R_x^*, as the maximum revenue from X. Assignment
of base Y *together with a maximum rate limit* of t_y will, of course,
yield that same revenue at smaller welfare loss, just as the traditional
analysis assures us. The orthodox tax analysis, therefore, could be
looked on as implicitly assuming an appropriate maximum rate
constraint: the appropriate maximum rate must however be jointly
determined with the base to yield the desired level of revenue. The
equi-revenue assumption familiar from orthodox tax analysis only
becomes institutionally relevant if there are appropriate constitutional restriction to ensure that revenue cannot increase.

B. Rate Structure Limits

We have already noted the analogy between assigning Leviathan
some taxable base X and assigning Leviathan a monopoly franchise
in the sale of X. Carrying this analogy further, we should note that a
profit-maximizing monopolist can obtain larger profits from the sale
of X than those indicated in fig. 1, by various forms of discrimination: discrimination over units of X, or between different consumers of X. In the same way, the revenue-maximizing government
can use the rate structure effectively to discriminate over units of X,
and/or between different taxpayers. Such discrimination will increase
public revenue—and therefore appropriate restrictions on the *rate
structure* can be a means of tax limitation, just as maximum rate
limits can be.

Consider the simple two-person example set out in fig. 2. Individuals A and B have demand curves for the assigned tax base, X,
designated by D_A and D_B. The aggregate demand for X is D_T.
Suppose there is a legal restriction which requires *uniformity* of tax
treatment of A and B, in the sense that A and B must face the same
rate structure. The revenue-maximizing rate chosen will be t*, derived from the aggregate demand curve D_T and the associated marginal revenue curve. In the absence of the uniformity restriction,
however, Leviathan could impose the proportional rate on A which
maximizes the revenue obtained from A (shown as t_A in fig. 2,
and determined from D_A in the same ways as t* is from D_T) and the
corresponding rate on B which maximizes the revenue obtained from
B (shown as t_B in fig. 2). This would increase tax revenues since, by
definition, one is obtaining more revenue from each taxpayer than
with t*. Requiring uniformity as between taxpayers is, therefore, one
means of restricting total revenue.

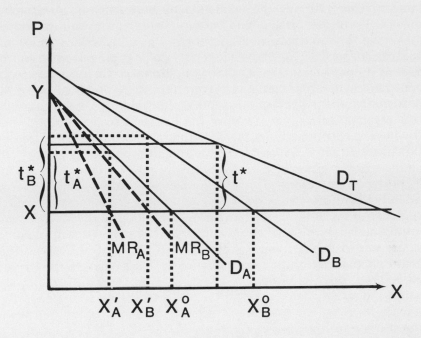

FIGURE 2

We should note that discrimination *among individuals* under a proportional rate regime does not have any efficiency advantages. The welfare loss for A is exactly half the revenue obtained from A; likewise, for B. Hence, the aggregate welfare loss remains one half of aggregate revenue.

Another form of discrimination is, of course, possible—this is discrimination over units of X. In the monopoly case, "perfect" discrimination, appropriating the entire consumer surplus of all consumers, is an analytically familiar possibility. Here, precisely the same possibility appears. By setting a rate structure for each individual which follows that individual's demand curve,[15] Leviathan can obtain as tax revenue the entire consumer surplus from X of each taxpayer. The rate structure for A, for example, would involve an initial rate infinitesimally below XY for the first unit of X and decline over the range to a zero rate at X_A^0. Each taxpayer would face a different *regressive* rate structure, and virtually all consumer surplus would be appropriated as public revenue.

Constraints which outlaw regressive rate structures may be used to restrict government revenue take. Suppose that regression is permitted,

but uniformity in the rate structure as between individuals is required. Then, the revenue-maximizing rate structure can be derived
as in fig. 3. We construct D_A^+ in this figure by taking twice the
vertical difference between D_A and the dollar marginal cost line and
adding it to the dollar line. Thus, the distance XZ is exactly twice
XY. This line depicts the revenue per unit of X obtained while the
rate structure follows D_A — for B will consume the units taxed on
this basis as well as A. Clearly, in the range up to F where D_A^+ and
D_B intersect, the revenue obtained from the rate schedule based on
D_A exceeds that obtained from the rate schedule based on D_B,
because in the latter case only B would purchase units of X. Beyond
F, the opposite applies. The uniform rate structure which maximizes
revenue therefore follows D_A up to F and D_B thereafter and is
depicted in fig. 3 by the heavy line. We should note the sudden jump
in the marginal rate at F. Under this rate structure, A will consume
at X_F and B at X_B^0 : there is therefore a standard welfare loss imposed by the uniformity constraint—in this case equal to the triangle
HLE.

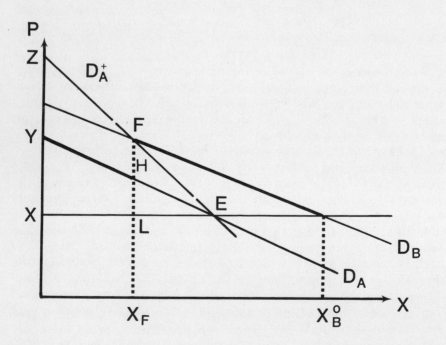

FIGURE 3

What emerges clearly from this discussion is that requirements of uniformity in the rate structure applying to different individuals and requirements which restrict regressivity in the rate structure of particular taxes may be used to restrict the revenue capacities of a Leviathan government, along with or independently of base limits or direct revenue limits.

In evaluating the desirability of rate structure restrictions, however, a certain amount of care must be exercised. We should note that the perfectly discriminating regressive tax structure involves a zero welfare cost. Suppose that, under a proportional rate structure, the tax base assigned yields the level of public goods supply the citizenry wants. Since permitting a regressive rate structure would increase revenue levels, it might seem that this should be undesirable. However, it need not be. Consider fig. 1. The maximum revenue R^* obtained under the revenue-maximizing proportional tax, t^*, is exactly half the aggregate surplus given that D_X is linear, and the total cost in terms of consumer surplus from X forgone, which includes the excess burden is $\frac{3}{2} R^*$. Allowing the 'perfectly discriminatory' regressive rate structure to be applied to X would therefore double the level of revenue and hence of public goods supply, and increase the cost in terms of consumer surplus forgone by one third. It seems that only if the demand for public goods supply is extremely inelastic will the imposition of restrictions to prevent regression be desirable. We should note, however, that this proviso is strictly applicable to the case where the perfectly discriminatory tax rate structure is feasible: if *imperfectly* discriminatory tax rates are likely to be applied, then restrictions on the rate structure are more likely to be desirable. In any case, the advantages of discrimination only appear when discrimination *over units* (i.e. via a regressive rate structure) is applied: discrimination *between individuals* in and of itself implies no reduction in excess burden per dollar of revenue, under revenue-maximizing government behavior.

Summary and Conclusions

There can be little doubt that tax limitation is and will remain an important issue of current economic policy.

In this paper, we have tried to suggest a setting within which the issue may be examined along with some indication as to how the public-finance specialist may contribute to the analysis. The taxpayers' revolution can only be satisfactorily understood in constitutional terms and by appeal to a model of political process that is captured neither by the 'benevolent despot' model of conventional policy analysis, nor by the median voter model that dominates the public choice alternative. We have suggested a *non-benevolent* despot model, that we have called 'Leviathan.' And in order to offer an analysis of alternative tax limitation possibilities, we need to examine ways in which Leviathan can be constrained by elements of the 'fiscal constitution.'

The formal analysis of the fiscal constitution, both in its positive and normative aspects, remains in its infancy. In this paper, we have done little more than set the stage for discussion.[16] We have, however, in the process attempted to indicate how the analytic discussion of tax limitation, in its diverse possible guises, might go.

If there is a policy conclusion to be drawn from this discussion it is perhaps that there is more than one way to skin the government cat, and the alternatives are not necessarily all equally good. And we need to be reminded that much which passes for informed tax advocacy—indeed, much conventional analytics—is systematically eroding many of the natural tax limits embodied in our current system. Attempts to broaden tax bases, on ostensibly legitimate equity and efficiency grounds, lead in directions that the modern taxpayer apparently does not wish to tread.

NOTES

[1]   Virtually, a two-to-one majority to favour.

[2]   The language here reflects our implicit contractarian perspectives. It would be possible to conceive of government as wresting power by brute force. Historically, this origin of government may be descriptively accurate in many cases. But conceptually and normatively, it is more useful to think of government as emerging from voluntary agreement among the members of a group, and then to ask what the *terms* of that agreement might be.

[3]   Or, more accurately, goods for which price exclusion is infeasible or prohibitively expensive.

[4]   Whether the requirement that taxes be general is itself sufficient to ensure acceptable political outcomes is, of course, dubious, as we show below.

[5]   Broadly interpreted to include the definition and collective enforcement of private property rights.

[6]   See, for example, J. M. Buchanan (1977).

[7]   Craig Roberts & Richard Wagner (1978) have recently used an observation along such lines to explain why power-maximizing governments do not abolish tax loopholes.

[8]   The significance of this assumption is that we can treat the tax per unit as a tax rate, t. The assumption is in no sense crucial.

[9]   We shall examine the significance of this assumption in the ensuing section on tax *rate* limitation.

[10]   While it is true that this result assumes linearity, it is also true that conventional measures of excess burden, such as those promulgated by Harberger (1971) implicitly assume linearity by considering only first order terms in the relevant Taylor series expansion. The linearity assumption here, then, should not be regarded as unduly objectionable.

[11]   This argument is developed more fully in Geoffrey Brennan and James Buchanan, (1978).

[12]   In a normative setting rather different from that adopted here.

[13]   Perhaps of the Simons type, see Henry Simons (1938).

[14]   As shown in Fig. 1 and the surrounding text.

[15]   More strictly, his indifference curve corresponding to zero consumption of X given his consumption possibilities.

[16]   In our forthcoming book, we shall explore many of the relevant issues in greater detail. See Brennan and Buchanan (1979 forthcoming).

REFERENCES

Geoffrey Brennan & James Buchanan: "Tax Instruments As Constraints On the Disposition of Public Revenues" *Journal of Public Economics* June 1978 p. 301-318.

—————: "Taxation for Taxpayers: Constitutional Control of the Taxing Power" (forthcoming 1979).

James Buchanan: *Freedom in Constitutional Contract* Texas A&M Press 1977.

Arnold Harberger: "Three Basic Postulates for Applied Welfare Economics" *Journal of Economic Literature* Sept. 1971 pp. 785-797.

Thomas Hobbes: *Leviathan* London, J.M. Dent, Everymans Library 1943.

John Stuart Mill: *Essays on Politics and Society,* Vol. XIX of Collected Works Toronto University Press (1977).

Craig Roberts & Richard Wagner: "Tax Reform Mongering: Common Ignorance or Political Fraud" Paper presented at the Southern Economic Association Meetings, Washington 1978.

Henry Simons: *Personal Income Taxation* University of Chicago Press 1938.

7

The Expenditure Effects of Grant-in-Aid Programs

James A. Wilde*

A NUMBER of recent articles in this Journal and others have dealt w'+h grant-in-aid programs and their effects on expenditure levels.[1] These have been of both an empirical and a theoretical nature. However, the empirical articles have failed to consider whether the results presented make intuitive sense, and the theoretical ones have largely neglected the total dimensions and characteristics of such programs. This paper presents a basic model for use in analyzing how grant-in-aid programs could be expected to influence the expenditure levels of recipient governments.[2]

Consider two important dimensions which grants-in-aid exhibit. They can be either *specific* or *general*, depending on whether or not the donating government selects the expenditure category for which the aid must be spent. Grants can also be *matching* or *non-matching*, depending on whether the amount of aid given is or is not a function of the recipient government's own financial contribution to the aided expenditure. Given this classification, the analysis focuses on the relative effects of three different types of grants: general non-matching, specific non-matching, and specific matching.[3]

The frame of reference to be used is the decision-making body of the governmental unit which receives a grant-in-aid. This may be a school board, a city council, a board of county commissioners, or a state legislature, all to be referred to here as the local government. The donating unit will be the central government. Assume that this

* The author is Assistant Professor of Economics, University of North Carolina. This paper is adapted from his doctoral dissertation, which was directed by Professor Richard A. Musgrave. The author is highly appreciative of Professor Musgrave's assistance and acknowledges the financial support of the Brookings Institution.

local governing body has a set of preferences for goods and services, both social and private; and that such preferences are consistant. Such consistency would mean that a normal indifference map could be taken to represent those preferences.[4] In addition assume that the local government seeks to maximize the utilities inherent in that set of preferences, subject to given prices of private and social goods and the resources available to it. Those resources consist of the sum of the incomes of the individual citizens in the locality minus the taxes paid by these citizens to other governmental units plus the money that the local government is able to collect from external sources, either as taxes or as grants-in-aid.

The Model

Figure 1 presents such an indifference map for a local government, with units of one social good X on one axis and resources for all other social and private uses (in dollar terms) on the other axis.[5] Known initial prices of X and all other goods provide an initial budget line *PP'* and initial equilibrium at A, in the absence of any grant-in-aid. Now let the central government give a specific non-

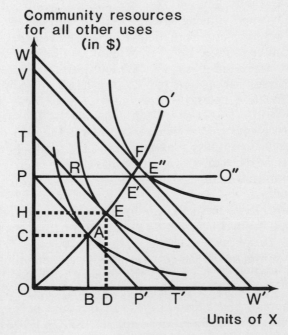

FIGURE 1

matching grant of PT (in dollars) which must be spent on X. The budget line now confronting the local government is PRT′, PR being the number of units of X that PT dollars will buy and representing the income-in-kind influence which the specificity of the aid implies. With the kinked budget line PRT′, equilibrium is at E. The grant has stimulated purchases of X by BD.

Consider a general non-matching grant of equal dollar amount, PT. Since it is general, this grant money can be spent on X or anything else, thus confronting the community with budget line TT′. Equilibrium would be again at E, the stimulus to X-spending being exactly the same as if the aid had been given specifically for X. Clearly this aid, whether general or specific, has boosted expenditures in other areas by the amount of CH. In this case only a fraction $\left(1 - \frac{CH}{PT}\right)$ of the aid tied to X actually went to that social good, the rest leaking into non-designated areas. How large this leak might be depends on the slope of OO′, the income-consumption curve which includes points A and E, or in other words on the marginal propensity of this community to spend its resources on X.

The inability of a specific grant of PT to cause any greater expenditures on X than a general grant of PT continues until the aid reaches amount PV. Beyond that the specificity of the grant has a "deflective effect," causing greater deployment of resources to X than if the aid had not been tied. For instance a specific grant of PW will produce budget line PE″W′ and equilibrium at E″, while an equal-amount general grant yields equilibrium F on budget line WW′. The charge that specific aid ties the hands of recipient governments in allocative decisions thus may or may not be true. The existence of any deflective effect depends on the marginal propensity to consume that social good and on the size of the grant relative to the community's expenditures in its absence. It is easy to know when the deflective effect has taken over; for then the locality's own funds are all devoted to other uses (it finds itself somewhere along E′E″O″) and only grant money is used for the aided function. Even in that case, there has been an effective leakage of specific aid into other uses equal to the original spending on X, namely CP in figure 1.

Figure 2 summarizes the relative effects of general and specific non-matching aid. OZ represents the expenditures on X in the absence of aid, equal to CP in figure 1. ZZ′ suggests the consequences of general grants, only a fraction of which would be expected to go to expenditures on the single social good X. ZZ″ indicates the analogous effects of specific grants, which would be identical to general aid up to amount ZY (equal to PV in figure 1). At that point the leakage of grant money into other uses (the vertical distance between ZZ'' and 45° line ZF) has reached the original expenditures on X. Further leakage is prevented as specific aid is wholly devoted to X at the margin and ZZ'' diverges from ZZ'. It is clear that grant leakage is absent if the community would not have purchased X were the aid not given. Only in the latter case would 100 percent of the specific grant be channeled to the aided function.

Figure 3 presents the case of specific matching grants. Once again the initial budget line and equilibrium are PP' and A respectively. In the case of a single matching rate in an open-ended program the local government is simply faced with a lower effective price for social good X, e.g. new budget line PP''. In this instance the central government has agreed to bear $\frac{P'P''}{OP''}$ of the costs of the local program for X. More units of X have been purchased, but spending on all other local goods has also risen, a leakage of CH. However, reference to the price-consumption line PAEW indicates that such leakage will not always occur. For instance if the initial price of X facing this local government had been higher, providing an initial equilibrium on the elastic portion of PAEW at say L, a central

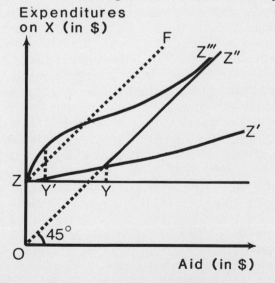

ZZ'	applies to general non-matching aid.
ZZ''	applies to specific non-matching aid.
ZZ'''	applies to specific matching aid (open-ended).

FIGURE 2

government plan to bear part of the costs of X could reduce local spending on all other goods, in effect a seepage into the aided function rather than a leakage from it.

Figure 2 summarizes the expenditure effects of specific matching aid in curve ZZ'''. It assumes that the community was initially in the elastic portion of its demand for X, for ZZ''' starts by rising above 45°-line ZF, indicating that expenditures on X increase by more than the amount of aid received. Unitary price-elasticity corresponds to aid ZY', beyond which leakage occurs at the margin. As PAEW approaches PQ' in Figure 3, ZZ''' approaches 45°-line OZ'' in Figure 2. The maximum possible leakage (in the limit) is again the initial expenditure on X. The asymptotic approach of ZZ''' to ZZ'' reveals that for large aid programs, there would be little allocative difference between specific matching and non-matching grants. Note that since the price-consumption line PAEW must always lie to the right of income-consumption line OAO' beyond the initial point A in Figure 3, ZZ''' will always lie above either ZZ' or ZZ'' in Figure 2. Thus for given dollar amounts of aid, matching grants will provide more stimulus to the aided function than non-matching specific or general grants.[6]

The situation in which the local government initially would have spent nothing on X does not alter the basic conclusions already reached. Non-matching specific aid would go solely to X with no leakage into other uses, the deflective effect taking hold immediately. Matching grants would provide a seepage into X from other uses, no matter what the matching rate offered by the central government. General non-matching grants may or may not result in any spending for X. Figure 4 summarizes this case.

In the above discussion of matching aid, it was assumed to be open-ended, with the central government placing no ceiling on its donations. This is hardly the typical circumstance in today's fiscal federalism. Returning to Figure 3, suppose the central government adopted matching rate $\frac{P'P''}{OP''}$ but agreed to help finance only OB' units of X, or equivalently placed a ceiling on its aid of PT. The community faces budget line PRT', with units of the aided function beyond OB' costing the full market price. Equilibrium is at E' on the income-consumption curve, just the same as for equal-amount non-matching grants, either general or specific. A statutory aid ceiling of PV provides a budget line PR'V' and equilibrium at R'. The latter matching grant yields more expenditures on X than equal-amount non-matching grants but less than an open-ended grant with the same matching rate. Clearly grant ceilings greater than PW' are not effective restraints on the decisions of this local government. In short

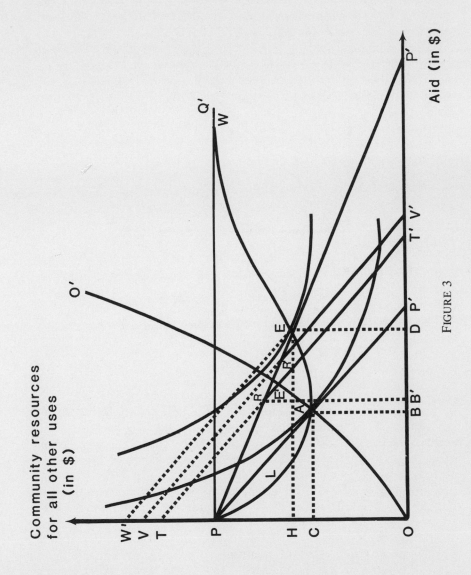

Community resources
for all other uses
(in $)

Aid (in $)

FIGURE 3

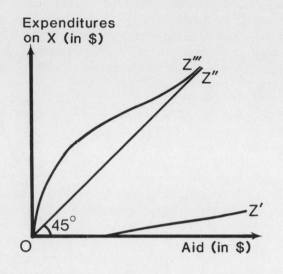

OZ′   applies to general non-matching aid.
OZ″   applies to specific non-matching aid.
OZ‴   applies to specific matching aid (open-ended).

FIGURE 4

while open-ended matching aid has an effect on expenditures through price-elasticity, closed-ended grants can have considerably less influence. In the extreme the latter may only produce income effects. Great care should be taken in the analysis of such closed-ended cases.

The analysis of grant-in-aid programs is far from complete until consideration is also given to the tax side. Many states have statutory requirements of budget balance, and stabilization developments would probably make a central government reluctant to launch a new grant program without planning roughly equivalent additional revenues, *ceteris paribus*. Even the Heller-Pechman tax-sharing proposal, while involving no new taxes, is viewed as a fiscal alternative to a tax cut. Therefore it seems justifiable to assume that a grant program will have an equal tax revenue side.

The effects of taxes on aided-function expenditures are less complex than the grant side. The levying of a tax to pay for a grant program has the effect of reducing the money resources available to the community. So long as the tax is not based on expenditures for X or for its possible substitutes, it can be viewed merely as a negative general grant from the central government. This involves a vertical shift downward in whatever new budget line is appropriate to the grant side of the program.

Assume for the moment that the community under consideration receives in grants exactly the same amount of dollars as its citizens paid in taxes to the central government to finance the program. Were the grants of a general non-matching form, the locality would end up at the initial equilibrium, with no different spending totals than prior to the program. The same might be true for specific non-matching aid, unless the deflective effect was operative. Note, however, that the deflective effect enters at lower amounts as taxes push point P down. If the grant is an open-ended matching one, expenditures for the aided function will be stimulated to the extent of the substitution effect. A closed-ended matching grant could have anything from a zero effect to a substitution effect, depending on the height of the ceiling.

Where communities are in surplus (grants greater than taxes) or deficit within the grant program, consequences for spending on X should be clear from the above analysis. But for all communities in the federal system these surpluses and deficits must be equal if the central fisc has balanced its grant budget. Attention is thus focused on the effects on X-expenditures of the whole program, considering all communities and both sides of the budget. In this context, general non-matching grants cannot stimulate spending on X unless some communities are in program-surplus, and then only if the surplus localities have a higher marginal propensity to spend on X than do the deficit localities. Once again the specific non-matching grant has the same results unless the deflective effect is operative in one or more communities. Specific matching programs may stimulate X-expenditures if it can be substituted for other goods and if grant ceilings are not restrictive.[7]

Qualifications

The above framework is admittedly a simplified one. It would be naive to believe that governments behaved in just such a fashion. However, one should not discard the insights of this model without determining whether they would be fundamentally upset by reference to reality. This paper now turns to such issues.

1. *Redistribution.* The possible substitution of central for local taxes that could result from a grant program would likely mean a redistribution of income in the community. This redistribution might prompt an altered demand for social goods, which if followed by the governing body would change the indifference map. What type of change this meant would depend on which taxes were involved in the substitution and the social-goods preferences of different taxpayer groups. It would be impossible to rigorously incorporate such a possibility into the above model.

2. *Democracy.* It is virtually certain that local governments do not reflect perfectly the preferences of their citizens, whether this is because of institutional difficulties of gathering information or conscious lack of democracy. It seems likely that this condition has existed for some time, and that its effects are included in past expenditure patterns. Thus use of the latter in forecasting the effects of grants should be valid and accurate so long as the aid itself does not alter the local power structure or preference revelation mechanism.[8]

3. *Externalities.* The existence of inter-community spillovers of the benefits of social goods is often cited as the rationale for grant programs. The above model does not take this into account. For the sake of completeness, it might be desirable to redefine the resources available to the community to include such externalities, both positive and negative. That amendment should not, however, change the fundamental logic of the model. Nor should the fact that a grant is given to allow for externalities seem to change the reaction pattern of a locality. A 50 percent matching grant designed to express the central government's interest (because of spillovers to other localities) will have its effect through a reduced effective price to the locality, not because spillovers have finally been recognized.

4. *The grant is something special.* Grants have been referred to "outside money," which having been raised by someone else can be utilized in a different way from locally-raised funds. One allegation is that grant money is spent less efficiently, in terms of value of services received. If situations of that sort exist, they are compatible with the above model, which essentially aims at the allocation of revenues between aided function and all others. The implicit assumption of uniform conversation of dollars into units of a social good is not crucial. Another belief is that grants will be totally devoted to the aided function because that is the donor's objective. This notion presumes clearly defined central government aims and an acquiesence to central preferences, neither of which may be present.

5. *Tax illusion.* It could be argued that central government taxes to support grant programs are not visible to the local government and thus not part of their reactions. This would mean that the downward shifts in the budget line which tend to reduce aided function expenditures do not in fact occur. It would seem difficult to argue that central taxes for grant programs are ignored without implying that central taxes for other purposes were similarly disregarded. The latter is too large a lack of democracy or preference relevation to be plausible.

6. *Tax competition.* It is widely held that there is considerable competition among states and among localities for both residents and businesses, all of which has a negative effect on the tax rates and hence expenditures of these governments. Harold Groves has commented that "the institution of aid and shared taxes . . . increases expenditure . . . because it reduces interterritorial competition."[9] While this is not the place for a complete discussion of tax competition, the latter would seem to have financial relevance for firms or families in terms not of absolute tax rates but of tax rate differentials as applied to the tax base. Such downward tax pressure as exists should already be reflected in the localities' histories, so that past data should accurately predict grant results. The introduction of an aid program can be expected to result in a tax competition as fierce as ever, though carried on at a lower level of local tax rates than previously.

7. *Transfer payments.* If the aided function is a transfer payment area such as public assistance, the above model would probably need considerable modification. This stems from the fact that such payments are not alternatives for other (exhaustive) uses by the community, as the negatively-sloped budget line implies. Aid to dependent children could be used to buy bread, which would be part of the y-axis. However, transfer payments could be viewed as alternatives and the model left as it is if one assumed that decision-making of local governments took place with reference to only the non-transfer-payment population.

Summary and Implications

An attempt has been made to draw on standard economic analysis of individual behavior and apply it to a governmental unit. While it is doubtful that the model accurately portrays public decision-making, it offers one view of what rationality in that area might mean. To the extent that the model is realistic and the qualifications discussed not overly disruptive, the following implications appear to be valid.

1. Specific non-matching aid may have no different allocative effects than general non-matching aid. In such situations it would be invalid to assert that the specific non-matching grant tied the hands of the recipient government. Hence the inter-community redistribution of income inherent in the plan would be a more significant outcome than the expenditure stimulus. In fact the grant's specificity could be a political guise for that less apparent redistribution.

2. If specific non-matching grants are larger than what the locality would spend on the aided function in their absence, the specificity provisions may have allocative significance. This case can easily be identified, for then none of the community's own revenue sources would be supporting the aided function; it would be solely grant financed.

3. Only in the case where the local government would not have funded the aided expenditure in the absence of a grant can one expect 100 percent of a non-matching grant to be channeled in effect to that area. The possible lack of importance of the specificity provision may reduce the expenditure stimulus to that fraction which is the marginal propensity of the community to spend on the aided function. Realistic acknowledgement of the tax side of a grant program should reduce this fraction still further. Thus the overall stimulus of a specific non-matching grant program may be positive, negative or zero, depending on the differential incidence of central and local taxes, the extent of tax exportation and varying marginal propensities to spend on the aided function.

4. It is likely that much less than 100 percent of a general non-matching grant program or tax-sharing plan would be devoted to social goods. The boost to the public sector may be positive, negative or zero, depending on differential tax incidence, tax exportation, and varying marginal propensities to spend on all social goods.

5. Only specific matching grants could be expected to increase expenditures by more than the amount of aid given. Since price-elasticity may be considerably below unity and the tax side of the program should reduce this influence to a substitution effect alone, the overall program stimulus of matching aid might be very small. As with other aid, this stimulus will also depend on varying tax incidence, tax exportation and marginal propensity to spend.

6. What is nominally matching aid may have only the influence of general non-matching aid where closed-ended provisions are

involved. Care should be taken to identify those cases.

7. For large amounts of aid, there may be insignificant allocative differences between specific matching and non-matching programs.

8. The situation in which grants will have their greatest simulatory possibilities is one in which the local government has not previously undertaken the aided function.

NOTES

[1] See the list of references at the end of this article, most of which are of this nature.

[2] No attempt is made here to discuss the normative aspects of this subject. The appropriate design of grants-in-aid clearly depends on the goals of the donor unit of government, as has been developed elsewhere. For discussion in this area see references (2), (6), (7), (8), (15), (20), (21), (23).

[3] Since a truly general grant should permit the local government to use the funds for transfer payments to its citizens, analogous to tax cuts, a general matching grant clearly is impractical, since it would have no limit.

[4] It should be noted that this indifference map resembles that of an individual in being convex to the origin and non-intersecting, but is not assumed to be a "social indifference map" or part of a "social welfare function." This map is not assumed to represent the true preferences of the citizenry, discussion of this and other over-simplifications being reserved for the second part of the paper. Without making this consistency assumption, the problem takes on an element of irrationality and becomes unmanageable. The formulation used here is similar to that found in Scott (20). The difficulties involved with social indifference maps have been discussed frequently. Since this is not a normative analysis, search for such a framework is unnecessary. However, the aggregation problem is not totally avoided here if the governing body has more than one decision-making participant.

[5] "Socal good" is used here in the Musgravian sense, see reference (16), pp. 9-17. The framework seems applicable also to merit goods. However, the model may have to be amended where the aided function is a transfer payment as is discussed below.

[6] This should shed some light on the Thurow-Nichols-Cotton-O'Brien discussion of earlier issues of this Journal, references (9), (17), (23), (24), (25).

[7] Without discarding the assumption that the budget of the grant program is balanced, additional stimulus to spending on X might result if central taxes could be more easily exported outside of the Federal system than the local taxes they replaced.

[8] However, there may be some potential for change in the grant provisions which require community participation in project planning. Once again this might alter the indifference map.

[9] As quoted in Harvey Brazer, (4), p. 22n.

REFERENCES

Roy W. Bahl, Jr. and Robert J. Saunders, "Determinants of Changes in State and Local Government Expenditures and Intergovernmental Flows of Funds," *National Tax Journal,* 17 (March, 1964), pp. 75-85.

R.N. Bhargava, "The Theory of Federal Finance," *Economic Journal*, 63 (March, 1953), pp. 84-97.

George A. Bishop, "Stimulative Versus Substitutive Effects of School Aid in New England," *National Tax Journal*, 17 (June, 1964), pp. 133-143.

Harvey Brazer, *City Expenditures in the United States*, National Bureau for Economic Research (Occasional Paper No. 66), New York, 1959.

Harvey E. Brazer, "The Federal Government and State-Local Finances," *National Tax Journal*, 20 (June, 1967), pp. 155-164.

Albert Breton, "A Theory of Government Grants," *Canadian Journal of Economics and Political Science*, 31 (May, 1965), pp. 175-187.

James M. Buchanan, "Federal Grants and Resource Allocation," *Journal of Political Economy*, 60 (June, 1952), pp. 208-217.

James M. Buchanan, "Federalism and Fiscal Equity," *American Economic Review*, 40 (September, 1950), pp. 583-600.

John Cotton and Thomas O'Brien, "Unconditional Versus Matching Grants: Further Comment," *National Tax Journal*, 21 (March, 1968), pp. 103-104.

Glenn W. Fisher, "Interstate Variation in State and Local Government Expenditure," *National Tax Journal*, 17 (March, 1964), pp. 57-74.

L.R. Gabler and Joel I. Brest, "Interstate Variations in Per Capita Highway Expenditures," *National Tax Journal*, 20 (March, 1967), pp. 78-85.

Ernest Kurnow, "Determinants of State and Local Expenditures Reexamined," *National Tax Journal*, 16 (September, 1963), pp. 252-255.

Elliot R. Morss, "Some Thoughts on the Determinants of State and Local Expenditures," *National Tax Journal*, 19 (March, 1966), pp. 95-103.

Elliot R. Morss, "Tax Sharing: Good and Bad Reasons for its Adoption," *National Tax Journal*, 20 (December, 1967), pp. 424-431.

Richard A. Musgrave, "Approaches to Fiscal Theory of Political Federalism," in National Bureau for Economic Research, *Public Finances: Needs, Sources and Utilization*, New York, 1961.

Richard A. Musgrave, *The Theory of Public Finance*, McGraw-Hill, New York, 1959.

Alan Nichols, "Unconditional Versus Matching Grants: Comment," *National Tax Journal*, 20 (September, 1967), pp. 344-345.

Jack W. Osman, "The Dual Impact of Federal Aid on State and Local Government Expenditures," *National Tax Journal*, 19 (December, 1966), pp. 362-372.

Seymour Sacks and Robert Harris, "The Determinants of State and Local Government Expenditures and Intergovernmental Flows of Funds," *National Tax Journal*, 17 (March, 1964), pp. 75-85.

A.D. Scott, "The Evaluation of Federal Grants," *Economica*, 19 (November, 1952), pp. 377-394.

Anthony Scott, "The Economic Goals of Federal Finances," *Public Finance*, 19 (no. 3, 1964), pp. 241-288.

Ira Sharkansky, "Some More Thoughts About the Determinants of Government Expenditures," *National Tax Journal*, 20 (June, 1967), pp. 171-179.

Lester C. Thurow, "The Theory of Grants-in-Aid," *National Tax Journal*, 19 (December, 1966), pp. 373-377.

Lester C. Thurow, "Unconditional Versus Matching Grants: A Reply," *National Tax Journal*, 20 (September, 1967), p. 346.

Lester C. Thurow, "Unconditional Versus Matching Grants: A Further Reply," *National Tax Journal*, 21 (March, 1968), p. 105.

8

A Theoretical View of
Revenue - Sharing Grants

Ronald C. Fisher*

ABSTRACT. *A theoretical model of revenue sharing grants including central government and subnational taxes is developed and used to show the grant effects on subnational jurisdiction expenditure and welfare. The individual distributional effects of the grant program and the nature of the incentive for change in expenditure introduced by a tax effort factor in the allocation formula are detailed. The analysis indicates that expenditure effects are not determined solely by interjurisdictional income redistribution and that tax effort allocation will stimulate greater expenditure increases in low income and high effort jurisdictions and cause welfare losses in high income and low effort jurisdictions.*

I. Introduction

REVENUE sharing, general support intergovernmental grants have in recent years become a significant feature of fiscal federalism in the United States, so that it is important to clearly identify the expected effects of this type grant on government expenditures. While there is now a substantial theoretical literature examining the expenditure stimulating effects of alternative intergovernmental grant forms,[1] in this paper, the theoretical view of revenue sharing grants is extended in several ways. First, a revenue sharing grant program is viewed as a two-phase operation, with the central government first collecting funds from the entire nation or state and then, in a second phase, redistributing those funds to the subnational jurisdictions. Second, revenue sharing grants with an equalizing function, such as allocation by tax effort, introduce an incentive for expansion of the public sector via a price effect (Goetz, 1967).

* Department of Economics, Michigan State University.

Because revenue sharing grants have generally not been considered in this manner in the theoretical literature, in this paper I present a unified and theoretical discussion of the effects of revenue sharing grants on subordinate jurisdiction public expenditure and welfare. It is an explicit goal to integrate three separate aspects of a complete theory of intergovernmental grants—the distributive effect of a central tax system, the incentive effect of interdependent jurisdictions competing for grant funds, and the effects of a collective choice mechanism to translate individual demands into public decisions. This approach should be considered as an opposite alternative to the analysis of free grant funds in the standard consumer choice framework.

The basic model is set out in Section II. The question of the individual distributional effects of revenue sharing type grants when full central government financing is specified is considered in Section III. In Section IV, the nature of the incentive for change in public expenditure that is introduced by a tax effort factor in the allocation formula is considered. Conclusions and policy implications are discussed in Section V.

II. General Model

Assume that each individual i chooses to distribute a fixed amount of income, I_i, between private consumption goods, X_i, and local public goods, G_j. Individual preferences over these two goods are given by a utility function, $U_i = U_i(X_i, G_j)$, which is monotonic and strictly quasiconcave. Individuals also pay taxes both to the central government and to the one subordinate jurisdiction in which they reside.

Each subnational government, which is the recipient of a revenue sharing grant, selects a level of public expenditure from the set of residents' optimal public expenditure levels and collects taxes sufficient to finance the selected expenditure. There are no spillovers of local public goods or local taxes. Each jurisdiction j faces a local budget constraint,

$$G_j = T_j + M_j$$

where T_j = local taxes in jurisdiction j;
M_j = revenue sharing grant to j.

The distribution of local tax burdens is exogenous to the model. Every individual's local tax share, h_i, is predetermined and assumed constant. This means that the given local tax distribution is not altered in response to federal redistributive programs. Bradford and Oates suggest that school district financing by property taxation represents a fixed tax share system.

A central government collects taxes from all individuals and redistributes those funds to the subnational jurisdictions in the form of revenue sharing grants. I assume that the introduction of a new grant program or an increase in an existing one is accompanied by an increase in federal taxes sufficient to fully finance the change in grants.[2]

Because the grant program is financed by central government taxes, the central government budget must satisfy the identity

$$\sum_{j=1}^{L} M_j = \sum_{i=1}^{N} C_i$$

where M_j = revenue sharing grant to jurisdiction j, defined for all jurisdictions, $j = 1, 2, \ldots, L$.

C_i = central government tax for individual i, defined for all individuals, $i = 1, 2, \ldots, N$.

An essential feature of a revenue sharing program compared to other grant systems is, therefore, that the amount of funds to be shared is predetermined in some way.

The individual choice problem, then, is to maximize

$$U_i (X_i, G_j)$$

subject to two constraints:
Private consumption constraint:

$$X_i = I_i - h_i T_j - C_i \tag{1}$$

Local government budget:

$$G_j = T_j + M_j . \tag{2}$$

By solving the local government budget for T_j and substituting that expression into the private consumption constraint, the individual's maximization problem reduces to

$$\text{Max } L = U_i(X_i, G_j) + u[X_i + h_i G_j - I_i - h_i M_j + C_i] \tag{3}$$

The solution to this problem yields demand functions for X and G for each individual. Discussion of the effects of any particular revenue sharing program requires that one specify a mechanism to determine the distribution of grant funds among the subnational jurisdictions and a collective choice mechanism for the subnational jurisdiction.

III. Revenue Sharing with Exogenous Allocation

Central government funds can be allocated among subnational jurisdictions according to a predetermined formula, the factors of which are considered exogenous to local government choice. Let m_j be the allocation coefficient of jurisdiction j, that is the fraction of the grant program funds to be received by jurisdiction j. Note that $0 < m_j < 1$ and $\sum_{j=1}^{L} m_j = 1$. The grant to jurisdiction j is M_j = $m_j F$, where F = funds to be distributed as revenue sharing grants. Since the program is financed by central government taxes,

$$F = \sum_{i=1}^{N} C_i.$$

The allocation coefficients, m_j, will vary under different revenue sharing plans. For example, revenue sharing grants could be distributed on a per capita basis, in which case m_j would simply be the fraction of the nation's population residing in j. Other programs of this type are allocation based on per capita income and allocation proportional to the origin of central government tax receipts. The latter might be called pure revenue sharing; the central government imposes a tax and serves as the collection agent for local governments.

The effects of this type of revenue sharing program on any individual depend only on the effects on the individual's budget constraint, (3). The constraint becomes

$$X_i + h_i G_j - h_i m_j F + C_i - I_i = 0.$$

Assuming fixed local tax shares and non-inferior pure local public goods, the revenue sharing program will increase, not affect, or decrease an individual's desired amount of public expenditure depending on whether

$$h_i \, m_j \, F \gtreqless C_i, \text{ respectively.} \tag{4}$$

This result has a straightforward interpretation. The left-hand side is the amount the individual would have had to pay through the local tax structure to provide revenue equal to the grant; the right-hand side is his actual central government tax payment to finance the revenue sharing program.

If local expenditure decisions are made as if by majority voting, the public expenditure of any subnational *jurisdiction* will increase because of the revenue sharing program only if there is an increase in the median of the set of desired levels of public expenditure.[3]

In other words, if an individual pays less taxes to the central government to finance the grant than he would pay in local taxes to make the same amount of revenue available to his local government, that individual is effectively better off and thus desires a larger quantity of public good.[4]

Allocation by Central Government Tax Origin

An important feature of this approach to grant theory is illustrated by an example of pure revenue sharing. Suppose that the central government returns individuals' central government tax payments, in the form of grants, to the government in the subnational jurisdiction where they were collected. With this allocation system, (4) reduces to

$$h_i \gtreqless \frac{C_i}{\displaystyle\sum_{i \text{ in } j} C_i} \tag{5}$$

The introduction of a revenue sharing system of this type, accompanied by a corresponding increase in central government taxes, would increase an individual's desired amount of local expenditure if his local tax share is greater than his share of central government taxes among those individuals in his jurisdiction. Although there is no change in marginal tax price and no change in aggregate jurisdiction resources, there are individual differences in tax burdens in the central and local tax systems that result in individual income effects. This analysis indicates, then, that if all central government tax collected in a jurisdiction is returned as a revenue sharing grant there may be stimulative or depressing effects on local public expenditure, depending on the relative burdens of the two tax systems and the local choice system.

Some Other Implications

1. This view of revenue sharing provides an empirical method of predicting the effect of any program. As long as the allocation formula does not cause interjurisdictional redistribution, then one need only compare an individual's share of local taxes with his share of central taxes collected in the jurisdiction to determine whether he is an implicit gainer or loser of income from the program. For example, there is some evidence that the complex allocation system in the current form of United States general revenue sharing leaves several states without significant resource gains or losses.[5] In those cases, given an assumption of local tax incidence, comparison of local tax shares and locally collected federal tax shares provides a measure of the redistributive effect of the program.

2. This model implies a necessary distinction between the effect of a grant on a subordinate jurisdiction and on its members. Individuals' costs of the grant program are distributed according to central government tax burdens, while individual's implicit resource gains are distributed according to subnational tax burdens. Consequently, even though the revenue sharing grant to a jurisdiction may be greater than the sum of central taxes paid by that jurisdiction's members, some individuals can find themselves in a less favorable situation because they have high central tax liability compared to local taxes. Therefore, aggregate jurisdiction allocations are not sufficient to determine the effect of the grant on public expenditure. A jurisdiction may be a net recipient (contributor) of resources in aggregate and still select a smaller (greater) amount of public expenditure.

IV. Revenue Sharing with Endogenous Allocation (Tax Effort)

Many revenue sharing programs, including that enacted by Congress, include a measure of subnational jurisdiction tax effort in the allocation formula. In that way, higher local taxes in any one jurisdiction lead to a larger grant to that jurisdiction. Conversely, the use of the revenue sharing grant to reduce local taxes results in a decrease in future grant levels for this jurisdiction, *ceteris paribus.*

This type of revenue sharing program is characterized as follows. The tax effort of jurisdiction j, E_j, is represented as

$$E_j \equiv \frac{T_j}{\sum_{i \text{ in } j} I_i}$$

where $T_j = G_j - M_j$. Thus the per capita revenue sharing grant to jurisdiction j is

$$M_j = \frac{E_j}{\sum\limits_{j=1}^{L} E_j} \; F$$

where F is the total amount of funds to be allocated.

Because each jurisdiction's grant depends on the tax effort of all other jurisdictions, it is necessary for each individual to adopt a behavioral assumption characterizing the expected actions of all other individuals and jurisdictions. In this presentation I assume that each individual believes all jurisdictions other than his own will maintain the level of local taxes from the preceding fiscal period.[6]

With this assumption, the general model can easily accommodate revenue sharing with tax effort allocation.

The solution shows that the desired level of public expenditure for each individual must satisfy

$$\frac{\partial U_i}{\partial G_i} = -\mu \left(h_i - h_i \frac{\partial m_j}{\partial G_j} F \right) \; .$$

In other words, the optimal public expenditure for each individual is that for which the marginal benefit equals his marginal cost in taxes. The crucial variable is $\frac{\partial m_j}{\partial G_j} F$, the increase in jurisdiction j's grant for each unit increase in its local public expenditure, *ceteris paribus,* which is a function of all jurisdiction public expenditure levels, all jurisdiction income measures, and the size of the revenue sharing fund.[7]

In effect, each jurisdiction has a desired amount of public expenditure for each different amount of expenditure in the other jurisdiction as shown by the set of reaction functions represented in Figure 1. An equilibrium, G*, is obtained when each jurisdiction's desired amount of public expenditure is consistent with the other jurisdiction's desired expenditure. It is expected that this reaction process will occur over several periods and, if conditions continually change, may never actually achieve the equilibrium. Nevertheless, the model suggests the direction of effects of the revenue sharing program, at least in the long run.

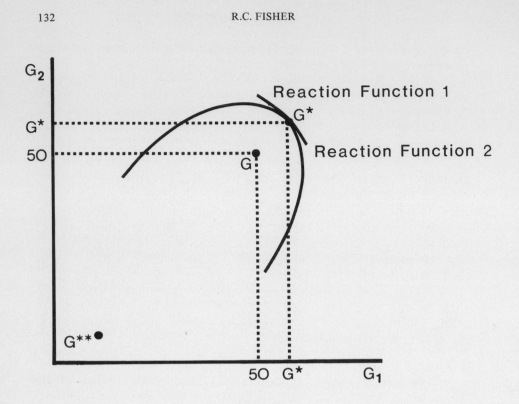

FIGURE 1

A. A Special Case

It seems best to proceed to consider revenue sharing in the context of this model by an example. Consider a world of two subnational jurisdictions each with a single individual as a member. Further assume that these two individuals are identical in all respects, and that utility is a multiplicative function of the private and public goods.

Individual one's problem is to maximize

$$X_1^a \, G_1^b + \lambda \left[X_1 + G_1 - I_1 - m_1 \, F + \frac{F}{2} \right]^8,$$

where

$$m_1 = \frac{G_1 - m_1 \, F}{G_1 - m_1 \, F + (G_2 - m_2 \, F)}$$

because $I_1 = I_2$ and

assuming that $G_2 - m_2 F$ is constant. The individual in jurisdiction two faces an identical problem.

Note that because in this simple example the jurisdictions (individuals) are identical, both select the same quantity of public good, pay equal federal taxes, and receive equal revenue sharing grants.

It is relatively easy to show (see appendix) that the equilibrium amount of public expenditure is greater with the revenue sharing program than without it for both jurisdictions, even though neither jurisdiction has a net increase in resources from the program. The increase is due solely to the incentive effect of the grant.

A numerical example is illustrative. Let $a = b = 1/2$, $I_1 = I_2 = 100$, $C_1 = C_2 = 10$, and thus $F = 20$. The pregrant amount of public expenditure in each jurisdiction is $G_1 = G_2 = 50$. Assuming the level of local taxes immediately after the revenue sharing begins as constant for each jurisdiction, one can calculate the equilibrium amount of public expenditure under this revenue sharing program from either reaction function using the given parameter values and applying the equilibrium conditions. That equilibrium amount is $G^* = 52.76$. A revenue sharing program with tax effort allocation equal to 10 percent of national income has induced about a 5-1/2 percent increase in local expenditure without any redistribution of income.

When revenue sharing funds are allocated solely by tax effort and if all individuals act on the assumption that other jurisdictions' local tax effort will remain constant, all jurisdictions are induced to increase their level of local public goods. In the case where all individual public good preferences and resources are the same, the final equilibrium will involve no interjurisdictional redistribution and thus no gain or loss of resources by any jurisdiction. Thus, while resources remain at the pregrant level in each jurisdiction, the perceived opportunity to win free grant dollars from other jurisdictions induces every jurisdiction to allocate more of their fixed resources to public consumption and thus reduce private consumption.

Since the attempts to win free grant dollars are unsuccessful, from a local viewpoint the revenue sharing program makes every individual worse off. While it may seem strange that tax effort allocation would be used if it has the potential to make all jurisdictions worse off, the more likely result, if jurisdictions are not identical, is that some are hurt while others are made better off, as shown below.[9]

B. Extension and Generalization of the Results

1. In dealing with identical individuals one is certain that each
will take the same action and thus that no jurisdiction will gain
relative to any other. It seems more reasonable to assume, however,
that jurisdictions, or more correctly the individuals that compose
them, may differ by tastes, income, or the distribution of local
tax burden.

Suppose still that revenue sharing grants are allocated solely on the
basis of tax effort and that there are only two jurisdictions. The
effect of the grant on local public expenditure now depends upon
two factors: the initial net gain or loss of income and the marginal
gain of grant funds from an additional unit increase in public expenditure. I have already shown that all jurisdictions will face a
positive incentive, although now a jurisdiction may face the opposing forces of possible grant gains from increasing public expenditure
and simultaneous decreases in income, if one's central taxes are
greater than the grant received.

The initial grant to any jurisdiction depends upon its allocation
coefficient, m_j, which in turn depends upon relative tax effort.
Local tax effort can vary because of differences in local taxes or
local income. A basic relationship between the initial grant amount,
represented by m_j, and the incentive to change public expenditure,

$\frac{\partial m_j}{\partial G_j}$, is apparent. The strength of the incentive varies inversely

with income and with effort, *ceteris paribus*. Consider two single
individual jurisdictions that differ only by income. Although they
initially have equal tax effort, a one dollar increase in local taxes in
the lower income jurisdiction has a greater percentage effect than a
similar dollar increase in the higher income jurisdiction. Similarly,
among two jurisdictions with equal income but different tax effort
(and thus different amounts of local expenditure), a one dollar
increase in local taxes in the low effort jurisdiction has a greater
percentage effect than in the other. Thus a jurisdiction initially with
lower tax effort receives a smaller grant, but may face a greater
opportunity to gain grant funds by increasing its local taxes. Conversely, such a jurisdiction need increase its local taxes less than
higher effort jurisdictions to make an equivalent dollar gain in grant
funds at the margin.

To consider the relationship between the redistributive and incentive effects of tax effort allocated revenue sharing when juris-

dictions are not identical, I present two variations of the numerical example in the previous section.

Case A: Suppose there are two jurisdictions each with a single individual such that $I_1 = 100$, $I_2 = 80$, $U_1 = U_2 = X^{1/2} G^{1/2}$. With no grant program $G_1 = 50$ and $G_2 = 40$. Note that tax effort is the same in the two jurisdictions.

Case B: There are two jurisdictions each with a single individual such that $I_1 = I_2 = 100$, $U_1 = X_1^{1/2} G_1^{1/2}$, $U_2 = X_2^{3/4} G_2^{1/4}$. These individuals differ only tastes so that they differ in tax effort. Before the grant program is introduced $G_1 = 50$ and $G_2 = 25$.

TABLE 1

Effect of Tax Effort Allocation
When Jurisdictions Differ by Income and Tastes

	Case A* $a = b = 1/2$		Case B* $I_1 = I_2 = 100$	
	$I_1 = 100$	$I_2 = 80$	$a = b = 1/2$	$a = 3/4$, $b = 1/4$
Initial grant share, m_j	.50	.50	.67	.33
Initial incentive, $\dfrac{\partial m_j}{\partial G_j}$	.005	.006	.003	.009
Central government tax	11.11	8.89	10.	10.
Expenditure before revenue sharing	50.	40.	50.	25.
Expenditure after revenue sharing	52.5	42.9	54.4	27.9
Percentage charge expenditure	5.0	7.3%	8.8%	11.6%
Change in utility	decrease	increase	increase	decrease

* $U_1 = U_2 = X_j^{1/2} G_j^{1/2}$.

** $U_1 = X_1^{1/2} G_1^{1/2}$; $U_2 = X_2^{3/4} G_2^{1/4}$.

The initial amounts of public expenditure and the revenue sharing allocation factors are shown in Table 1.[10]

Suppose, in each case, that the central government begins a revenue sharing program distributing grants entirely on the basis of tax effort. Let the size of the grant program be F = 20, financed by a proportional central government tax on income.

For Case A, tax effort is initially equal, so that each individual receives an equal grant. The richer individual pays a greater amount of central government taxes. The increase in grant dollars from an increase in public expenditure, represented by

$\frac{\partial m_j}{\partial G_j}$, is larger for the poorer individual. Thus while the poorer indi-

vidual makes an initial income gain and the richer individual faces an income loss, the poorer jurisdiction must increase public expenditure less than its competitor to maintain its income distribution position with respect to the more wealthy jurisdiction.

The result is an increase in public expenditure in both jurisdictions. Note that the richer jurisdiction increases public expenditure in spite of incurring an income loss because the incentive effect overwhelms the income effect. Both the income loss and the increase in G serve to make him worse off. The poorer jurisdiction has a net income gain, so both the incentive effect and the income effect operate to increase public expenditure. Although both jurisdictions begin with equal tax effort, only the jurisdiction with lower income benefits in a welfare sense from the revenue sharing program.

In Case B, both individuals pay equal central government taxes while the tax effort of jurisdiction one is twice as great as jurisdiction two. Consequently, the revenue sharing grant to one is also twice as great as the grant to two. Note also that the marginal gain in grant funds from increasing local public expenditure is greater for the *low* effort jurisdiction. Therefore, at the start of the grant program, individual two faces an income loss but must increase G less than his competitor to make an equivalent gain in grant funds. In contrast, individual one is an income gainer but must react more than individual two to maintain his income position with the grant program in operation. These incentives are reinforced by the taste differences between these jurisdictions.

As shown in Table 1, the positive incentive on public expenditure for both jurisdictions remains. For individual one, the income effect and the incentive effect operate together to generate a large increase in G_1 and to make this individual better off. For individual two, the incentive effect dominates the opposite income effect so that public expenditure still increases serving to make him worse off. Note that this action allows him to avoid further loss of his central government taxes through the revenue sharing system. The effect of revenue sharing with tax effort allocation in this case is to increase all jurisdictions' public expenditures and to make jurisdictions which have relatively greater preference for public consumption better off while hurting those jurisdictions which favor more private consumption.

2. The basic examples used above are easily extended to larger numbers of jurisdictions. Suppose there are L jurisdictions, each with a single identical, individual resident. A comparison of the equilibrium public expenditure for various values of L with that of the two jurisdiction example will show the effect of an increase in the number of jurisdictions on the tax effort incentive. I assume that the total size of the revenue sharing program increases to keep individual central government tax payments constant. In this way, regardless of the number of jurisdictions, the revenue sharing program is a constant share of national income.

Assuming the parameters of the previous example, $a = b = 1/2$, $I_j = 100$, $C_j = 10$, and $F = 10L$, calculation of G_i^* for various values of L is straightforward and shown below:

L	G^*	Incentive Induced Increase	Percentage Increase
1	50	— —	— —
2	52.76	2.76	5.5%
10	54.59	4.59	9.2%
100	54.96	4.96	9.9%

As before, since the individuals are identical, at the equilibrium $G_i^* = G_j^*$ for all j and $m_j = 1/L$. It appears that the examples with only two jurisdictions *understate* the stimulative impact of tax effort allocation revenue sharing if the number of jurisdictions is large (as long as the revenue sharing program is fixed in relative size). However, the incentive effect does approach a limit as the size of the nation rises. This occurs because the incentive depends both on the marginal gain from increasing tax effort and the total size of the grant program. As the number of jurisdictions increases, the marginal gain to each jurisdiction falls less than proportionately while the size of the grant program rises just proportionately to keep the program constant in relative size. Thus the expected dollar gain to each jurisdiction from increasing their tax effort, the product of the above two factors, increases. These results have an important policy implication. If one desires to minimize the incentive for a larger public sector inherent in this type of revenue sharing program, jurisdictions should compete for grant dollars with the smallest feasible number of other jurisdictions.

V. Conclusions and Implications

This research indicates that in terms of the effect of a lump-sum grant on expenditure, distinction between individuals and governments is important. Whether an individual's desired level of public expenditure increases, decreases, or remains constant depends on whether his local tax share is greater than, less than, or equal to his federal tax share weighted by the inverse of the jurisdiction's allocation factor. Depending then on the income distribution and the voting system in a jurisdiction, it is possible and even likely that a jurisdiction will alter its level of public expenditure even if there is no jurisdiction income loss or gain in the tax/grant transfer.

The important factor is the distributive effect of the progressive federal tax relative to state or local taxes with different incidence. Through the tax substitution that occurs, revenue sharing is a means of making the overall tax systems more progressive, although this is accomplished only at the expense of altering the existing public/ private consumption mix in subnational governments.

While revenue sharing is often presented as a pure lump-sum transfer and redistributive system, there is an expenditure incentive effect introduced by the inclusion of tax effort in the allocation formula. Tax effort allocation introduces an element of interjurisdictional competition into the grant program resulting in an incentive for increasing public expenditure beyond that stimulated by income redistribution. Even if full federal financing is considered, tax effort allocation causes an increase in public expenditure in *all* jurisdictions, although the greatest increases can be expected in jurisdictions with relatively lower per capita personal income and higher tax effort. Thus, if the tax effort incentive is intended to stimulate subnational jurisdiction public expenditure, it will do so best in jurisdictions that already have relatively large public sectors and in jurisdictions that are relatively poor. This seems a curious type of subnational government expenditure stimulation. More important, the incentive introduced by tax effort allocation can serve to make all jurisdictions worse off, although more likely there will be a decrease in welfare of higher income jurisdictions (among those with equal effort) and of lower effort jurisdictions (i.e., those that prefer private consumption among those with equal per capita incomes).

Although the incentive effect of tax effort allocation is recognized in the theoretical literature, there remains a skepticism about its practical effect. Maxwell (1973) argues that "the most formidable reason why the bonus (or penalty) will have a weak and diffused effect over time is the *relative* nature of tax effort. If increased effort by state X merely keeps pace with that of all states, state X will not secure a bonus . . . In short, the bonus for taxing more and the penalty for taxing less are reduced by the uncertainty of the outcome . . . ."

This discussion shows directly that the strength of the incentive will increase when the number of jurisdictions directly competing rises (as long as the size of the revenue sharing pie increases proportionately). It is precisely the fact that there is a large number of jurisdictions competing which motivates the existence of the incentive. Only in this situation will any one jurisdiction be totally uncertain about the behavior of its competitors and therefore totally sure that its own action will not affect competitor's behavior.

Policy Implications for the Structure of Revenue Sharing

Since there is only a small, negative correlation between jurisdiction revenue sharing grants and per capita personal income, it is often argued that revenue sharing as presently structured is only mildly redistributive. This analysis suggests, however, that if the measurement were properly made, revenue sharing as presently structured would show up as a much stronger redistributive force. This results from (i) the consideration of each jurisdiction's cost in federal taxes, and, (ii) the implicit redistributive gain to some individuals because of the relatively greater progressivity of the federal tax structure. Indeed, Nathan *et al.* (1975) show that net state per capita revenue sharing entitlements (that is, per capita revenue sharing grants less per capita federal taxes) are significantly negatively correlated to state per capita personal income. Of course, even this measure understates the redistributive effect of general revenue sharing because it ignores the interpersonal equalizing tendency of the federal personal income tax at work within each state. Thus as a redistributive device revenue sharing surely has more than a modest equalizing tendency.

In addition, this research suggests that the incentive for public expenditure increases introduced by tax effort allocation may be quite strong, although this depends crucially on the size of the revenue sharing program. Depending on the rationale for including tax effort in the allocation formula, it may be valuable to consider alternatives to tax effort allocation, particularly if any revenue sharing program is large or is to be increased in size or relative importance. If the goal of tax effort allocation is to encourage increases in general subnational public spending for some valid national purpose, then it should be retained. However, since tax effort itself may be a proxy for preferences, one should recognize that the largest increases in public spending are likely to occur in jurisdictions that have previously revealed a preference for a relatively larger public sector. If, however, tax effort is included in the allocation formula as a distributive device—to provide more aid to central cities, for example—then this goal would be more efficiently served by eliminating tax effort as an allocation device and adopting a direct approach weighting revenue sharing in favor of cities.

If tax effort is to be retained as a factor in the allocation formula, then this research suggests two ways to minimize the public expenditure incentive. First, once the total revenue sharing fund is divided among the states, the incentive for expenditure increases at the local level will be smaller if local jurisdictions compete within county areas rather than within the entire state or the entire nation. Thus the present allocation structure of U.S. General Revenue Sharing, for whatever reason it was adopted, is a type of "second best" allocation structure. Second, a tradeoff of incentives introduced by tax effort may be possible. To the extent that tax effort understates revenue effort in any jurisdiction, there is an incentive for shifts in financing methods to raise tax effort without increasing total public expenditure. Assuming jurisdictions would shift to taxes from charges more quickly than raising expenditures (and total revenue), then one must ask which distortion is less preferable. If "tax effort" were supplanted by "revenue effort," then jurisdictions could only increase grants by increasing expenditures. Therefore, the incentive toward tax financing in the present system is to some degree an alternative to the incentive for public expenditure increases.

One should also note that the incentive resulting from tax effort allocation can be counterproductive to other government objectives. If, for example, state financial aid to local governments is allocated according to the tax effort and local tax or expenditure limits exist, then the grant program creates an incentive to increase local effort or expenditure while the limit may be intended to prevent just that.

Is revenue sharing "equivalent to passing a taxpayer's own money from one pocket to the other" as Goetz (1972, p. 78) has suggested? Not exactly. First, for most individuals the amount taken out of the first pocket is either less or more than the amount put into the other. Second, by attempting to minimize the amount lost in this particular transfer, individuals are induced to give up further resources to public consumption. This research does suggest that through structural change—particularly elimination of tax effort as an allocation factor—the relative attractiveness of general revenue sharing may be enhanced.

[Appendix deleted]

NOTES

The author acknowledges the valuable contributions and encouragement of Vernon Henderson and Allan Feldman. Thanks also to Daniel Rubinfeld and the Editor for their helpful comments on an earlier version.

[1] See Goetz (1967), Wilde (1968), Teeples (1969), Bradford and Oates (1971), Goetz and McKnew (1972), Sheshinski (1977), Courant, Gramlich, and Rubinfeld (1978).

[2] Other federal expenditures are constant. Alternatively, the grant could be financed by decreases in other expenditures or increased debt.

[3] Similar results were noted by Greene (1972) and Heins (1971). Heins' work was important in developing my approach, although this work formalizes and extends the analysis.

[4] This occurs solely from an income effect. There is no change in the marginal tax price of public expenditure as long as the grant is less than the total public expenditure of a jurisdiction. Courant, Gramlich, and Rubinfeld as well as others have recently shown how fiscal illusion can generate a price effect for lump-sum grants. See Courant, et al., (forthcoming).

[5] See Nathan, Manvel, and Calkins (1975).

[6] That is, individual's *believe* that other jurisdictions will not react to tax changes in their jurisdiction. This is a valid assumption if there are a large number of subnational jurisdictions or if there are counter-veiling competitive forces.

[7] Although jurisdiction tax changes affect the size of its revenue sharing grant, the effect is different from a traditional matching grant in which local taxes are matched by federal funds at a fixed rate. In the revenue sharing case the matching rate is not constant but depends on the reaction of all jurisdictions. For elaboration on this point and direct comparison of revenue sharing and matching grants, see Fisher (forthcoming, 1980).

[8] I assume $0 < a < 1$; $0 < b < 1$. Cobb-Douglas utility functions are used for simplicity. None of the results depend on this form of the function.

[9] Because collective choice of the type and magnitude of federal grant program is not specified, there is no explicit explanation of why tax effort

142   R.C. FISHER

allocation is selected if all individuals are made worse off. Several possibilities
are (i) that individuals do not correctly perceive the effects of the revenue
sharing program, (ii) that the program goal is an increase in local public expenditure (for income redistribution by public expenditure perhaps), or (iii) that
public officials support the revenue sharing concept because they perceive lower
political costs to revenue collection in this manner. This seems a fruitful area
for research.
[10] Because the exact equilibrium is not easily calculated, an iterative procedure is used to determine public expenditure with revenue sharing.

REFERENCES

Barr, James and Otto Davis, "An Elementary Political and Economic Theory of
    the Expenditures of Local Governments," *Southern Economic Journal,*
    XXXIII, 2 (October 1966), pp. 149-165.
Bradford, David and Wallace Oates, "Towards a Predictive Theory of Inter-
    governmental Grants," *American Economic Review,* LXI, 2 (May, 1971),
    pp. 440-448.
————, "The Analysis of Revenue Sharing in a New Approach to Collective
    Fiscal Decisions," *Quarterly Journal of Economics,* LXXXV, 3 (August,
    1971), pp. 416-439.
Courant, Paul, E. Gramlich and D. Rubinfeld, "The Stimulative Effects of
    Intergovernmental Grants: or Why Money Sticks Where it Hits," in *Papers
    of the Committee on Urban Public Economics,* forthcoming.
Fisher, Ronald C. "A Theoretical Analysis of General Revenue Sharing Effects
    on Subordinate Government Public Expenditures," Unpublished Ph.D.
    dissertation, Brown University, 1976.
————, "Expenditure Incentives of Intergovernmental Grants: Revenue
    Sharing and Matching Grants" in *Research in Urban Economics, A Research
    Annual,* Vol. 1, JAI Press, Inc., forthcoming, 1980.
Goetz, Charles, "Federal Block Grants and the Reactivity Problem," *Southern
    Economic Journal,* XXXIV, 2 (July, 1967), pp. 160-165.
————, *What is Revenue Sharing?* Washington, D.C.: The Urban Institute,
    1972.
————, and Charles McKnew, "Paradoxical Results in a Public Choice
    Model of Alternative Grant Forms," in J. Buchanan and R. Tollison, eds.,
    Theory of Public Choice, Ann Arbor: University of Michigan Press, 1972.
Greene, Kenneth, "Some Institutional Considerations in Federal-State Fiscal
    Relations," in J. Buchanan and R. Tollison, eds., *Theory of Public Choice,*
    Ann Arbor: University of Michigan Press, 1972.
Heins, A. James, "State and Local Response to Fiscal Decentralization," *Ameri-
    can Economic Review,* LXI, 2 (May, 1971), pp. 449-455.
Maxwell, J.A., "Tax Effort as a Determinant of Revenue Sharing Allotments,"
    Harvard Journal on Legislation, X, 4 (December, 1973).
Nathan, R., R. Manvel and S. Calkins, *Monitoring Revenue Sharing,* Washington,
    D.C.: The Brookings Institution, 1975.
Sheshinski, Eytan, "The Supply of Communal Goods and Revenue Sharing,"
    in M. Feldstein and R. Inman, eds., *The Economics of Public Services,*
    London: The MacMillan Press, Ltd., 1977.

Teeples, Ronald, "A Model of a Matching Grant-in-Aid Program with External Tax Effects," *National Tax Journal,* XXII, 4 (December, 1969), pp. 486-496.
Wilde, James, "The Expenditure Effects of Grant-in-Aid Programs," *National Tax Journal,* XXI, 3 (September, 1968), pp. 340-348.

9

The Demand for Municipal Goods

A Review of the Literature from the
Point of View of Expenditure Determination

W. Patrick Beaton*

FOR MANY YEARS, planners have puzzled over the fiscal pressures that residential, commercial and industrial activity has placed on municipal budgets.

Ruth Mace's now classic review of the relevant planning literature reaches the conclusion that, as of 1961, our level of empirically useful knowledge was extremely low. She found that the research then in existence was poorly designed. As examples of this, she observed that the then extant studies (1) aggregated all commercial and industrial activity, thus overlooking what may have been significant differences among different classes of business activity, (2) neglected the pressures for new residential development and start-up costs for schools, and (3) ignored the deleterious effects of inappropriate or improperly located business activity. (Mace, 1961).

Mace's criticisms suggest that to properly explore the issues centering on the fiscal impact of development activities, two levels of research must be mounted. First, the full range of potential fiscal pressures that can affect the local budget-making process must be uncovered. Second, these pressures must be assessed for their influence on the future growth or viability of the neighborhood and the city. The pressure of events has directed most research toward the latter, the estimation of specific expenditure multipliers that attempt to measure expenditures generated by new housing or commercial development.

*Research Professor, Center for Urban Policy Research, Rutgers University.

Most of the early work in the area of municipal cost has been based solely on average cost considerations (Burchell and Listokin, 1978). Work of this genre identifies for a specific point in time the municipal and school district expenditures per citizen or pupil and, after holding the effect of inflation constant, projects total expenditures through forecasts of population or school enrollment. The great benefit of this type of analysis is its relatively clear cost-assignment process. Its disadvantage vis a vis accurate cost forecasts is the omission of all market considerations. Changes in the costs of government, demands by citizens, and changes in the structure of the local business community and their impact on the local budgets are totally overlooked.

One of the major lines of improvement toward the understanding of the local governmental expenditure-setting process by planners has come out of the municipal expenditure determinant literature (Sternlieb et al., 1973). This work, which is largely statistical in both its empirical method and in its conceptual underpinnings, seeks to find the best equation that will link a set of municipal, social, economic and governmental characteristics with local governmental expenditure levels. The equation, usually linear in form, is estimated from municipal expenditure and demographic data using regression techniques. The resulting regression coefficients are used as expenditure multipliers, each showing the expenditure increment associated with the increase in one unit of each independent variable. The reasonableness of each of the coefficients is then judged on the bases of congruence with received economic, geographic, social and political theory.

Although the equations generated through this procedure are quite successful in explaining in a statistical sense the variation in municipal or school district expenditure levels, the arguments to the expenditure determinants equation have no direct link to theory. As a consequence, the coefficients derived from the analysis may in reality be functions of unspecified exogenous and endogenous variables and, thus, used for forecasting marginal municipal expenditures only with a high degree of risk.

The third branch of municipal cost analysis is derived from the theories of public goods (Samuelson, 1954), public choice or voter sovereignty (Mueller, Dennis C., 1976), and microeconomic theory. The integration of these lines of theory has been recently undertaken by several sets of authors.

This body of theory seeks to uncover the full range of fiscal measures facing local government, and in a sense addresses Mace's

primary criticism of the use of expenditure determinants. In the
review to follow, I shall examine work that focuses on the municipal production function, the characteristics of the citizen's utility
function, and the specification of terms not normally considered
a part of the private market model.

The Demand for Municipal Goods: A Focus on the Municipal Production Function

The structural model proposed by Borcherding and Deacon
(1972) (BD), while integrating the supply and demand side of the
municipal goods and services market, focuses attention on the
supply side. The market-type solution for the quantity and price
of municipal goods is diagrammed in Figure 1.

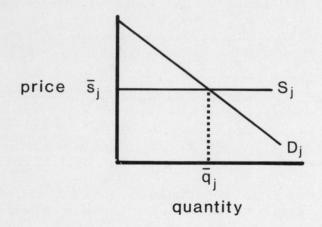

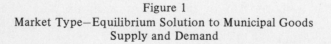

Figure 1
Market Type—Equilibrium Solution to Municipal Goods
Supply and Demand

where

S_j = supply schedule
D_j = demand schedule
s_j = equilibrium price of municipal goods
q_j = equilibrium quantity of municipal goods
j = jurisdiction

The traditional downward-sloping demand schedule is met with a horizontal supply schedule. That is, the quantity supplied is assumed to be capable of change without the need to change the price. However, each jurisdiction is assumed to have a different equilibrium solution. In the case of the demand function D_j, quantity is presumed to be a function of price and income:

(1) $\quad q_j = A s_j^{\eta} y_j^{\delta}$

where, in addition to the above symbolism,

y = median voter income,
A = equation constant,
η, δ = price and income elasticities respectively, with ($\eta < 0$) and
($\delta > 0$).

In the individual utility maximization model, the arguments to the demand equation are easily specified; this is not the case with its municipal goods analogue. Each argument must be examined in the light of the somewhat unique problems posed by aggregate decision making and the public goods character of the municipal product. Before doing this, however, let us examine the supply function. As indicated in Figure 1, municipal goods are supplied at a constant price (s_j) as perceived by the voter-consumer and derived from the marginal cost (C_x) which is a function of wages (w^{β}):

(2) $\quad s_j = f(C_x)$

(3) $\quad C_x = a' w_j^{\beta}$

where

a′ is the equation constant, and is a constant derived from the municipal goods production function.

It should be recalled that market equilibrium occurs in perfectly competitive markets where the marginal cost schedule, which is the supply schedule, intersects with the demand schedule.

Determination of Supply

The BD structural model specifies as the municipal production function a continuously differentiable, linearly homogenous Cobb-

Douglas production function. Factor inputs to the municipality (as the production unit) are exogenously determined at constant input prices:

$$(4) \quad X_j = a_j L_j^{\beta} K_j^{1-\beta}$$

where $0 < \beta < 1$,

X = physical output of municipality
L = labor inputs
K = capital inputs
w = wages
r = rental rate

Due to the properties of the Cobb-Douglas production function, the marginal cost function as modified by BD can be easily derived. Since price equals marginal cost, and input factor prices (w, r) are assumed constant, a change in total cost must be a function of L and K. One way to show this is as follows: total costs at equilibrium (TC) must equal the sum of the products of factor input quantities and factor prices (assumed constant):

$$(5) \quad TC = Lw + Kr;$$

while on the output side total costs must equal total quantity times market price:

$$(6) \quad TC = XC_X .$$

Two problems face the analyst: first there is the problem of placing the marginal cost in terms of marginal changes in the input variables, and second the problem of identifying the conditions of the factor inputs such that production costs will be minimized.

First, from the Cobb-Douglas production function, it is useful to show how changes in capital and labor affect the marginal product. That is, given the production function in Equation 7,

$$(7) \quad X = aL^{\beta} K^{1-\beta}$$

the marginal product of labor is:

(8) $\dfrac{\partial X}{\partial L} = a\beta L^{\beta-1} K^{1-\beta} = a\beta\left(\dfrac{K}{L}\right)^{1-\beta}$

and, the marginal product of capital is:

(9) $\dfrac{\partial X}{\partial K} = aL^{\beta}(1-\beta)K^{-\beta} = a(1-\beta)\left(\dfrac{K}{L}\right)^{-\beta}$

The important point to note from this is that for each additional unit of X produced, factor inputs must be consumed in the ratio (K/L). The specific level of capital K and labor L can be derived by optimizing the use of factor inputs in face of a budget constraint.

It has now been shown that as production increases, each unit of increase is brought about by a fixed ratio of factor inputs, and that the input factors will be used to the extent that their marginal product ratios equal their respective factor price ratios. The problem is now to return to specify the supply function in terms of the input factors; that is, an output term must be placed in terms of inputs.

The Cobb-Douglas marginal product functions have an interesting property that greatly simplifies the task of linking outputs with inputs. That is, the ratio of the marginal products to their respective average products are constants:

(10) $\dfrac{\partial X/\partial L}{X/L} = \dfrac{a\beta L^{\beta-1} K^{1-\beta}}{aL^{\beta} K^{\beta-1}/L} = \beta$

(11) $\dfrac{\partial X/\partial K}{X/K} = \dfrac{aL^{\beta}(1-\beta)K^{-\beta}}{aL^{\beta} K^{\beta-1}/L} = 1-\beta$

The constants are clearly the partial elasticities of municipal outputs with respect to factor inputs.

The final component of theory needed for a solution to the supply equation is a link between an input price and the output. To do this we shall sketch the procedure used to identify optimal output in terms of input qualities and their factor prices.

Graphically, the optimal solution can be seen in Figure 2. Isoquant curve Q_0 intersects at the tangent with the budget constraint or iso-cost curve, giving maximum output X_0 at factor inputs $(\overline{K}, \overline{L})$ and factor prices (w, r).

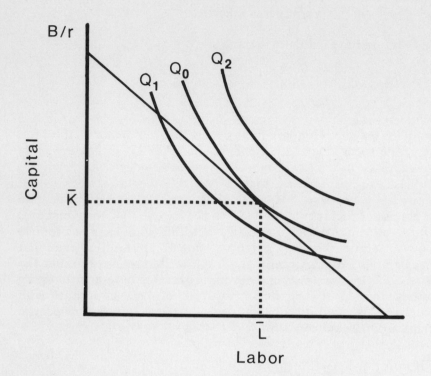

FIGURE 2
Optimal Input Combination under Budget Constraint

Conceptually, the technique used to find $(\overline{K}, \overline{L})$ is in this case the construction of a Lagrangian function and the simultaneous solution: $(\overline{K}, \overline{L}, \overline{\lambda})$ where $\overline{\lambda}$ is the Lagrangian multiplier. The optimization problem can be set up by using the production function as the objective function, a budget constraint equation where prices are assumed constant:

(12) $B = wL + rK$

and combining both in a Lagrangian function $F(L, K, \lambda)$:

(13) $F = aL^{\beta} K^{1-\beta} + \lambda (wL + rK - B)$

Minimization of the cost through the budget constraint equation involves solving the first order conditions:

$$(14) \quad F_L = a\beta L^{\beta-1} K^{1-\beta} + \lambda w = 0$$

$$(15) \quad F_K = aL^{\beta}(1-\beta)K^{-\beta} + \lambda r = 0$$

$$(16) \quad F_\lambda = + wL + rK - B = 0$$

and solving for λ :

$$(17) \quad -\lambda = \frac{a\beta L^{\beta-1} K^{1-\beta}}{w}$$

$$(18) \quad -\lambda = \frac{aL^{\beta}(1-\beta)K^{-\beta}}{r}$$

As an outgrowth of this operation, the relationship between the isocost and isoquant functions at the optimal point of production can be seen. By equating equations 17 and 18, the input price ratio is found to be equal to the ratio of the marginal physical products; the latter expression is termed the marginal rate of technical substitution. This

$$(19) \quad \frac{w}{r} = \frac{a\beta L^{\beta-1} K^{1-\beta}}{aL^{\beta}(1-\beta)K^{-\beta}} = \frac{\partial X/\partial L}{\partial X/\partial K}$$

relationship is interpreted to mean that the chief administrative officer of the municipality, acting as an entrepreneur, will, in order to minimize costs for a given output, trade off the use for factor inputs (L, K) in such a way that the ratio of their contribution to production at the margin will equal their input factor price ratio. If the solution were to be carried out to completion, the optimal values of $\overline{K}$, $\overline{L}$ and $\overline{\lambda}$ could be obtained.

We have seen from equation 19 that the factor price ratio is equal to the marginal rate of technical substitution at optimal levels of production. What is now needed is a way of determining the value of each factor price in relation to total or marginal costs. The theoretical solution to this problem states that the municipal corporation in an effort to optimize its use of resources will consume that quantity of a variable factor of production up to the point where the value of the marginal product equals the input factor cost. This statement is placed in the context of labor and capital inputs in equations 20 and 21:

(20) $\partial X / \partial L \ C_x = w$,

(21) $\partial X / \partial K \ C_x = r$,

where:

C_x = marginal cost or output price.

It must be noted here that planners should be aware of the work of both Niskanan (1971) and Courant, Gramlich, and Rubinfeld (1979) who have alternative approaches to the cost-output link within the municipal corporations.

Since the ratio of the marginal physical product to the average physical product is a constant, as shown in equations 10 and 11, marginal cost (the supply function) can finally be expressed in terms of outputs and inputs:

(22) $\beta \left\{ X / L \right\} C_x = w$,

(23) $(1 - \beta) \left\{ X / K \right\} C_x = r$,

and

(24) $L = \dfrac{\beta X C_x}{w}$,

(25) $K = \dfrac{(1 - \beta) X C_x}{r}$.

These terms can now be substituted into the production function (Equation 26) and the equation solved for the marginal cost term (Equation 27):

(26) $X = a L^{\beta} K^{1 - \beta} = a \left\{ \dfrac{B X C_x}{w} \right\}^{\beta} \left\{ \dfrac{(1 - \beta) X C_x}{r} \right\}^{1 - \beta}$

$$(27) \; C_x \; = \left(\frac{1}{a}\right)\left(\frac{w}{\beta}\right)^{\beta}\left(\frac{r}{1-\beta}\right)^{1-\beta}$$

At this point BD make an important simplifying assumption: labor's wages are assumed to vary across jurisdictions:

$$(28) \; w_j \; \neq \; w_{j+1} \;\; ;$$

however, rental rates for capital are assumed to be constant across all jurisdictions:

$$(29) \; r_j \; = \; r_{j+1} \;\; ;$$

thus, Equation 27 simplifies to:

$$(30) \; C_x \; = \; a'w^{\beta}$$

where the constant,

$$a' = \left(\frac{1}{a\beta}\right)\left(\frac{r}{1-\beta}\right)^{1-\beta}$$

The marginal cost for municipal goods production is expressed as a power function with the single argument being municipal employee wages.

This completes our review of the BD analysis of the municipal supply functions. We shall now turn our attention to their development of the municipal demand function.

Determination of Demand

As indicated earlier, two problems unique to the market solution to the supply and demand for public-municipal goods must be addressed: first, the description and quantification of municipal goods, and second, the decision-making process that aggregates individual choices for packages of municipal goods into a single bundle over the effective period of the collective decision.

Municipally supplied goods such as police, planning or park services are clearly different in nature from the common private good such as the family auto, clothing or food. The former is provided collectively and may or may not be consumed or be capable of consumption by the individual at any given moment for legal-social reasons; on the other hand, goods purchased by the individual

on the private market can in general be consumed when and in the
manner chosen by the individual. From such observable differences
as these, the mutually exclusive definitions of purely public and
purely private goods have emerged (Samuelson, 1954). A private
good in its polar extreme can be completely parceled out to individuals and independently consumed; a public good is provided in
such a manner that each unit produced can be consumed equally
by each and every individual within the society without diminishing its quality or quantity. This conceptualization has allowed
Samuelson to specify the equilibrium conditions for the production
of public goods: public goods should be produced up to the point
where the marginal social cost of removing goods from the private
goods market equals the marginal rate of substitution of public goods
from private goods in terms of utility in consumption (see Holcombe).

In practical terms, such a definition is difficult to apply to
municipal goods and services. Polinsky (1974) has identified four
dimensions along which imperfections may blur the distinction
between pure public and private goods:

(1) The spatial area permitting consumption; (2) nonsymmetry in
consumption, i.e., some characteristics of the individual consumer
alter the consumption of public goods; (3) excludability from
consumption by barriers other than jurisdictional boundaries; and
(4) rivalry or congestion in the consumption of the public goods.

The degree to which any jurisdiction may produce goods that
are less than perfectly public is for the most part an empirical
question. The most common approach to the specification of the
private-public goods issue is to assume nondiscrimination in the
provision of municipal goods such that each individual receives an
average share of the municipal good on its specific public-private
goods continuum. This is shown in Equation 31 as:

$$(31) \quad q = \frac{X}{N^{\alpha}}$$

where N is the population,

   X is the number of units of municipal goods produced,

   q is the number of municipal public goods consumed by an
      individual, and

   α is the degree of privateness found within municipal goods:
      $0 < \alpha \leqslant 1$

As the coefficient α approaches 1, factors are thought to be at work within the municipality that for any one of Polinsky's four reasons result in an increasingly private type of good. This in essence is the procedure used by BD to address the public-private nature of municipal goods.

The problem of price is the last theoretical issue to be dealt with by BD. In a perfectly competitive private market, equilibrium occurs at the point where the marginal cost curve intersects the demand curve; in the long run where firms can enter and exit the market, marginal cost (C_x) equals price (s). In the short run, where $C_x \neq s$, profits or losses can be obtained by the firms, creating movement into to out of the market.

In the public sector, jurisdictions do not normally enter and exit the market for public goods. Thus, a gap would be thought to exist between these two measurable quantities. However, while marginal cost can be handled with neoclassical production theory, the concept of price must be reformulated to take into consideration the structurally distinct payment mechanisms that exist within local government. In the private market, a buyer and seller are related through a "quid-pro-quo" situation; this good is delivered in exchange for that amount of money. In the municipal sector, revenues are commonly derived through the property tax, an institution not directly tied with the provision of municipal goods to the taxpayer. Thus, price to the taxpayer-consumer must take into consideration not only production costs but also taxpayer burdens. Public choice theory (See Holcombe) suggests that the decision of the median voter will determine or be the jurisdiction's choice as to budget policy or other policy issues; in the case of budget policy, the median voter is usually considered to be the owner of that parcel of residential property having the median value. It must be noted that non-property-tax revenue is usually considered as income to the jurisdiction; however, nonresidential property tax revenue has still further complicating factors surrounding its use in determining municipal budget policy. These issues will be treated later.

The BD approach to the tax-price problem is somewhat simplified in that total expenditures are hypothesized to be spent equally on all members of the jurisdiction's population. Thus, the average burden is the average or per capita expenditure level, and the tax price (Equations 32 and 33), commonly thought of as resources spent per unit of good, is the average per capita expenditure level per municipal public good produced.

$$(32) \ s \ = \ \frac{C_X X}{Nq} \ .$$

$$(33) \ s \ = \ C_X N^{\alpha - 1}$$

The final element to be added to the demand function is income. Most commonly, the income characteristic driving demand is considered to be personal income and is entered into the demand function in a manner similar to that done in the private-sector model. Municipal revenue derived from external sources such as intergovernmental aid can, as shown by Wilde (1968), however, enter as the demand function as income distributed to all members of the jurisdiction, or revenue having both an income and a tax effect depending on the matching provisions tied to its use by the donor level of government.

This completes the theoretical development of the municipal goods supply and demand. The original demand equation can now be solved for an equilibrium point where supply has been integrated into the tax price term by recursive methods:

$$(34) \ \overline{q} \ = \ A\bar{s}^{\eta} y^{\delta} \ .$$

In review, the quantity of municipal goods consumed at equilibrium has been derived through the use of a Cobb-Douglas production function in which the tax-price term incorporates the optimizing behavior of the municipal corporation in maximizing output while minimizing costs. Factor inputs to the municipal production function are assumed to be traded continuously until the marginal rate of technical substitution is equated with the factor-cost ratio; this property also permits the determination of marginal cost as a function of factor inputs. The public goods nature of municipal goods has been incorporated into the tax-price term as a determinant of demand, and lastly income has been incorporated directly into the demand function.

Each jurisdiction is recognized to possess a simple equilibrium condition, as shown in Exhibit 1. However, when comparing a set of jurisdictions, a system of supply and demand curves must be considered. In order to see this, we need to untangle the interdependencies due to the individual jurisdiction's supply- and demand-oriented behavior versus apparent simultaneity due to the comparison of several jurisdictions in one analytic space.

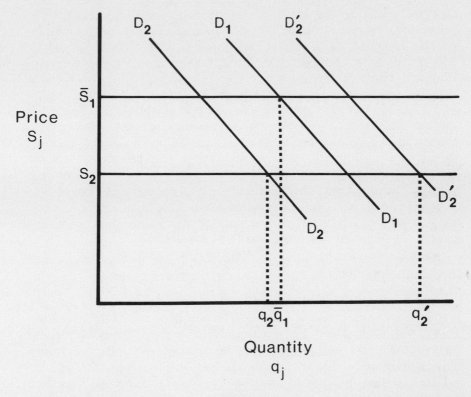

FIGURE 3

Municipal Goods Determination: The Market Model

Within each jurisdiction's decision-making process, three independent behavioral equations can enter the picture: (1) the production function; (2) the marginal cost function; and (3) the demand
function.

The remaining functions are either definitions or mixtures of the
above. Since the tax price equation is a combination of definitions
as well as the marginal-cost function, its behavioral characteristics
are derived from the latter. Since price is a function of exogenously
determinant wages, there is a clear path of causation resulting in
values for tax price.

Similarly, the demand equation contains the terms price and
income, and is internally consistent in terms of causal structure.
The interaction between supply and demand will produce an outcome ($\bar{s}_1$, $\bar{q}_1$) such as shown in Figure 3.

However, when several jurisdictions are compared in the same analytic space, an apparent source of indeterminancy exists. The price equation in Equation 32, for example, contains two endogenous variables: X, C_X; q is definitionally determined through X and the exogenous variable N. Thus, tax price (s_j) can change not only for behavioral reasons but also because of differences across jurisdictions in the values of the definitionally determined values of X_j or N_j. For example, the value of $s_j = s_2$ shown in Figure 3 is due to differences in C_X, N and X between jurisdictions 1 and 2. Since the change in s_j can be due to each of these influences and not behaviorally influenced by q_j the demand equation's location is due to exogenous factors such as income and the market solution is derived through the intersection of the jurisdictionally shifted supply curves s_2 and a jurisdictionally specific demand curve $[D_2$ or $D]$. Clearly when dealing with several jurisdictions, multiple supply and demand functions must be considered.

Municipal Expenditures

The final step in the BD model is the combination of supply and demand equations into a municipal expenditures model. Two alternative formulations of the expenditure function commonly appear in the literautre: total municipal expenditures and per capita municipal expenditures. The BD model utilizes the per capita form. Per capita municipal expenditures (e) are obtained through the definitional equation.

(35) $e = sq$

We recognize s and q as endogenous variables defined through the structural model shown in Equations 33 and 34. The reduced form of this equation, where only exogenous variables appear to the right of the equals sign is more efficient from the point of view of expenditure determination. Given the functional value of C_X shown in Equation 30, the basic expenditure equation is shown in Equation 36.

(36) $e = A'w^{\beta(\eta+1)}y^{\delta}N^{(a-1)(\eta+1)}$

The equation contains each of the fundamental economic influences needed to explain public expenditures in a municipality where the decision-making process includes both voter-citizen taxpayers who wish to maximize the benefits they individually received from both public and private sector and a municipal corporation whose sole concern is to minimize input costs for each level of output and selects the level of output corresponding with the demand of the citizen with the median income level within the jurisdiction.

Municipal Goods: A Focus on Demand

The structural model developed by Borcherding and Deacon placed an emphasis on the production process and the construction of a marginal cost supply function. The model we shall now investigate has been developed by Theodore Bergstrom and Robert Goodman. While it is quite similar in all of its basic assumptions and range of concerns to the former model, it focuses on the demand for municipal goods.

Five basic assumptions underly the model:

(1) Unit costs: C_{xj} are constant within each jurisdiction (j) but not necessarily across jurisdictions;

(2) The citizen's (i) tax share, τ_j, is the function of the total cost of municipal expenditures paid by "i". It can vary by income, wealth or other individual characteristics but not through formal or legal arrangements with the jurisdiction.

(3) The consumer (i) living in jurisdiction (j) faces a tax price $(\tau_i C_{xj})$ for a known quantity of municipal goods and services.

(4) For each jurisdiction, the quantity of municipal goods demanded, X_j, is equal to the median of the quantities demanded by its residents.

(5) The jurisdiction chooses the level of production of X_j that corresponds to the tastes of the voters with the median income.

In outline form, Bergstrom and Goodman (BG) first develop the conditions for optimal individual choice between private and municipal goods, assume a perfectly inelastic supply of municipal goods, specify a demand function and finally define the municipal expenditure functions. We shall now proceed through this sequence.

The point of departure for (BG) is the individual's effort to maximize utility in the consumption of private (P_i) and public goods (X_j):

(37) $U_i = f(X_j, P_i)$

subject to budget constraint:

(38) $y_i = P_i p + \tau_i C_{xj} X_j$

Analogous to the theory of production applied by Borcherding and Deacon, (BG) assume an analytic public goods-private goods space equally dense throughout with convex indifference curves permitting the use of an optimizing technique such as the use of a Lagrangian function (Equation 13) that will maximize U_i given income and prices. Given the mix of public-private characteristics within municipal goods, (BG) incorporate the degree of privateness in good X by the relationship:

$$(39) \quad q = \frac{X}{N^\alpha} \, ,$$

which is identical in meaning to that structured by (BD) in Equation 31. The revised budget constraint function is:

$$(40) \quad y = P_i p + \tau_i C_{xj} N^\alpha q$$

and price (s) is defined as:

$$(41) \quad s = \tau_i C_{xj} N^\alpha$$

The actual use of the budget constraint function is limited in practice to the specification of the price term $(\tau_i C_{xj} N^\alpha)$. This is, of course, essential to building a voter's demand function for municipal goods. For example, as the tax price of the municipal good increases from s_1 to s_3, the budget line shifts toward smaller levels of public goods consumption (q_1 to q_3), and the point of the optimal mix of consumption shifts in a similar manner from e_1 to e_3. This is shown in Figure 4, where the point of equilibrium shifts from high consumption levels of both goods in e_1 to greatly reduced levels of public goods at e_3, and due to the income effect associated with the price change in municipal goods, a reduction in private goods. If the behavior exhibited by the ith citizen is that of the median voter, a demand function for municipal goods can be constructed; this is shown in Figure 5.

The construction of the demand side is completed with the specification of the form of the function. As in the case of (BD), a constant elasticity model is proposed with the arguments being tax price and income.

$$(42) \quad q_i = a s_i^\eta y_i^\delta$$

The only essential difference between this and the (BG) model is the price term. In the current formulation, tax price is specified as the fraction $[\tau_i N^\alpha]$, of the unit or marginal cost of municipal

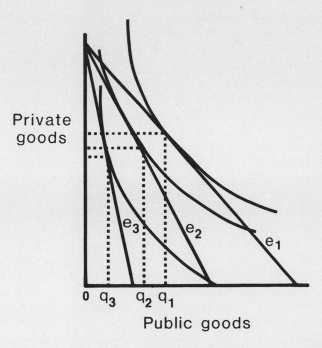

Private goods

e_3 e_2 e_1

0   q_3 q_2 q_1

Public goods

FIGURE 4
The Effect of a Price Change in Municipal Goods on the Optimal Quantity
of Private and Public Goods Consumed by Citizen i in Jurisdiction j

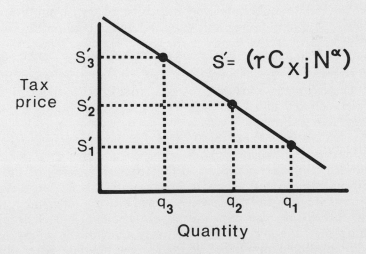

Tax price

S'_3

S'_2

S'_1

$$S' = (\tau C_{Xj} N^{\alpha})$$

q_3 q_2 q_1

Quantity

FIGURE 5
The Demand for Municipal Goods for Jurisdiction j

goods production $[C_{xj}]$, that is paid by the residential property-tax payer (Equation 41). In the Borcherding and Deacon model (Equation 33), the tax price term is total expenditures per capita $[C_x X/N]$ per unit of municipal public good $[q]$. Even though Borcherding and Deacon derive marginal cost through optimal production tradeoffs between labor and capital, their tax price is really an expenditure price on a per capita basis. Alternatively, their view may be one of assuming that citizens view all revenue sources as ultimately equally burdensome upon them whether the sources be intergovernmental and nonresidential property taxes or non-property taxes. Bergstrom and Deacon on the other hand relate tax price directly to the payment of revenues to the jurisdiction by the residential taxpayer, thus implicitly requiring all other revenues that are needed for a balanced budget to be viewed as cost-less income. These issues are partially addressed in the examination of Helen Ladd's work later in this chapter as well as that which is taken up in later chapters dealing with tax incidence, shifting and tax burden, and intergovernmental aid.

Returning to the Bergstrom-Goodman demand function, when expressed in its reduced form the equation is:

$$(43) \quad q = a(\tau_i C_{xj} N^\alpha)^\eta y^\delta.$$

The supply side is treated in much less detail in this model than it is in the (BD) model; however, the constant cost assumptions are the same, yielding a comparable supply-demand equilibrium solution for (BG) as is shown in Figure 1 for (BD). From a behavioral point of view, the models are the same from this point on; however, due to differences in the sequence of development (where municipal goods per citizen is extended to municipal goods per jurisdiction), the final demand equations and expenditure equations appear to have a different form.

It is recalled from Equation 36 that the Borcherding and Deacon model expresses municipal goods and expenditures in a per capita function, leaving the extension to the total population of the jurisdiction an algebraic effort on the part of the user. Bergstrom and Goodman integrate the extension process into the demand equation and therefore into the expenditure equation within their model. Recalling that the relationship between individually consumed or usefully consumed municipal goods by the median voter and the total package of municipal goods has been defined by the equation:

$$(44)\ q = \frac{X}{N^{\alpha}}$$

the total packaged municipal goods produced can be defined in terms of individually consumed goods as:

$$(45)\ X = q_i N^{\alpha}\ .$$

The demand equation for voter i (Equation 42) can replace q_i in this equation to give a demand for municipal goods that is jurisdiction-wide. This is:

$$(46)\ X = a(\tau_i C_{xj} N^{\alpha})^{\eta} y^{\delta} N^{\alpha}\ .$$

Finally, total expenditures (quantity times price) can be derived as:

$$(47)\ E = C_{xj} X = a\tau^{\eta} C_{xj}{}^{\eta+1} N^{\alpha(\eta+1)} y^{\delta}\ .$$

From the view of the utility maximizing voter, the total municipal budget (or functions such as police, fire, etc.) can be expressed as a function of four exogenous variables: tax share, unit cost of production, population size and personal income. These arguments are of course found in the reduced form equation (Equation 47); however, the truly meaningful relationships must be derived from the basic structural equations: the behavioral equation 42 (demand) and identities for public goods (Equation 37) and tax price (Equation 38). Although other factors may be present, from the point of view of demand theory developed by BD, all of the basic classes of demand determinants are incorporated into the model: prices, incomes and the degree of publicness exhibited by the total package of municipal goods. Not explicitly treated are the substitution effects with related goods, non-income-related tastes and preferences, and demand factors not directly attributable to individual citizens. This conclusion can be equally well attributed to the (BD) model as well. Both models explicitly treat the demand for municipal goods and services through the eyes of the median voter; this voter in turn is concerned solely with tax price (as variously defined) and personal income. No allowance except through the equation constant is allowed in theory for other phenomena within the jurisdiction. All other factors that may influence the demand for municipal goods are after-the-fact additions to the basic equations. For example, Borcherding and Deacon derive a logarithmic per capita expenditure equation of the form:

(48)   ln   (per capita expenditures)

$$= \ln A + B \ln w^{\beta} + C \ln N + D \ln y$$

where A, B, C, D are equation constants composed of the structural parameters of the model.

Recognizing the need to include other environmental factors in the model, an urbanization index (U) and land area index (L) are appended to the equation:

(49)   ln   (per capita expenditures)

$$= \ln A + B \ln w^{\beta} + C \ln N + D \ln Y + E \ln U + F \ln L.$$

In a similar fashion, Bergstrom and Deacon expand their individually oriented municipal goods demand function:

(50)   ln   (total municipal expenditures)

$$= \ln a' + b \ln \tau + c \ln C_{xj} + d \ln N + e \ln y$$

(where a', b, c, d and e are equation parameters composed in part of the basic structural parameters)

shown in Equation 51 to include factors such as housing tenure (H), business activity in the form of the employment-to-residence ratio (B), and several other factors, by augmenting Equation 50 with these factors to form Equation 51:

(51)   ln   (total municipal expenditures)

$$= \ln a' + b \ln \tau + c \ln C_{xj} + d \ln N + e \ln y + f \ln H + g \ln B...$$

Left unanswered in these formulations are the proper criteria by which phenomena, so important to the urban planner (such as commerical or industrial activity, multifamily rental housing, etc.), should enter into the demand and expenditure functions. In part these questions are addressed in the work of Helen Ladd (1976); it is to this work that we now turn.

Municipal Demand Functions and Tax Base Composition

A major contribution to the understanding of municipal expenditures and budget policy comes from the work of Helen Ladd (1976). Ladd has explored the role of nonresidential activity on both the revenue or tax price side of the budget as well as on the expenditure side. In this review, we shall focus on the former.

As in the previous cases, Ladd's model involves an individual utility maximizing process (Equation 52) subject to budget constraint (Equation 53); to establish the municipal budget:

(52) $U = U(X, S, H)$,

(53) $Y = P_x S + tP_h H + dP_h H$,

where   X is private goods consumed per family,
        S is municipal goods consumed per family,
        H is units of housing stock per house,
        P_h is price per units of housing stock,
        P_x is price per unit private goods, and
        t is municipal tax rate.
        d is a housing depreciation rate.*

Here, three classes of consumables are placed in the optimization process: private goods net of housing services, municipal public goods, and the flow of services derived from homeownership in jurisdiction j. Ladd modifies this budget constraint term in order to explore the budgetary impact of nonresidential development. Recall the Bergstrom and Goodman budget constraint (Equation 54).

(54) $y_i = P_i p + \tau_i C_{xj} X_j$.

Public goods were explicitly placed in the equation (X_j) as was their resource costs (C_{xj}) and the median voter's tax share (τ_i). Ladd's budget constraint is comparable in its allocation of the median family's income to municipal goods. However, its form has been modified; instead of total cost being based on tax price and quantity consumed, the cost to the family is based on the revenue requirements of local government as totally met by a real property tax. Thus, total municipal goods costs to (BG) are equivalent to the tax levied on the median voter's family:

(55) $\tau_i C_{xj} X_j = tP_h H$.

In order to maximize utility in terms of S, Ladd establishes an additional identity:

*This model is simplified somewhat by assuming total rivalry in municipal goods consumption.

(56) $tB = SCn$

where   B is the municipal property tax base,
          C is the unit resource cost of municipal goods and re-
             sources, and
          n is the number of service consuming units (families) in
             the jurisdiction.

In a sense this is a balanced budget identity in that the left side is
an expression of the total revenue needed to meet total municipal
expenditures, which in turn is the expression of the right side of the
equation. The value of this definition is its ability to bridge the
revenue-output relationship and to place the output to be maximized subject to budget constraint into the budget constraint (Equation 57).

(57) $Y = P_x X + SCn/B \ P_h H + dP_h H$

The proper specification of the tax-price term in the municipal-
goods demand equation can be determined through such means as
the Lagrangian technique. In this case the Lagrangian function
F is

$$(58) \ F = F(X, S, H) + \lambda \left(P_x X + \frac{\left(CnP_h H \right)}{B} \left\{ S + dP_h H - Y \right) \right.$$

The marginal rate of substitution of S for X can be derived from the
solution process, with the recognition that:

$$(59) \ \frac{\partial U}{\partial S} = \frac{\partial F(X, S, H)}{\partial S} + \frac{\lambda C_n P_h H}{B} = 0 \ ,$$

$$(60) \ \frac{\partial U}{\partial X} = \frac{\partial F(X, S, H)}{\partial X} + \lambda P_x = 0 \ ,$$

and solving for λ:

$$(61) \ \frac{\partial U/\partial S}{CnP_h H/B} = \frac{\partial U/\partial X}{P_x}$$

producing the result that the marginal rate of substitution equals the price ratio. The price of municipal public goods under the conditions required by Ladd is:

$$(62) \quad P_s = \frac{CnP_h H}{B}$$

This relationship is expressed in terms of the average units of housing for the median voter where:

$$(63) \quad H = H_m \ .$$

However, since total residential property value is expressed as average units of housing per household times price per unit, a method must be established whereby the average and median are related. This is done in Equation 64:

$$(64) \quad H_m = \frac{H_a H_m}{H_a} \ .$$

The price term: Ps, can now be rewritten as:

$$(65) \quad P_s = \frac{CnP_h H_a}{B} \cdot \frac{H_m}{H_a}$$

In this form, price from the point of view of the median voter can be seen to possess three types of terms:

C: unit or marginal cost of production of the municipal goods,

$nP_h H_a/B$:   the fraction of the property tax base that is residential (R) and

H_m/H_a: the ratio of the housing stock owned by the median voter to that of the average ownership unit.

In conclusion, the median voter's demand for municipal goods is derived from the three elements in the price term and income. In general functional form, the demand function is:

$$(66) \quad S = f\left(Y, C, R, H_m/H_a\right) \ .$$

Returning to Ladd's initial utility and budget constraint functions, several additional influences on the demand for municipal goods can be seen. Although difficult to measure empirically, the theory embodied in these equations points clearly to the tradeoffs voters can make between municipal public goods (S) and private goods (X):

$$(67) \quad \frac{\partial U/\partial S}{\partial U/\partial X} = \frac{P_s}{P_x} \; ,$$

and similarly, the tradeoffs in demand between municipal goods and the housing services provided the median voter:

$$(68) \quad \frac{\partial U/\partial S}{\partial U/\partial H} = \frac{P_s}{P_h} \; .$$

Since the consumption of private goods and housing services are alternative ways for the median voter to gain utility, the price of each of those goods (P_x, P_h) can also appear in the demand function. Given, as is shown in 67 and 68, that the marginal rates of substitution are equated with the respective price ratios when an optimal mix of goods is consumed, then any change in the price ratio will be transmitted via price, income and substitution effects into the consumption of municipal goods. As a consequence, as municipal goods become too expensive relative to the utility gained by the median voter, there will be a desire to consume the relatively less costly private goods or housing services. This finding may involve rejection of tax levies, tax ceilings, or expenditure ceilings (see Brennan and Buchanan) or long-term intrametropolitan shifts in residential location, such as hypothesized by Tiebout (see Holcombe). These influences can be incorporated in the municipal demand function as:

$$(69) \quad S' = f\left(Y, C, R, {}^{H}m/H_s, P_x, P_h\right)$$

where changes in both P_x and P_h as well as in personal income Y should be directly proportional to changes in S'; whereas, the municipal goods price-related elements C, R and H_m/H_a should be inversely related to changes in S'. Returning to Ladd's initial concern with the effect of tax base composition on the median voter's demand for municipal goods, we find from Equation 65 that the fraction of the tax base that is residential is an element of the tax-price term to the median voter. As a tax price, we can conclude that as that fraction increases in value, the fraction of the cost of a unit of service increases and, given median voter optimizing behavior in the face of budget constraint, this rising price will produce a substitution effect—private goods and housing goods for municipal goods—and an income effect—a reduction in consumption of all three classes of goods.

As a point of departure, Ladd's theoretical contribution suggests a further fiscal phenomenon. The substituting effect indicates that there may be a greater consumption of housing services after the tax-price increase; as this occurs, however, the property tax will take an increment of this growth in housing value causing the benefit maximizing voter to make an additional substitution, this time out of housing and into purely private goods. This can be seen as one of the theoretical links between fiscal policy and urban decline. It then follows that the reduced benefit level associated with a given jurisdiction will encourage the resident voter to move, thus linking the Tiebout model with that derived from microeconomic theory.

The Research Agenda: Environmental Influences

The demand functions for municipal goods and their corresponding expenditures functions are the focus of at least four types of improvements. The first arena for further research deals with a reexamination of the median voter's utility function.

Privatization of Municipal Services

The initial direction for further research is to be found in the impact of private sector alternatives to the production of municipal goods. This area of research is suggested in Ladd's utility function. (See Equation 52). Vehorn (1979) has explicitly dealt with this issue with respect to fire protection. The median voter's utility function is defined as:

$$(70) \quad U_m = U_m (q, s, X, Q)$$

where q = public fire protection
s = private fire protection
X = all other private goods
Q = all other public goods

Given an appropriate budget constraint, it can be seen that at voter equilibrium, public and private delivery of the same types of benefit providing service must both be considered for the proper specifications of the municipal goods demand function.

Identification of Supply and Demand Functions

A second focal point for further research is the basic causal logic buttressing the structional models of the demand for municipal goods. Most demand functions have employed what has been called the "Walrasian" type function. This type of function is supported by a causal mechanism that states that tax price is exogenous to quantity demanded. This is possible because the structional models assume constant marginal costs based on a homethetic production function and constant factor prices. Jhun and Yoo (1978) suggest to the contrary that a Marshallian-type demand function is most proper to the study of municipal demand. The Marshallian-type demand function models price as endogenously determined by quantity demanded. This concept reverses the direction of causation within the structural models, and at the empirical level (a subject not touched in this review) significantly alters the process of estimating the demand and a supply coefficients for each demand function.

The justification for the use of the Marshallian function is based on the notion of the Samuelson pure public good. If a good is a pure public good, the marginal cost for its consumption by a new citizen is zero. In such a case, society's marginal rate of transformation of private goods into public goods can be viewed as the societal marginal cost of public good consumption, while the sum of each individual's willingness to trade private goods for the public good (marginal rate of substitution) becomes the societal demand function for the public good. Samuelson's analysis defines an equilibrium position, it does not identify a behavioral process. This makes questionable the use of this approach to the identification of municipal demand functions; further, municipal goods are rarely if ever thought of as pure public goods. Problems of congestion (Hochman, 1982), rivalry, and various forms of exclusion (Oakland, 1969) suggest that municipal goods are far closer to the purely private than the public good. If this is the case with municipal goods, the Samuelson equilibrium definition no longer holds leaving its use as a justification for the shift in causalty in doubt.

The basic concern of Jhun and Yoo is still a relevant empirical and theoretical issue. William Fox (1980) broadens the analysis by identifying what may be assumed to be the basic elements of causation within the expenditure-tax share nexis.

The partial equilibrium approaches described above are of the general form:

Expenditures = (tax share, population, income...)

Fox contends that given the ability of individuals to adjust their property holdings within a jurisdiction, such as is suggested in the Tiebout model, it is necessary to look at the role expenditure policies may have on the tax share of the median voter.

Tax Share = g (expenditures)

If these policies can be shown to have measurable affects on the tax-share term, a system of simultaneous equations must be used to properly explain long-run municipal expenditures. Fox identifies each potential source of municipal intervention in the value of the individual's tax share by applying the tools of differential calculus to several basic budgetary equations.

Mathematically, the term to be decomposed is the derivative of tax share (TS) with respect to municipal expenditures (E):

(71) dTS/dE .

From the point of view of the average voter within the jurisdiction, tax share is the combination of two terms—the residential voter's tax base (b) and the jurisdiction's tax rate (r). In order to properly examine the separate effects of expenditure change on b and r, a total differential must be defined:

$$(72) \quad dTS = \frac{\partial TS}{\partial b} db + \frac{\partial TS}{\partial r} dr$$

That is, the total change in tax share is the sum of the product of the marginal change in tax share with a change in the tax base (holding r constant) and the marginal change in tax share with a change in tax rate (holding b constant).

From the point of view of the underlying causal process, the total differential must first be expressed as:

$$(73) \quad dTS = \frac{\partial(br)}{\partial b} db + \frac{\partial(br)}{\partial r} dr \quad ,$$

and each argument b and r of the tax-share term decomposed into its fundamental exogenous terms for long-run studies. The average tax-base term b is composed of the total residential assessed value within the jurisdiction R and the population supporting that value: p,

$$(74) \quad b = \frac{R}{p} \ .$$

The tax rate term is derived from the basic balanced budget equation:

$$(75) \quad E = bpr + Br + I$$

and

$$(76) \quad r = \frac{E - I}{bp + B}$$

where in addition to the previously used definitions

B is the aggregate business tax base, and
I is intergovernmental aid.

Assuming that Equations 75 and 76 contain all of the relevant fundamental causal factors, each component of the total tax share differential can now be differentiated.

The first term:

$$(77) \quad \frac{\partial (br)}{\partial b} \, db = r \, \frac{\partial \left(\frac{R}{p}\right)}{\partial b} \, db$$

allows the partial effects of a change in b on R and p holding r constant to be determined. Using the quotient rule:

$$(78) \quad r \frac{\partial \left(\frac{R}{p}\right)}{\partial b} db = \frac{p \frac{\partial R}{\partial b} - R \frac{\partial p}{\partial b}}{p^2}$$

The second term can be resolved in a similar fashion:

$$(79) \quad \frac{\partial (br)}{\partial r} \, dr = b \, \frac{\partial \left(\frac{E\text{-}I}{bp+B}\right)}{\partial r} \, dr$$

and:

$$(80) \quad b\frac{\partial\left(\dfrac{E-I}{bp+B}\right)}{\partial r}\,dr = b\left\{\frac{\dfrac{\partial E}{\partial r}-\dfrac{\partial I}{\partial r}}{pb+B} - (E-I)\left\{\frac{p\dfrac{\partial B}{\partial r}+b\dfrac{\partial p}{\partial r}+\dfrac{\partial B}{\partial r}}{(pb+B)^2}\right\}\right\}$$

Combining these findings into one marginal tax share equation we find:

$$(81)$$
$$\frac{dTS}{dE} = r\left(\frac{p\dfrac{\partial R}{\partial b}-R\dfrac{\partial p}{\partial b}}{p^2}\right)\frac{db}{dE} + b\left\{\frac{\dfrac{\partial E}{\partial r}-\dfrac{\partial I}{\partial r}}{pb+B} - \left(\frac{\dfrac{\partial p}{\partial r}+\dfrac{\partial b}{\partial r}+\dfrac{\partial B}{\partial r}}{(pb+B)^2}\right)(E-I)\right\}\frac{dr}{dE}\ .$$

The key terms from Fox's point of view are the seven partial derivatives. An expenditure policy that affects the per capita residential tax base, which in turn changes aggregate residential property values or population size, will produce a nonzero marginal tax share. Similarly, an expenditure policy that affects tax rate, which in turn changes expenditures, intergovernmental aid, population, residential tax base or business tax base, will add to the size of the marginal tax-share term. A nonzero value for the marginal tax-share term will necessitate the use of a system of simultaneous equations for the model of municipal goods demand.

Reexamination of the Nature of Municipal Goods

The third area for study to be examined in this review is that of structural models. The models incorporated in this review have all had one common basis: the municipal decision-making process is modeled as if the utility function of the median voter controls the demand for municipal goods, while production is optimized in terms of input allocation and costs. This model views municipal government as a relatively transparent production entity. Models such as Niskanen's utility-optimizing bureaucrat (see Holcombe), and the role of public employee power in affecting the supply function (see Courant, Gramlich & Rubinfeld) add in the former case an entirely new conceptual dimension onto the basic median-voter model, and in the latter case significantly expand the scope of price effects on the demand for municipal goods.

Finally, there is that ever-present, if rarely recognized, problem of the definition of municipal goods and services. The Samuelson concept of a pure public good as well as its modification in specific cases through the used concepts such as rivalry, congestion, jointness in consumption and the like, treat the citizen as a passive consuming entity whose benefit is a function of the physical product of municipal government. The problem with this thinking, brought out by Bradford, Malt & Oates (1969), is the relationship between the units in the municipal production function and those within the citizen's utility function.

Many goods and services purchased in the private market have a clearly predictable link between the purchase of a unit of the item (goods or services) and the benefit to be derived therefrom. For example, an appointment with a dentist will assure the patient, with a high probability of success, that the following 6 months will be cavity free; similarly, the purchase of a stereo receiver at a given price level will be closely associated with the quality of musical benefit derived by the consumer over time.

In a similar fashion, the output of local government can be viewed as the actual services (patrols, plans, street repairs, etc.) sold to the citizens in return for the payment of taxes. In the case of the repair of streets, removal of trash, provision of water, etc., the units of production and the level of benefit are conceptually comparable. However, in the case of police patrols, or the activities of the planning and fire or health departments, Bradford, et al. argue that the consumer-citizen is more interested in events not taking place (crime, fire, disease) than in the actual output—i.e., persons performing assigned tasks: patrol, standby, inspection, etc. To the extent that there is a difference between the direct output of municipal government and the desired but indirect output, judgment as opposed to rational conclusions must be used to link price, and income with output. I shall explore this problem to a greater extent in the topic to follow.

Municipal Supply and Demand:
The Search for the Proper Decision Making Center

In the work reviewed in this paper, demand for municipal goods has been specified from the point of view of the individual taxpayer-consumer. Public choice and neoclassical demand theory best explain the governmental decision process when strong knowledge of municipal prices and benefits desired by the individual for its goods exists. Yet to be deductively explored are the problems entailed in having multiple subgroups of individuals within the jurisdiction each with unique demands on local government. While it is true that median voter demand functions can be weighed with an index of their relative influence: as for example, percent of citizens who are elderly, Black or renters, the individualistically oriented theory states that any unique demands from these potential interest groups must first be recognized and placed in the median voter's benefit-cost calculus and only then impressed on municipal goods production.

Another related problem facing this type of demand function is the incorporation of nonresidential and therefore nonvoter service demands into the demand function. Typically, service demands emerging from employment centers such as industrial or commercial firms are added onto the median-voter demand functions. Although these clearly are business-related phenomena which do impinge on the median voter's awareness, such as externalities or synergistic effects of business and community characteristics, both explored by Ladd (1976), there remains to be incorporated in the demand function the direct influences of the business community for service generation.

The incorporation of those phenomena into the demand function for municipal goods raises interesting theoretical issues. The decision-making center in the preceding analyses has been the dominant or controlling voter within the jurisdiction. It is difficult, however, to see how or why the direct demands of the business sector should effectively focus on the median voter's utility function. One response to this concern is to opt for theoretical simplicity and to accept the model as our current best theoretical representation of a complex phenomenon. Another approach similar to the above is to assign the general characteristics of the individual utility-maximizing process to an aggregate community-preference function (Bahl, Gustely and Wasylenko, 1978). A more radical approach to this problem is to shift the focus from the median voter to the institutional structures of local government. Where the standard approach to explaining municipal goods supply and demand is to posit a market completely responsive to the constrained optimizing behavior of the median voter, William Niskanen posits the existence of a utility-maximizing bureaucrat whose utility function may be different from that of the median voter but whose objective function can be viewed as the maximization of the budget given the constraint that the budget must be equal to or greater than the minimum total costs of supplying the output expected by the bureau's sponsor. Furthermore, the bureaucrat is viewed as offering the municipal corporation a total package of goods and services in exchange for a total budget whereas the median voter accepts a unit of good or service at a given tax price.

Given that the bureaucrat is in a position central to the acquisition of information and its use vis a vis the bargaining process with the sponsoring group (city council), the pressure is to expand the budget in order to produce to the point where marginal benefits are zero while marginal costs are positive. Thus, it may seem questionable to use the marginal valuation of the median voter to represent the demand for municipal goods. The resolution of these extremes is suggested in the work of Courant et al. (1979).

Finally, it is suggested by Wallace Oates (1981) that many of the phenomena subsumed under the term "environmental influences" should be arguments to the municipal production function. This view supports further efforts to expand and integrate the work of Borcherding & Deacon (1972) and Niskanen (1971). However, this view also directly points toward the need for improved definitions of the municipal decision process as well as municipal output. Relating Niskanen's thinking with that of Bradford, Malt & Oates (1969) is perhaps the most critical problem in that the link between the production of direct output and the citizen-consumer's perception of the municipal output is the least well understood component in the model.

The particular type or quality of direct output has been judged to be highly significant in producing the desired indirect good. In the case of security or protection from crime, it is viewed that the production of a larger direct output (deployment of additional police officers) will have a crime deterence effect which in turn will increase the citizen's feeling of security. Ladd's work on expenditure demand brings out this conceptual issue (1976).

The perception of security (P) is hypothesized to be inversely related to the presence of business activity: (B)

$$(82) \quad \partial P/\partial B < 0$$

while in turn the presence of police manpower (S) increases the feeling of security:

$$(83) \quad \partial P/\partial S > 0 \; .$$

Ladd's work focuses directly on the security-insecurity related externalities produced by the presence of business actively within a community. That is, security (P) is an argument in the utility function of citizen i, along with the consumption of all other goods and services X.

(84) $U_i = U_i(P, X)$

Security or protection from crime or auto accidents (P) is viewed as an indirect output of the municipal corporation. The security production function (the link between direct and indirect output) is viewed as a function of police services (S), the direct output, and the environmental influence, business activity B.

(85) $P = f(S, B)$

This equation shows that the demand for police services (S) is clearly a derived demand based ultimately on the demand for protection (P). If the relationship between service delivery and protection is positive, the citizen will continue to support the delivery of police services; however, if the rate of change in perceived protection per unit police output per unit business activity becomes negative:

(86) $\dfrac{\partial P^2}{\partial S \partial B} < 0$,

then utility is lowered: i.e., $\partial P_i / \partial S < 0$

(87) $\partial U_i / \partial P < 0$.

A finding similar to this has been reported by a Police Foundation Study. In the Kansas City Experiment (Kelling et al., 1974), changes in preventive patrol activities were found to be unrelated to neighborhood crime rates. Although there are claimed to be methodological flaws in this experiment (Larson, 1975), nonetheless site-specific production functions for crime reduction must be based on inputs other than pure manpower with the information-related "threat of apprehension" being possibly the dominant factor (Cook, 1980).

In terms of the demand function, however, citizen support for the municipal budget policy may be withheld. To the municipal bureaucracy, however, the protection production function may remain unchanged.

(88) $\partial P / \partial S > 0$

This results in a confrontation of forces whose analogy in the operation of the private market does not exist and points up the need for further research.

Final Thoughts

Over the years the planning profession has shown a tendency to avoid theoretical paradigms and to rely on the use of brute empiricism in its technical analyses. One hurdle in the increased use of theoretical models is the issue of applicability. The presentation of the scholarly works reviewed in these pages has been done for the purpose of revealing both the economist's logic and his mathematical tools as applied to the study of municipal government. The study and use of this body of knowledge requires a certain openness and flexibility of mind, one that can accept a separation from concrete urban issues long enough to explore in almost game-like fashion a body of theory. The challenge here is the acceptance of the discipline required in the development and use of a structural model. The elements of this discipline include the clear use of well-defined terms (defined from the point of view of the theoretical paradigm), the willingness to accept logical and mathematical operations to simulate real world processes and finally, and perhaps most important, the insight necessary to bridge the gap from the model back to the planning problem.

REFERENCES

Roy W. Bahl, Richard D. Gustely, and Michael J. Wasylenko, "The Determinants of Local Government Police Expenditures: A Public Employment Approach," *National Tax Journal,* Vol. XXXI, No. 1 (March 1978) pp. 67-79.

Theodore G. Bergstrom and Robert P. Goodman, "Private Demands for Public Goods," *American Economic Review,* Vol. 63, No. 3 (June 1973) pp. 280-96.

Thomas E. Borcherding and Robert T. Deacon, "The Demand for the Services of Non-Federal Governments," *The American Economic Review,* Vol. 62, No. 4 (December 1972) pp. 891-901.

D.F. Bradford, R.A. Malt, & W.F. Oates, "The Rising Cost of Local Public Services: Some Evidence and Reflections," *National Tax Journal,* June 1969, pp. 185-202.

Robert W. Burchell & David Listokin, *The Fiscal Impact Handbook* (New Brunswick, N.J.: Center for Urban Policy Research, Rutgers), 1973.

Philip J. Cook, "Punishment and Crime: A Critique of Current Findings Concerning the Preventive Effect of Punishment," *The Economics of Crime,* Edited by Ralph Andreano and John J. Siegfried Wiley, 1980, pp. 161-68.

William F. Fox, "The Public Good Demand Function: A Comment," *Public Finance Quarterly,* Vol. 8, No. 2 (April, 1980) pp. 237-44.

Oded Hochman, "Congestable Local Public Goods in an Urban Setting," *Journal of Urban Economics* II, 290-310 (1982).

U-Jin Jhun and Jang H. Yoo, "The Public Good Demand Functions: Tax Share as a Dependent Variable," *Public Finance Quarterly,* July 1978, pp. 277-85.

G. Kelling, T. Pale, D. Diekman & C. Brown, *The Kansas City Preventative Patrol Experiment: A Summary Report.* The Police Foundation, Washington, D.C., 1974.

Helen F. Ladd, "Municipal Expenditures and the Composition of the Local Property Tax Base," *Property Taxation Land Use and Public Policy,* Edited by Arthur D. Lynn, Jr. (Madison: University of Wisconsin), 1976.

R. Larson, "What Happened to Patrol Operations in Kansas City: A Review of the Kansas City Preventive Patrol Experiment," 3, *Journal of Criminal Justice,* 1975, p. 267.

Ruth L. Mace, *Municipal Cost-Revenue Research in the United States: A Cricical Survey of Research to Measure Municipal Costs and Revenues in Relation to Land Uses and Areas, 1933-1960.* (Chapel Hill: Institute of Government, University of North Carolina), 1961.

Dennis C. Mueller, "Public Choice: A Survey," *Journal of Economic Literature* (June, 1976) Vol. XIV, No. 2, pp. 395-433.

William A. Niskanen, Jr., *Bureaucracy and Representative Government* (Aldine: Atherton, Chicago) 1971.

William H. Oakland, "Joint Goods," *Economics,* August 1969, pp. 253-68.

Wallace E. Oates, "On Local Finance and the Tiebout Model," *Papers and Proceedings, The American Economic Review,* May 1981, pps. 93-97.

A. Mitchell Polinsky, *Collective Consumption Goods and Local Public Finance Theory: A Suggested Analytic Framework* (Washington, D.C.: The Urban Institute), April 1974.

Paul A. Samuelson, "The Pure Theory of Public Expenditure," *Review of Economics and Statistics* 36 (Nov. 1954), pp. 387-89.

George Sternlieb, *et al., Housing Development and Municipal Costs* (New Brunswick, N.J.: Center for Urban Policy Research, Rutgers), 1973.

Charles L. Vehorn, "Market Interaction Between Public and Private Goods: The Demand for Fire Protection," *National Tax Journal,* March 1979, pp. 29-39.

and conclude that higher public sector growth may be the result. A related argument is made in the paper by Thomas Borcherding, Bush, and Robert Spann, who suggest that bureaucrats view public goods as yielding higher (wage) income as well as utility from consumption. If public employees perceive this added dimension as a reduction in the price of public goods, then public employees will opt for a larger public sector.

While certainly not complete, this brief overview of the literature is suggestive. A number of reasons have been given as to why public sector growth might get out of control, without much discussion of the possible checks on governmental growth. As Buchanan and Tullock themselves state, "Presumably there is some limit on this process, but it has not been determined either theoretically or empirically" (p. 150).

In this paper we attempt to respond to the theoretical gap recognized by Buchanan and Tullock by providing a model that permits explicit analysis of some of the issues just raised. The context of the model is a local government beset by growing political and economic power of its own employees on one side, and the threat of mobility of the private sector on the other. As regards the former, it is natural, but not necessary, to view the process in terms of a cohesive public employee union that can bargain for uniform (and high) public wages, and also can choose to vote for a larger public employee work force (though we will see that this particular behavior can be suboptimal). In terms of the classic seller-buyer dichotomy that underlies almost all of economics, to the extent that public employees or their unions gain political power over the budgetary behavior of the jurisdiction, the problem becomes interesting because the suppliers of public goods are in part their own demanders, with the private sector having little to do but pay the bills.

Section I presents the assumptions of the model. Of particular importance is the assumption that public employees have some control over both their own wages and the level of public output. Section II shows how the size of the government budget and its composition between wage rates and employment are determined, first when the private sector workers are the dominant electoral bloc, and then when public sector workers assume control. The main object of interest in this latter case is the ratio of government spending to total income of the community, which will be shown to depend ultimately on the sensitivity of private sector location decisions to the cost of government services. In Section III we deal explicitly with how the competing demands of public and private sector employees might be resolved by a majority rule voting process, noting that public employee bargaining power can alter the level of public employment and public expenditures even when these employees are a minority of the total voting population. This has important implications for the median voter theory, at least in its simplified form, because it argues that even when the median voter is a private employee, the presence of public sector market power will result in a level of public sector expenditures which is influenced by public sector voting power as well as bargaining power. At the same time, the influence of public employees should be a good deal less than is often claimed in the popular press, because the threat of outmigration by private employees constrains the size of the public budget. In addition, for a given public budget, as the employee work force gets large, public wages must fall. Finally, in Section IV, we conclude by summarizing the implications of the analysis for the question of the controllability of public budgets and suggest some further policy issues that might be examined.

I. Assumptions of the Model

To clarify the analysis which follows, we first list the assumptions used in the paper, grouping them by topic.

ASSUMPTION 1. *Employee Optimization:* All actions in the model are employed in either the public or private sector,[4] and maximize utility functions with the arguments private consumption (C) and public output (E_g). The latter is measured exactly by the level of public employment. This assumption is the basis for the voting and private spending behavior of all employees.

ASSUMPTION 2. *Mobility and Tastes:* We assume that all private sector employees have identical tastes for public and private output, and all public sector employees have identical tastes, though the tastes of the public and private employees will in general not be the same.[5] Since a major theme of the paper is the effect of private sector mobility on the size of the government budget, we assume that although private employees have identical tastes for output, their underlying desires to live in the community vary randomly. When things become sufficiently disadvantageous, those members of the private work force with the weakest desires to live in the community will leave.[6]

ASSUMPTION 3. *Goods and Labor Markets:* We make what might be known as small-country assumptions regarding the behavior of goods and labor markets. Private sector workers produce consumption goods (C) which are sold on a national market at a fixed price which we normalize at unity. All returns from the sale of these consumption goods are distributed equally to the private employees (E_p). Hence the private wage bill W_p (the private money wage) times E_p equals the gross value of private output (C).[7] Over the relevant range, there are no diminishing returns to private sector labor, so W_p remains constant. All private sector workers are assumed to supply labor inelastically as long as they remain in the community.[8]

ASSUMPTION 4. *The Public Sector:* We assume that the government must always balance its budget. Total revenues, the product of a tax rate and the tax base, must equal total expenditures, the product of the number of government employees (E_g) and their annual money wage rate (W_g). The nominal tax base is simply total community wage income (both private and public). The tax rate on income is assumed to be proportional and uniform across all employees, though the model could easily be adapted to cases of progressive or regressive taxes. The level of government output (E_g) is determined by the majority voting of utility-maximizing citizens.

ASSUMPTION 5. *Income and the Tax Base:* Since all income in the community is wage income, total income may be represented by an index of wages (W*) times total employment ($E = E_g + E_p$).[9] Thus,

(1) $W^*E \equiv W_p E_p + W_g E_g$

Note that when government employees have no bargaining power, $W^* = W_g = W_p$. With bargaining power, W_g can exceed W_p, and W* becomes a weighted average of wage rates in the two sectors.

In the competitive case where employees have no bargaining power, all wages are taken as given and the tax base is fixed and independent of the composition of output between the public and private sector. When employees have bargaining power, upward changes in W_g will alter W*E for two offsetting reasons: a) since private wage rates are fixed by the price of consumer goods, increases in W_g at a given E_g will tend to raise W*E through the $W_g E_g$ term; and b) since private employees are allowed to leave the community in response to monopolistic behavior by public employees, declines in E_p at a given W_p will lower $W_p E_p$ and thus W^*E.

II. The Model

The results of the model are described by first calculating outcomes when private employees are the dominant voting bloc—giving the standard outcome of prevailing public finance theories. We then contrast these results to those that are obtained when public employees are given control over public output, public wages, or both together.

A. Private Employees

Private sector employees are assumed to maximize a utility function of the form

(2) $U_p = U_p(E_g, C_p)$

where U_p is the level of utility achieved by private employees when optimizing with respect to the level of public sector employment and private consumption of private employees (C_p). The utility function is maximized subject to the budget constraint

(3) $W_p = C_p + P_p E_g$

where P_p is the price that the private employee must pay for the hiring of an additional public servant, and the private employee is assumed to be a price taker with respect to both private consumption goods and public employment.

The price paid by a private sector employee for a unit of public output is equal to the product of the cost of a public employee (the public sector wage, W_g) times the *share* of community-wide taxes paid by the private sector voter. If taxes are assessed on a per capita basis for all N residents of the jurisdiction, this price (W_g/N) is independent of the income of the private sector employee. However, with out assumption of a proportional income tax,[10] the share of wages the private sector voter must pay is W_p/W^*E, where W^*E is the tax base of the community.[11] The price of a public employee is thus given by

(4) $P_p = W_g W_p / W^*E$

After substituting (4) into (3), we obtain the budget constraint for the private employee:

$$(5) \quad C_p = W_p \left(1 - \frac{W_g E_g}{W^*E}\right)$$

The private employee assumes that the tax base W^*E and the prices he faces are not affected by his actions and maximizes (2) subject to (5). Solving the first-order condition yields

$$(6) \quad \frac{U_1}{U_2} = \frac{W_g W_p}{W^*E} = P_p$$

This is the standard result (appropriate for both voters in political elections and private consumers) that the individual will desire to consume that amount of public goods which equates the marginal rate of substitution with the price ratio.

In the case of the CES utility function, for example, the utility function is

$$(7) \quad U_p = [aE_g^{-r} + (1-a)C_p^{-r}]^{-1/r}$$

and the optimal level of public employment of condition (6) is

$$(8) \quad E_g = \left\{ \left[\frac{a}{1-a}\right]^{-1/(1+r)} \left[\frac{1}{W_p}\right]^{r/(1+r)} \left[\frac{W_g}{W^*E}\right]^{1/(1+r)} + \frac{W_g}{W^*E} \right\}^{-1}$$

where $r = (1-s)/s$, s being the elasticity of substitution, and a is the distribution parameter. It is easy to show that E_g is homogeneous of degree zero in all prices. In addition, $\partial E_g / \partial W_g$ will always be negative. The desired level of public employment arising from equations (6) and (8) is equivalent to the level of public output resulting from the familiar median voter model in which the median voter is a private employee. (See, for example, James Barr and Otto Davis; Theodore Bergstrom and Robert Goodman; Borcherding and Robert Deacon.)

B. Public Employees

The constrained maximization exercise for public employees is very similar. Employees are assumed to maximize

(9) $U_g = U_g(E_g, C_g)$

subject to

(10) $W_g = C_g + P_g E_g$

where C_g is the private consumption of the public employees and P_g is the tax price facing public employees; i.e.,

(11) $P_g = W_g^2/W*E$

At this point an important difference arises between the analysis for the public and private sectors. The difference is that while private sector employees take both public and private wages as given and choose their consumption of public goods (and thereby private goods as well), public employees are assumed to have greater choice. We analyze three cases. First, analogous to the private employee optimum, we consider public sector optimization when the public sector wage (W_g) is fixed. Second, we assume that E_g is fixed, and solve to find the wage rate public employees would set if they had unlimited bargaining power. Third, we combine the first two to find the optimum when E_g and W_g are simultaneously determined. Unless otherwise incidated, in all cases it is assumed that the public sector employees acting in concert are aware of the effects of their policies on the tax price which they face (equation (11)).[12].

For a given value of W_g, the optimal level of public employment for public sector employees is found through a straightforward extension of the private employee optimization exercise by substituting (10) and (11) into (9) and maximizing with respect to E_g:

(12) $\dfrac{U_1}{U_2} = \dfrac{W_g^2}{W*E} = P_g$

or in the case of a CES utility function:

(13) $E_g = \left\{ \left[\dfrac{b}{1-b}\right]^{-1/(1+r)} \left[\dfrac{1}{W_g}\right]^{r/(1+r)} \cdot \left[\dfrac{W_g}{W*E}\right]^{1/(1+r)} + \dfrac{W_g}{W*E} \right\}^{-1}$

where b is now the distribution parameter for public employees, but where the elasticity of substitution, $(1/1 + r)$, is the same as in the private case. Comparing (13) with (8), we see that the level of government employment desired by public employees is greater than than desired by private sector employees when

$$(14)\left(\frac{W_g}{W_p}\right)^r > (\frac{1-b}{b})(\frac{a}{1-a})$$

In the usual case where $r > 0$ (demands for public expenditures are price inelastic), this condition is met with $W_g = W_p$ and $a < b$ (the basic demand shift parameter is higher for public employees), when $a = b$ and $W_g > W_p$ (the income effect of higher public wages outweighs the substitution effect), or when some combination of the two conditions holds. Differentiating both (8) and (13) with respect to W_g, we see further than

$$(15a) \quad \epsilon_p = (\frac{-1}{1+r})(1 + r\frac{W_g E_g}{W^*E})$$

$$(15b) \quad \epsilon_g = \epsilon_p + (\frac{r}{1+r})(1 - \frac{W_g E_g}{W^*E})$$

where ϵ_g and ϵ_p are the price elasticities of demand for public and private employees, respectively. Again, when $r > 0$ the public employee demand elasticity will be less negative than that for private employees because the public wage W_g now has a dual effect, raising the price of public goods while also raising the income of public employees.

The second case we consider assumes that E_g is fixed and finds the wage that government employees would prefer if they had unlimited bargaining power. Obviously the fact that employees prefer this wage does not mean they will get it, but it is still fruitful to go through the case to see how the government wage rate and wage bill will tend to move as employees gain bargaining power.

The main limitation on the public sector wage rate in this case is the mobility of the private sector. We assume that there is at least one other accessible community and that public sector wage behavior is not identical in all jurisdictions.[13] To delineate the behavior of private employees further, we assume that each individual's level of utility attained depends not only on the level of public output and private consumption, but also on the characteristics of the community per se (for example, terrain, accessibility to relatives). To summarize this fact, we assume that each individual obtains a *quasi rent* from residence in the community with its unique characteristics. We also assume that there is a distribution of quasi rents, with the quasi rent for each individual given by A^i so that the actual level of utility of individual i is

(16) $U_p^i = U_p (E_g, C_p; A^i)$

where each quasi rent A^i is drawn from a known probability distribution and is strictly separable with respect to the other arguments of the utility function. Assume that each employee decides whether to move by comparing his level of utility U_p^i to the level of utility achievable in the best of all other jurisdictions, $U_p^{'i}$. If U_p^i is greater than or equal to $U_p^{'i}$, the private employee remains in the community. If U_p^i is less than $U_p^{'i}$, emigration occurs.

To simplify the analysis we assume that the parameters A^i are chosen so that private employees can be ranked in terms of the level of quasi rents that they achieve in the original jurisdiction. Specifically, we assume that if $A^i > A^j$ for employees i and j, then $U_p^i - U_p^{'i} > U_p^j - U_p^{'j}$. Define A^* to be the minimum value of A^i for all private employees residing in the original jurisdiction, as shown in Figure 1. All citizens with A^i greater than or equal to A^* reside in the community; all with $A^i < A^*$ do not.

Now consider the impact of a change in the public sector wage rate W_g. The gross income earned by public employees ($W_g E_g$) obviously rises, but since the model is open to trade as well as migration, the price of goods sold by the private sector is fixed, as are the gross receipts earned ($W_p E_p$). Hence if there is no migration W^*E will rise, but so will the tax rate on private income $W_g E_g/W^*E$. This increase in the tax rate implies that the consumption of private employees, given by (5) will decline, as will the utility of these employees. This outcome is shown graphically in Figure 1 as a downward shift in the U^i schedule. The result is an increase in A^* to A^{**}, the emigration of all private employees with A^i between A^* and A^{**}, a decline in E, and a decline in W^*E if the percentage decline in E exceeds the percentage rise in W^*.

In the more usual case the rise in W_g will lead to a decline in E_g (according to first-order conditions (6) or (12) above). Private employees then lose utility directly from the drop in E_g and indirectly if C_p falls (i.e., the tax rate rises). This in turn will happen whenever $W_g E_g$ rises, or whenever demands for public services are price inelastic.[14]

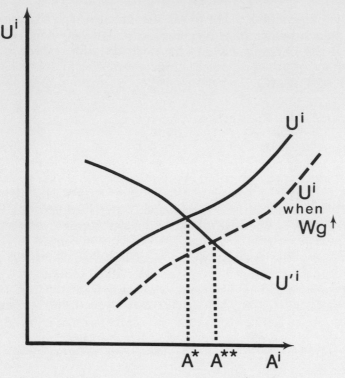

FIGURE 1. Mobility of Private Employees

As a general matter, then, we can assert that for relevant values of W_g, E_g, and W^*, private employment and earnings $(W_p E_p)$ will be negatively related to the public sector wage rate. If public sector employees are rational, they will take this mobility explicitly into account in determining their optimum wage levels, by recomputing the price of government services facing their members (equation (11)) as

$$(17) \quad P_g = \frac{W_g^2}{W^*E(W_g)}$$

where W^*E has been replaced by $W^*E(W_g)$, indicating that the tax base is a function of W_g.

It then becomes important to see how W^*E changes with W_g. There are two offsetting influences: a) the rise in W_g will alter the government wage bill $W_g E_g$ directly; and b) the rise in W_g will reduce private employment E_p and lower the private wage bill and hence the tax base available to public employees. We can summarize these influences by defining the tax base elasticity with respect to public wages as

$$(18) \ \eta = \frac{dW^*\!E}{dW_g} \frac{W_g}{W^*E}$$

$$= (W_p \frac{dE_p}{dW_g} + E_g + W_g \frac{dE_g}{dW_g}) \frac{W_g}{W^*E}$$

where the first term in the parentheses is clearly negative, the second is clearly positive, and the final term is probably negative but could actually go either way depending on who is setting E_g and the value of r (see equation (15b)). The highest η could be is + 1 (when $dE_p/dW_g = 0$ and when $W_p E_p$ is very small relative to $W_g E_g$), but there appears to be no lower bound on the elasticity.

In the case we are considering, E_g is fixed, the third term in the parentheses drops out, and public employees maximize W_g given this level of E_g. This is tantamount to maximizing

$$(19) \ C_g = W_g \ (1 - \frac{W_g E_g}{W^*E(W_g)})$$

which (differentiating with respect to W_g) yields

$$(20) \ \frac{W_g E_g}{W^*E} = \frac{1}{2 - \eta}$$

Hence the optimum solution is for employees to set the *entire* government budget as a share of the tax base. Other things equal, as the fixed level of government employment rises, the optimum wage declines. Further, when η is close to its highest attainable value of + 1, the share of the government budget in the total tax base, $W_g E_g/W^*E = t$, is close to unity: public employees take almost all of total output. But as η becomes negative, the share of government declines gradually. Indeed, in the opposite extreme case where the set of A^i for all private workers is sufficiently close to A^*, the private sector is so mobile and has so much bargaining power that the optimum public sector wage could get driven below the private wage. Again, we can rule out this outcome for logical

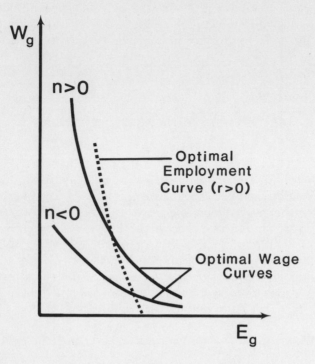

FIGURE 2. Optimal Wage and Employment Behavior with Mobility

reasons, because as soon as it begins to happen, public sector employees could also quit their jobs and work in the private sector. Hence (20) should be viewed as giving the upper bound on public wages and W_p as giving the lower bound.[15]

Next we consider the third case in which public sector employees are allowed to set E_g and W_g simultaneously. The first-order conditions (12) and (20) are the same, but now they must be solved simultaneously:

$$(21) \quad \frac{U_1}{U_2} = \frac{W_g}{E_g(2-\eta)}$$

This simultaneous equilibrium is summarized graphically in Figure 2, where in each panel the dotted line is the expenditure first-order condition (12) and the two solid lines are the possible wage first-order conditions(20), with the top line showing the situation where $\eta > 0$ and the bottom solid line showing the wage first-order condition

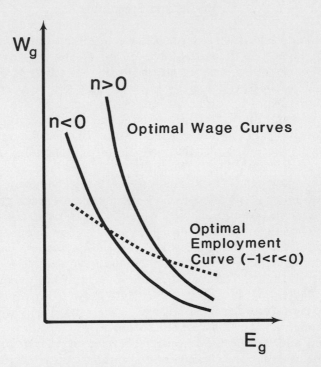

FIGURE 2. Optimal Wage and Employment Behavior with Mobility

when $\eta < 0$. As η becomes negative, the private sector is more mobile and the optimal wage for any E_g is shifted down. But the wage at which the ultimate intersection between the expenditure and wage condition takes place may be shifted either up or down, depending on public employees' price elasticity of demand for E_g (equation (15b)). If demand is inelastic (as in the left-hand panel), a community with a great deal of mobility (i.e., one in which η is negative) will have lower wages and a higher equilibrium level of government output than will a community with enough mobility so that η is exactly equal to zero. But if demand is elastic (as in the right-hand panel), a counterintuitive result arises: here the community with more mobility actually has a *higher* level of wages and a lower level of public employment than the community where not as much mobility is possible. Hence even though private sector mobility will constrain public employee wage demands at any given level of government employment, the full market equilibrium can lead to some surprising readjustments.[16]

III. Voting and Bargaining

In Sections I and II we described the determination by private and public employees of their desired levels of public employment. In this section we outline a resolution to the conflicting desires of private and public employees by introducing a simple majority-rule voting mechanism. In order to enrich the analysis we drop the assumption that the tastes of private and public employees are identical within groups, and instead assume that public and private employees have known distributions of tastes, which are in general different from each other. Thus, the analysis of desired levels of W_g and E_g now becomes an analysis of the levels desired by the median (or, more generally, the decisive) member of each group, and we assume that the chosen level of public output is equal to the desired level of the median voter.[17]

Consider first the case in which the public sector has a fixed amount of bargaining power and there is no mobility. Real wages in the public and private sectors are not necessarily equal—they could be higher in the public sector—but they are independent of current expenditure demands and the composition of employment in the community. In this case both sectors can be assumed to know W_g and W_p and vote for their optimal level of E_g, given for the private sector in equation (6) and for the public sector in (12) (where these now give the levels chosen by the decisive member of the respective groups). In general the two expressions imply different demands for public employment for three reasons: a) if relative wages differ, incomes differ and the income effect will lead to different public employment demands; b) if relative wages differ, tax prices differ and the substitution effect may lead to different demands; and c) the basic parameters of the utility function may not be the same.

If W_g is in excess of W_p, consideration a) would induce public employees to vote for larger public employment, consideration b) suggests smaller, and consideration c) is ambiguous, but probably dictates larger public employment. Regarding the latter, public employees might be sympathetic to the services they produce or have a job security motive where their own security depends on their seniority, which in turn would depend positively on the size of the public employee work force. As long as the substitution effect of higher public wages is small, and public employees have strong tastes for public output, they will vote for larger public employee work forces than will private employees, as shown in Figure 3.[18]

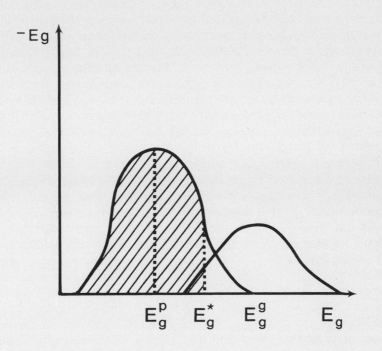

FIGURE 3. Distribution of Voters for Public Employment

In light of these considerations we assume the median private sector voter will want a smaller public work force (E_g^p) than the median public employee (E_g^g). As long as E_g is less than half of E, there will more private sector workers (larger area) and the voting mechanism will result in an employment level between E_g^p and E_g^g, closer to the median of the private employee distribution, where the shaded area includes exactly one-half of the total voters and E_g^* represents the vote of the median voter of the entire resident population. Note that the median voter is either a private employee with a strong taste for public output (relative to that of other private workers) or a public employee with a weak taste for public output (relative to that of other public employees).

The question becomes somewhat more intricate when we realize that wage bargaining strength might also be endogenous. Once the public employee work force rises to some critical level, these employees become strong enough to influence elections, and it does not take an extreme cynic to imagine political candidates attempting to bribe unions into supporting the "right" party either with high wage increases or with the promise of institutional changes that facilitate future union bargaining.[19] We might assume that when the public sector is very small, public employee wages are set competitively at W_p, but that as E_g grows, public employees have progressively more power in moving to their desired wage given in (20). But there is a catch here: recall that (20) implies $W_g = W*E/E_g$ $(2 - \eta)$. As soon as E_g rises to the value of $E/(2 - \eta)$, the *optimal* wage desired by public employees is equal to the wage received in the private sector. Hence the maximum ratio of W_g to W_p will be achievable at a value of E_g between 0 and $E/(2 - \eta)$. This is shown in Figure 4 as a result of a political weighting of the competitive wage line ($W_g = W_p$) and the optimal wage line of expression (20). If $\eta > 0$, the range of E_g/E for which $W_g > W_p$ will extend past $E/2$, implying that public sector workers could simultaneously have a small enough sector to raise their wages and a large enough voting bloc to achieve their wage and expenditure objectives. But in general η is probably less than zero and the optimum economic level of E_g, that at which W_g is maximized, is almost certainly a good deal less than the optimum political level of E_g (where the voting influence is strong enough that workers can achieve their wage first-order condition).

The preceding discussion is both similar to and different from Tullock's "Dynamic Hypothesis on Bureaucracy." Like Tullock, we have assumed that bureaucrats' political power is endogenous, and can be expected to be increasing in the fraction of the population which is employed in the public sector. But our analysis differs from his in one important respect: he suggests that bureaucrats will use an increasing fraction of their power to raise public sector *wages* as their employment rises. In our model this is not possible beyond some point, because the public employee's own *optimum* wage *decreases* as the level of public employment rises. Furthermore, the downward-sloping optimum wage curve is inherent in the technology of "exploitation" of the private sector—even if all of private sector income could be expropriated and there were no mobility (i.e., η approaches unity), the amount of such income available to each public employee must perforce be decreasing in the number of public employees. Thus, while we agree with Tullock that public employee *political power* will increase in the level of public employment, the ability of public employees to

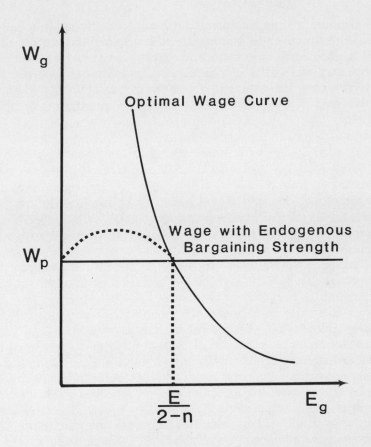

FIGURE 4. Relative Wages for the Public Sector

convert that power into high wages will be attenuated both by the mobility of the private sector and by the simple arithmetic of "dividing up the pie."

Putting things in this light implies that even a strong public sector union should ultimately be controllable. Since the total government budget desired by public employees is constrained by private sector mobility, public sector monopolies interested in maximizing the individual employee's wage will find it economically optimal to aim at a share of total employment that should be substantially less than E/2. As long as voting participation rates are the same among public and private sector employees, this assures that the public sector worker-voters will remain a minority. Moreover, there are two other constrains on behavior which temper public employee power even further: a) public employees themselves will be schizophrenic in the sense that their own public-private spending desires (equation (12)) may conflict with the E_g solution of Figure 4; and b) private sector employees may learn that increases in E_g increase the risk that the public sector can move toward its optimal wage curve, and these private employees may take this as another constraint in their own voting.

IV. Implications

At this point it may be helpful to return to the original message and pull together what this model has to say about it. The original fear was that as public servants are hired, they would become a steadily more dominant electoral force, elect politicians who would grant them steadily more market power, and the upshot of the rising levels of E_g and W_g would be steadily greater public budgets and higher tax rates. The public sector becomes dominant and the private sector is struggling, maybe unsuccessfully, for survival.

This model tries to put these fears in perspective by treating them analytically. The major conclusion is that as long as the private sector retains its right to leave the community, and as long as all communities are not suffering high and rising tax rates, public sector monopolies ought to be kept in check by the simple optimizing behavior of these same public employees.[20] It shows further that the optimum public wage depends inversely on the size of government employment. Adding public employees may increase the political strength of unions but it also decreases the wage they will desire to attain. Finally, on the demand side, both public and private voters in their expenditure demands will also be price sensitive. As public employees try to enforce higher levels of public sector wages, private voters will force down the share of public employment, which should reduce even more the chance the public sector monopolies will be able to raise wages and exploit the private sector.

NOTES

[1] Much of this rhetoric is contained in popular articles; see Norman MacRae and Jude Wanniski. The relevant formal empirical literature involves a discussion of Adolph Wagner's law by such authors as Richard Wagner and Warren Weber and Richard Bird.

[2] A related approach, emphasized by political scientists but rarely by economists, concentrates on the voting pressure of the clientele groups of government programs. One economist's treatment of this issue is by Richard Craswell.

[3]   The idea was treated in passing by Melvin Reder. See also John Pencavel. The empirical work of such authors as Ronald Ehrenberg and Gerald Goldstein, and Sharon Smith is also indirectly relevant.

[4]   Implicit in this assumption is the existence of some mechanism (such as a union) whereby public employees determine who will work in the public sector. It is further assumed that once in the public sector, all public employees get paid the same wage, which, due to the limitation on entry, could exceed the private sector wage. The model could be extended to deal with seniority rules of various kinds.

[5]   If an individual changes sectors, he is assumed to acquire the tastes associated with his current sector, either because of a socialization process or because he now has the same interests as others in his current sector. The assumption of identical tastes within sectors will be relaxed in Section IV, where we consider distributions of tastes. Even there, however, we retain the assumption that if an individual changes sectors his tastes are drawn from the distribution associated with his current sector.

[6]   We do not consider the potential mobility of public employees because our major interest is in private sector responses to the exercise of public sector market power. Whatever public employees are likely to do in response to the exercise of such power, it is unlikely that they will leave the community and thus abandon the fruits of their ability to exploit the private sector.

[7]   Nonwage income can be incorporated into the analysis by viewing the private wage W_p as the gross pretax income of private workers from all sources, including capital ownership and returns to entrepreneurial services.

[8]   It would be possible to incorporate a variable labor supply, but the qualitative results will differ little from those when private workers are free to leave the community.

[9]   In effect, we have assumed that both sectors produce output by means of a constant returns-to-scale one-factor technology. Explicit consideration of two-factor production functions in either one or both sectors would both complicate and enrich the model. For example, one could examine a situation in which factor intensities differed in the two sectors, in which case changes in the allocation of labor would induce changes in the private sector wage. While such possibilities could be important, for the sake of brevity we do not treat them here.

[10]   This approximates Joseph Pechman and Benjamin Okner's findings for the *U.S.* local government sector.

[11]   If wage rates are fixed in the public sector but not the same in both sectors, changes in E_g voted on by private employees will reallocate labor between the two sectors and make a slight alteration in the nominal tax base of the community and therefore in the tax price for private employees. We assume that private employees are unaware of this effect and simply take W*E as given.

[12]   We are implicitly assuming that each public employee is naive in that he does not account for the fact that cuts in public output (i.e.,E_g) will imply that there is a certain probability that a given public employee will lose his job and have his wage cut from W_g to W_p. Any attempt to account for this fully would substantially complicate the analysis. However, we might note that our discussion of bargaining strength in Section III does implicitly allow for control over the wage, and thus potential public sector benefits, to vary with the current size of the public sector.

[13]   As long as it is possible to incorporate entirely new jurisdictions, as it still is in many states, this assumption will be technically fulfilled; and as long as

there are many jurisdictions where relative public sector wages are low, the assumption will be fulfilled in practice.

[14]   The tax rate $W_g E_g / (W_p E_p + W_g E_g)$ obviously rises initially whenever $W_g E_g$ does. If $W_g E_g$ falls, there is a mathematical possibility that this fall in the tax rate would lead to a large enough utility *gain* from the increased C_p to offset the utility loss from the fall in E_g and actually encourage in-migration. This case makes no logical sense, however, because if the private sector could actually benefit from a higher W_g, it would already be paying such a wage.

[15]   With some algebraic manipulation, it can be shown that (21) is exactly equivalent to the first-order condition for the maximization of total tax revenue collected from the private sector, R_p. Since R_p can be written as $t W_p E_p$,

$$R_p = t W_p E_p = \frac{W_g E_g}{W^* E} (W^* E - W_g E_g)$$

$$= W_g E_g (1 - \frac{W_g E_g}{W^* E}) = E_g C_g$$

When E_g is fixed, as in this case, the revenue taken from the private sector will be exactly proportional to the consumption of public employees, and maximizing C_g is the same as maximizing R_p.

[16]   A plausible argument can be made that this case is unstable, while the inelastic demand case is stable. If, for example, moving expenditures were lowered so that η drops, W_g might begin falling as public employees recompute their first-order condition. This moves us toward equilibrium in the left-hand panel of Figure 2 and away in the right-hand panel.

[17]   It should be noted that voting is only one of several political mechanisms (say, campaign contributions) which might affect the determination of the level of public employment, and some of the other mechanisms are likely to be more effective from a political point of view. In addition to political mechanisms, there is also the possibility of resolving conflicting demands by using the familiar economic condition for optimal provision of public goods. In the context of our model, this would require finding the public sector wage W_g such that with proportional income taxes the levels of E_g chosen by both public and private employees would be the same; i.e., the tax prices for each group would be the Lindahl prices. In the *CES* example, this condition can be examined by making inequality (14) an equality and solving for W_g as a function of the relevant parameters. In the case where public employees have some wage-setting power, the notion of a Lindahl solsution seems to us to have little meaning, since the level of W_g is the instrument by which one party exploits another, and hence is hardly agreeable to the private employee.

[18]   Note that when utility functions are Cobb-Douglas (r = 0), the income and substitution effects exactly offset each other and the respective voting tendencies depend only on consideration c.

[19]   That this actually happens in the world can be seen from a discussion of the history of union wage negotiations in New York City, see Raymond Horton and Gramlich.

[20]   This does not mean to imply that public sector unions always perform their optimization calculations correctly. A plausible interpretation of the recent history of New York City, for example, would be that the municipal unions' estimate of η was well above the true value of that parameter. Moreover, in

constantly comparing their own wage levels to wage levels in other cities where the size of the public employee work force is smaller, these employees are hurting both the private sector (because the price of public services is raised) and ultimately themselves (because the tax base is falling).

REFERENCES

J.L. Barr and O. A. Davis, "An Elementary Political and Economic Theory of Local Governments," *Southern Econ. J.*, Oct. 1966, 33, 149-65.

T.C. Bergstrom and R.P. Goodman, "Private Demands for Public Goods," *Amer. Econ. Rev.*, June 1973, 63, 280-96.

R.M. Bird, "Wagner's 'Law' of Expanding State Activity," *Publ. Finance*, No. 1, 1971, 26, 1-26.

T.E. Borcherding and R.T. Deacon, "The Demand for the Services of Non-Federal Governments," *Amer. Econ. Rev.*, Dec. 1972, 62, 891-901.

——————, W.C. Bush, and R.M. Spann, "The Effects of Public Spending of the Divisibility of Public Outputs in Consumption, Bureaucratic Power, and the Size of the Tax-Sharing Group," in Thomas E. Borcherding, ed., *Budgets and Bureaucrats: The Sources of Government Growth*, Durham 1977.

J. Buchanan, "Why Does Government Grow?," in Thomas E. Borcherding, ed., *Budgets and Bureaucrats: The Sources of Government Growth*, Durham 1977.

—————— and G. Tullock, "The Expanding Public Sector: Wagner Squared," *Publ. Choice*, Fall 1977, 23, 147-50.

W.C. Bush and A.T. Denzau, "The Voting Behavior of Bureaucrats and Public Sector Growth," in Thomas E. Borcherding, ed., *Budgets and Bureaucrats: The Sources of Government Growth*, Durham 1977.

R. Craswell, "Self-Generating Growth in Public Programs," *Publ. Choice*, Spring 1975, 21, 91-98.

R.G. Ehrenberg and G.S. Goldstein, "A Model of Public Sector Wage Determination," *J. Urban Econ.*, July 1975, 2, 223-45.

E.M. Gramlich, "The New York City Fiscal Crisis:" What Happened and What is to be Done?," *Amer. Econ. Rev. Proc.*, May 1976, 66, 415-29.

Raymond D. Horton, *Municipal Labor Relations in New York City: Lessons of the Lindsay-Wagner Years*, New York 1973.

Norman MacRae, *America's Third Century*, New York 1976.

William A. Niskanen, "Bureaucrats and Politicians," *J. Law Econ.*, Dec. 1975, 18, 618-43.

——————, *Bureaucracy and Representative Government*, Chicago 1971.

Joseph A. Pechman and Benjamin A. Okner, *Who Bears the Tax Burden?*, Washington 1975.

J.H. Pencavel, "The Demand for Union Services: An Exercise," *Ind. Labor Rel. Rev.*, Jan. 1971, 24, 180-90.

M.W. Reder, "The Theory of Employment and Wages in the Public Sector," in Daniel S. Hamermesh, ed., *Labor in the Public and Nonprofit Sectors*, Princeton 1975.

S.P. Smith, "Government Wage Differentials," *J. Urban Econ.*, July 1977, 4, 248-71.

G.R. Tullock, "Dynamic Hypothesis on Bureaucracy," *Publ. Choice*, Fall 1974, 19, 127-31.

R.B. Victor, "The Effects of Municipal Unionism on Wages and Employment," unpublished doctoral dissertation, Univ. Mich., 1977.

R.E. Wagner and W.E. Weber, "Wagner's Law, Fiscal Institutes, and the Growth of Government," *Nat. Tax J.*, Mar. 1977, 30, 59-68.

J. Wanniski, "Taxes, Revenues, and the 'Laffer Curve'," *Publ. Interest*, Winter 1978, 50, 3-16.

11

Zoning and Property Taxation in a System of Local Governments

Bruce W. Hamilton*

IN THIS PAPER I will develop a model of the behavior of economic agents in a system of local governments. The model is very much in the spirit of the well-known Tiebout Hypothesis (1956) and many of Tiebout's original assumptions will be retained.

Much recent research in urban public finance has been concerned with the nature of the goods provided by local governments (in particular with various aspects of the 'publicness' of these goods), and the degree to which 'voting-with-feet' mechanism can distribute these goods Pareto optimally.[1] This paper is concerned not with the nature of the goods but with the nature of the mechanism itself, and I will discuss only peripherally such problems as economies of scale and spillovers. Toward the conclusion of the paper I will discuss in more detail the relationship between my work and the other literature in the field.

I believe that the major weakness of the Tiebout mechanism is that, whereas he has specified a device (namely migration), whereby consumers 'shop' for local public services, he has failed to endow his mechanism with a system of prices for the local public services. In the absence of constraints[2] on the consumption of these goods, they will be over-supplied or rationed by some inefficient method such as queueing. Also, in the absence of the constraints which will be built into my model, the Tiebout Hypothesis seems to be a formula for musical suburbs, with the poor following the rich in a never-ending quest for a tax base.

Casual empiricism suggests that the constraints missing from the Tiebout model are provided in the real world by various forms of

*The author is at the Urban Institute and The Johns Hopkins University, Baltimore. Received June 1974.

land-use restrictions which I classify under the heading of zoning. I shall therefore construct a model containing the basic Tiebout assumptions, and containing as well the following two assumptions: (1) local governments finance their operations solely with a proportional property tax (the tax rate may vary among communities) and (2) each community is authorized to enact a 'zoning ordinance' which states, 'No household may reside in this community unless it consumes at least some minimum amount of housing'.

Results to be Derived

With this model, it will be possible to derive the following results: (1) The local public service is distributed Pareto optimally, as suggested by Tiebout. (2) The property tax acts as an efficient price for the public service, and carries no deadweight loss; that is, it does not inhibit property consumption like a normal excise tax. (3) All communities are perfectly homogeneous with respect to house value. (4) Local governments are unable to engage in income redistribution. (5) In equilibrium, tax rates and levels of public service provision are not capitalized into property values.

Theoretical Model

Consider an urban area in which there are three goods; x_1, consumption of housing per family; x_2, the local public services (again, per family consumption) and x_3, a composite commodity consisting of the remainder of the household's consumption bundle. Each household has a utility function of the general form $U = (x_1, x_2, x_3)$. Households have no locational preference per se; they locate so as to maximize U. There are many communities in the urban area, each of which provides its residents with some amount of x_2, financed by a proportional tax on x_1 (i.e. the local property tax). A community must provide the same amount of x_2 to each of its residents, but the provision can vary among communities, as can the property tax rate.

The zoning ordinance is now specified as follows: No household may live in community i unless its consumption of x_1 is greater than or equal to x'_{1i}.[3]

Now we assume for the moment that x_2 is offered on the private market[4] at a price p_2, which is equal to the marginal cost of producing x_2. If production is perfectly competitive, p_2 is also equal to the average cost in the long run. The consumer maximizes his utility function subject to the constraint

$$Y = p_1 x_1 + p_2 x_2 + p_3 x_3 \, ,$$

deciding to consume some bundle (x_1^*, x_2^*, x_3^*). (This (Pareto optimal) allocation will be compared with the outcome under the system of local governments I have specified). We now return this household to the world in which x_2 is provided by local governments. The household looks for a community which will yield him the highest attainable level of utility. It can be shown that this search will lead the household to reside in a community whose minimum housing requirement x_1' is just equal to the household's actual x_1 consumption. If he lives in a community whose x_1' is less than his housing consumption (he cannot legally reside in a community where x_1' exceeds his housing consumption), he can increase his utility by moving to a community with a more restrictive zoning ordinance. (Recall that the zoning ordinance in the old community was not binding on him). This new community will have a higher tax *base* than the old one. It is thus in a position to provide a higher level of public service or a lower tax rate, or both. Thus, for any household which is consuming more x_1 than is required by the zoning ordinance of his community, there exists some move which will increase his utility. But this means that in equilibrium no household in any given community consumes more than that community's x_1'.

I have now shown that every household in a given community consumes the same amount of housing, pays the same amount in property taxes, and consumes the same amount of x_2. This implies that every household pays the average cost of the x_2 he consumes. Invoking the assumption that, for x_2, average cost = marginal cost = p_2, the household's consumption possibilities are restricted to the set $Y = p_1 x_1 + p_2 x_2 + p_3 x_3$. A community is defined in this space by the vector (x_1', x_2'),[5] the housing requirement and the public service provision. A consumption bundle is feasible for the household if, and only if, it satisfies the budget constraint and the x_1 and x_2 arguments define a community which exists. In particular, the utility-maximizing bundle under the free market regime, (x_1^*, x_2^*, x_3^*), is feasible if there is some community for which $x_1^* = x_1'$ and $x_2^* = x_2'$. To the extent that there exist (or can be established) communities of sufficient diversity in an urban area, the budget constraint faced by the household when x_2 is provided by local governments is identical with the constraint he would face if x_2 were provided (competitively) by the private market. The model is seen to yield a Pareto optimal allocation of resources, since the consumption bundle is identical with the private market result.[6] A somewhat surprising corollary is that the local property tax carries no deadweight loss, since deadweight loss always involves a departure from Pareto optimality. Note that it is not required that all residents of a community have the same income or the same utility function; it is only required that they all have the same x_1^*, x_2^*. And this is not an assumption of the model, but a result derived from the assumption.

The property tax in this model carries no deadweight loss because the tax payment bears no relationship to anything *except* the public services received from the local government. It is possible (by migration) to vary housing consumption without varying the total property tax bill and *vice versa*. That is, for any given level of property tax payment (not rate), and its implied level of public service provision, housing consumption can be varied as freely, and the same cost to the consumer, as if there were no property tax.[7] This simply means that the property tax is not considered a part of the price of housing, which in turn means it cannot impose a deadweight loss in the housing market. The property tax is seen to be a price for the public services received by the household. This price performs all the rationing functions that the price mechanism performs in the private sector.

Wallace Oates (1972) pointed out that if local governments finance their operations with a head tax, there will be efficiency in both the public and private sectors:

> This scheme (a head tax) would tend to receive excellent marks on. . . efficiency criteria. . . Since the tax price paid by the consumer reflects accurately the cost of the public goods he consumes, this system of finance introduces no incentives for inefficient behavior.

Oates further states that any other taxation scheme, such as a property tax, leads to deadweight loss and distortion of location preferences. The deadweight loss issue has already been discussed, and I will deal with location presently. The reason for the discrepancy between my results and the Oates conclusion is that, through the system of zoning ordinances I have specified, the property tax is essentially transformed into a head tax (with a different tax per head in each community).[8]

Adjustment and Dynamics: Capitalization

All that has been established so far is the existence of a solution to the constrained maximization problem which yields Pareto optimality. No demonstration has been offered that the system has any tendency whatsoever to approach such a point. Some light can be shed on this subject by asking what the system would look like in a state of disequilibrium. Assume that there are fewer dwelling units of a given (x_1, x_2) specification than are demanded by the population of the urban area. The dwelling units which do possess these desirable (i.e. demanded) characteristics will be sought after by an excessive number of households, and will earn a rent. In other words, the value of such property will be bid up. Landlords will have missed an opportunity to maximize the value of their property if they do not devote more land to the relatively scarce activity. Only when all (x_1, x_2) demand sets have been satisfied will all the potential gains have been realized. At this point, property values are completely uncorrelated with levels of public service provision, zoning restrictions, and property tax rates. That is, property tax rates and expenditure levels are not capitalized into property values. If such correlation exists, (that is, if certain (x_1, x_2) vectors earn rent) there is an incentive on the part of landlords to transfer land into those activities which yield relatively high rents. The disequilibrium situation (i.e. a scarcity of some particular type of community) can be characterized by either a positive or a negative correlation between land values and such explanatory variables as tax rates and public service expenditure. The direction of the correlation is determined by the types of communities which are in short supply.[9]

Extensions of the Model

Why Property Tax?

It can readily be seen that x_1, the good which is taxed and on which there is a minimum consumption requirement, is arbitrarily defined to be housing; formally, it could just as well be bagels or carrots instead.[10] In fact, the results hold if the tax is an income tax and each community has a minimum income requirement.[11] There are, however, some compelling empirical reasons for finding the property tax superior to most others, at least on the criteria of this model.

The model developed here can be characterized as follows: classify all households in a given urban area by local public service demand, and cross-classify them by housing demand. Each doubly-classified cell is a community.[12] The number of communities required in such a system to insure that every household can find a homogeneous community which suits his demand for x_1 and x_2 depends on (1) the distribution of demands for the public service, (2) the distribution of demands for x_1, the taxed good and (3) the correlation between the demand for x_1 and the demand for the public service. If the correlation between the demand for x_1 and x_2 is perfect, then the number of communities required to satisfy everybody's demand for x_1 and x_2 simultaneously is no greater than the number which would be required simply to satisfy everybody's demand for x_2.[13] It seems likely that the demand for housing and the demand for local public services are indeed highly correlated, so the tax on this good, as opposed to some other, leads to a relatively small number of communities in a given urban area. This is particularly important if returns to scale are significant in the provision of local public services. A problem with the income tax is that current income may fluctuate more widely over time than demand for x_2. Demand for public service may be highly correlated with *permanent* income but there is no ready way to tax that.

Another reason for the popularity of the property tax is undoubtedly the relative ease of enforcing the minimum consumption requirement. A minimum bagel requirement seems rather unenforceable, and a minimum income requirement sounds a bit unAmerican.

An Alternative to Zoning

Consider now the case where communities do not have zoning laws, but where property assessment rates vary in such a manner that all dwelling units within a given community have the same *assessed* value.[14] This scheme is, if anything, more efficient than the basic model described before. There is still no deadweight loss, since everybody pays the average cost of the public services he consumes, and since property consumption can be varied without changing one's tax liability. In this case, property consumption can be varied without penalty within a community rather than only by migration. The 'property' tax described here is not really a property tax at all but rather a form of head tax (everybody in a given community pays the same tax, regardless of property consumption). Within this framework, efficiency requires that there be enough communities to satisfy everybody's demand for public service, rather than enough communities to satisfy all the public service-housing pairs of demand. As has been indicated before, to the extent that there is not perfect correlation between demand for housing and for public services, this will tend to reduce the number of communities required.

Location

As was mentioned, a community is defined by its housing requirement and its public service provision; it does not as yet have a spatial component. This would seem to be a rather serious defect for a model which purports to describe optimality conditions for a system of communities. Communities, after all, do have rather important spatial components. Standard location theory, based on neo-classical rent theory, provides the framework for determining the optimal location pattern for residents in an urban area.

Yet in this model, the consumer is instructed to locate in the community where $x'_{1i} = x^*_1$ and $x'_{2i} = x^*_2$, and to ignore standard location-theory considerations such as the trade-off between commuting cost and the price of housing. At the level of pure theory, dealing with this problem is now rather straightforward.

To make this extension, classify all households in the urban area by demand for housing, and cross-classify them by public service demand, as was done above. Each doubly-classified cell is what we have referred to as a community. We can now cross-classify everybody again by location preference and call each triply-classified cell a community.[15] Again, the required number of communities may expand with each cross-classification since each resident must now find a community which satisfies three requirements rather than one or two. But we saw that if the variables used to cross-classify households are highly correlated with one another, then the number of communities required to satisfy three requirements is not much greater than the number required to satisfy one or two. And it can, on theoretical grounds, be argued rather strongly that location preference (as measured by most preferred distance from the CBD) is highly correlated with housing demand. In most models of urban structure, households with strong demand for housing (this is generally taken to mean households with relatively high income) are induced to endure the cost of commuting a relatively long distance to the CBD by the fact that land rents, and thus housing prices, are lower as one gets further from the CBD. The

stronger a household's housing demand, the more commuting he will
endure to live where housing prices are low. It can be seen that we
should expect a very high correlation between housing demand and
location preference.

Imperfections

The model may fail to describe reality for two general reasons:

1. The nature of the goods (various aspects of publicness) is such that the
   average-cost pricing mechanism worked out above does not imply Pareto
   optimality.
2. The mechanism itself fails to live up to the claims made for it here, and
   average-cost pricing of local public services is not achieved.

Nature of Goods

Buchanan and Goetz (1972) have argued that, even when they
'. . . examine the Tiebout adjustment in its most favorable setting'
(by which they mean costless migration, no interjurisdictional
spillovers and some unspecified mechanism whereby households
pay the average cost of the local public good), 'there remain inherent
inefficiencies in the Tiebout adjustment process'.

The first issue they address is that of the publicness of the goods
provided. If the cost of providing a given level of service to a marginal household is zero (or anywhere below the average cost), then
average-cost pricing is not identical to marginal-cost pricing and is
hence inefficient. Furthermore, under these conditions the average-
cost curve is not horizontal (with respect to additional members
of the community), so interjurisdictional migration imposes uncompensated costs and benefits on other members of the communities. This is because interjurisdictional migration, by changing
the scale of operation in the effected communities, alters the average
cost of public service provision. Buchanan and Goetz also argue that,
after some point, crowding of facilities raises the marginal cost of
provision above the average cost. Under these conditions the same
problems plague the system—the efficiency of average-cost pricing
and the existence of uncompensated external effects due to migration. In either case, the authors argue, the system is Pareto-sub-
optimal.

The second issue raised by Buchanan and Goetz is that of location.
They argue that the trade-off conditions between commuting costs
and the price of housing may well dictate a different residential

location than that dictated by foot-voting to obtain the most preferred public service bundle. I have argued above that, if impediments
to divisibility are not too severe, there can exist a system of communities which satisfies all the location criteria simultaneously.

Martin McGuire (1972) has pointed out that the combination of
publicness and crowding as properties of local public goods gives
rise to a standard U-shaped average-cost curve. At low levels of output (small community population) the marginal cost is near zero
and the average cost is high. An increase in the scale reduces the
average cost (fixed cost spread over a larger population), but beyond
some point the marginal cost rises above the average cost, as crowding becomes important. Exactly the same forces give rise to the U-
shaped short-run average-cost curve in standard production theory.
'Crowding' is merely a synonym for the law of diminishing returns.
It is impossible to produce enough wheat to feed the world in a
flowerpot for the same reasons that the world's swimming demands
cannot be satisfied by a single swimming-pool.

But if the average-cost curve for local public goods is U-shaped,
then, depending upon where the minimum point of the U occurs,
it may indeed be possible to have a set of communities for which
average cost equals marginal cost, and such that every household
can locate so as to satisfy both its location and public-service demands. There is a mechanism, namely capitalization of taxes and
benefits into land rents, which tends to drive the system toward
such a point.[16]

So the issues raised by Buchanan and Goetz are empirical. In a
frictionless world, where there are no interjurisdictional spillovers
and where migration is free, we cannot comment on the efficiency
of the Tiebout system until we know something of the magnitudes
involved in the production functions for local public services.

The Finance Mechanism

Buchanan and Goetz, McGuire, as well as Pauly (1970) and
others have assumed, either implicitly or explicitly, that local public
goods are financed by some unspecified mechanism whereby every
household pays the average cost of the service provision. My work
is concerned with the possible existence of a mechanism whereby
local revenue instruments approximate average-cost pricing. In the
process I have assumed away the important empirical problems discussed briefly above. The only other work I am aware of which
examines the problem of average-cost pricing is that of Ellickson

(1971). He points out that, in a Tiebout world, a local property tax is an efficient (average-cost) price if housing and local public services are sufficiently close complements in households' utility functions. Under these conditions households will voluntarily segregate themselves by housing demand and local public-service demand. The free-rider problem does not arise because households with a low demand for housing have little desire for local public service, and will make no effort to locate in communities with a high level of provision. This is similar to the proposition that, if left shoes were offered to consumers free, and the price of right shoes were doubled, the market for shoes would remain Pareto efficient. The zoning constraint introduced here removes the necessity of the assumption that demand complementarity will ensure voluntary segregation.

If we cannot demonstrate the lack of efficiency of the Tiebout mechanism by an appeal to pure theory, we certainly can do so by reference to the most casual empiricism. It is obvious that communities do not satisfy the public-service demands of all their residents; otherwise all municipal elections would be decided by unanimous consent. Communities are not perfectly homogeneous, so different households face different tax prices for public services. Communities produce an array of public services, not just the single one specified here. So the problems of reaching the minimum point of production functions and matching demand bundles with production bundles is multiplied many times over the single-good case presented here. The existence of interjurisdictional spillovers means that the solution would be suboptimal even if the other problems did not arise.

With regard to the mechanism itself, interjurisdictional migration is a very expensive means of clearing a market. Another problem that arises is that of community formation. As the population structure of an urban area changes, the set of communities required to satisfy public-service demands also changes. No effort has been made here (nor elsewhere that I am aware of) to describe the dynamic mechanism whereby the public-service/housing characteristics of communities change over time.

Conclusion

The inefficiencies inherent in the market-analog mechanism and in the publicness of the goods provided by local governments, are obviously severe—more so, undoubtedly, than in many portions of the private sector. Still, some of the most fruitful research in the field of local public finance is based upon the assumption that costs of local public services are shared equally among households. For this reason it seems useful to have a formal statement of the conditions under which our local political institutions give rise to such average-cost pricing, and of the effects of such institutions on housing markets and incentives for public-service consumption. In no way is the model developed here intended to rebut, or to deny the importance of, the problems pointed out by Buchanan and Goetz and others.

As a final disclaimer, I am not prepared to argue, on equity grounds, that local public services 'ought' to be distributed in accordance with market criteria. I consider the term 'Pareto optimality' to be descriptive rather than normative.

NOTES

[1]   See, for example, Pauly (1970) and Buchanan and Goetz (1972).

[2]   Actually, there are restraints on consumer behavior in the Tiebout model, but these restraints are not directed at the problem addressed here. Tiebout's Assumption 6 states in part, '. . . there is an optimal community size . . . defined in terms of the number of residents for which this bundle of services can be produced at the lowest average cost' (Tiebout (1956), p. 419). He goes on to say that, in order to achieve this optimal size, it may be necessary to impose land-use restrictions, agreement among realtors, or something of the sort. However, he further states that, if a community is faced with the necessity of restricting entry, and, depending on the forces lending to the U-shaped cost curve implied in Assumption 6, a second identical community can be formed to accommodate the overflow. So, except for the case of something like beach-front, which cannot be reproduced, there is no restriction in the Tiebout model on the number of people consuming any particular bundle of public services. And there is no hint of a restriction on the *kinds* of people consuming a given bundle. (By different kinds of people, I mean people with different income, family size, and so on. In other words, I mean people with different demands for public services.)

[3]   Formally, x'_{1i} should be a function of household size; that is, households with more members are required to consume more housing. The reason for this will become apparent.

[4]   To the extent that x_2 is a public good it cannot in fact be offered on the private market, since the non-exclusion character of public goods prevents the market mechanism from working. What is involved here, however, is simply a conceptual experiment where households reveal information contained in their utility functions.

[5]   At this point the definition of a community does not include a spatial component.

[6]   I assume in this section of the paper (along with Tiebout) that community formation is costless. However, it is not necessary that I assume that urban land is free. Later I will deal explicitly with the scarcity of urban land. Also, in a later section of the paper the assumption that community formation is free will be examined briefly.

[7] The mechanism of adjustment, i.e. migration, is undoubtedly quite costly. However, this is a discussion in comparative statics. The point I wish to make is that there is no necessary relationship between the property tax bill and real property consumption.

[8] In reality the true head tax would be more efficient, since this system would not require communities to be homogeneous with respect to house value, but only with respect to public service demand. The degree to which this would in fact lead to improved efficiency is discussed later.

[9] The empirical work by Oates, 'The Effects of Property Taxes and Local Public Spending on Property Values. . . ," (1969), indicates that property value is significantly correlated with public service provision and tax rates in his sample. As I have indicated here, and discussed at length elsewhere (forthcoming), I believe Oates observed this result because his sample was in a state of disequilibrium.

[10] As an historical footnote it should perhaps be pointed out that Louis XVI raised a substantial share of his revenue through the famous *taille,* or salt tax, and at the same time imposed a minimum-salt-consumption requirement on the peasants. Some historians claim that this was one of the direct causes of the French Revolution. The reader is invited to draw his own conclusions.

[11] Of course the membership of individual communities will not be the same under the regime where bagels are zoned and taxed as under the regime where property is zoned and taxed. But it is true that the results laid out in Section II still hold.

[12] This formulation of the model is due to Professor Gregory Chow.

[13] This was pointed out to me by Professor D.M. Jaffee. Ellickson (1971) has carried this line of reasoning one step further, pointing out that if housing and public service are sufficiently close complements, an efficiently stratified set of communities will emerge through voluntary associations among consumers.

[14] There is strong evidence that, within a community, assessment ratios vary inversely with house values. In other words, there tends to be less of a spread in assessed value than in true market value within a community. See for example New Jersey Tax Policy Committee (1972).

[15] When location is introduced, it is necessary to be a bit more precise. The demand for housing is no longer a number, but rather a function relating demand for housing to distance from CBD. The existence of equilibrium can be demonstrated as follows: allow each household to simultaneously satisfy its housing demand and equilibrium distance from the CBD, ignoring for the moment public service considerations. Such a process is described by E.S. Mills (1967). Now take everybody who has chosen to live at a given distance from the CBD, and sort them out according to their (x_1, x_2) demand. Within this framework, the demand for housing is a number rather than a function, since the independent variable of the function (distance from the CBD) has been held constant. Now we can define each (x_1, x_2) pairing at a given distance from the CBD as a community, and similarly at all distances from the CBD.

[16] Finally, it should be noted that the U-shaped cost-curve is short-run (i.e. fixed facility size) and the location of the minimum point can presumably be altered in the long run to satisfy consumer demand.

REFERENCES

Buchanan, James and Goetz, Charles (1972) Efficiency Limits of Fiscal Mobility. *Journal of Public Economics.*

Ellickson, Bryan (1971). Jurisdictional Fragmentation and Residential Choice. *American Economic Review Papers: Proceedings,* May 1971.

Hamilton Bruce (forthcoming). The Effects of Property Taxes and Local Public Spending on Property Values: A Theoretical Comment. *Journal of Political Economy.*

McGuire, Martin (1972). Private Good Clubs and Public Good Clubs: Economic Models of Group Formation. *Swedish Journal of Economics,* Vol. 4, pp. 85-99.

Mills, Edwin S. (1967). An Aggregative Model of Resource Allocation in a Metropolitan Area. *American Economic Review,* pp. 197-210.

New Jersey Tax Policy Committee (1972). *Report of the New Jersey Tax Policy Committee,* Trenton.

Oates, Wallace E. (1969). The Effects of Property Taxes and Local Public Spending on Property Values: An Empirical Study of Tax Capitalization and the Tiebout Hypothesis. *Journal of Political Economy,* 77, pp. 957-970.

Oates, Wallace E. (1972). *Fiscal Federalism,* Harcourt Brace Jovanovich. New York.

Pauly, Mark V. (1970). Optimality, 'Public Goods', and Local Governments: A General Theoretical Analysis. *Journal of Political Economy,* pp. 572-585.

Tiebout, Charles (1956). A Pure Theory of Local Public Expenditure: *Journal of Political Economy,* 64, pp. 416-424.

12

A Property Rights Approach
to Municipal Zoning

William A. Fischel*

MUNICIPAL ZONING in the United States began early in this century, and nearly all local governments in metropolitan areas now have ordinances. They include detailed regulations on the initial development and changes in the use of land and buildings. As part of the community's "police powers," zoning may be supplemented by other regulatory devices such as building codes, health laws, and subdivision regulations. Insofar as these devices affect land use, they will be considered as part of zoning in this essay.

The purpose of zoning is usually described as regulating external effects among land uses so as to provide a more efficient allocation of activities. The problem we shall be concerned with is its apparent failure to do this very well. In particular, there is evidence that zoning is too exclusive. Empirical investigations by several economists suggest that zoning tends to exclude land uses which have rather small effects on neighboring properties.[1] Several studies have noticed the substantial differentials in land prices which zoning creates [Mieszkowski 1973]. Studies in metropolitan Boston [Orr 1975] and in New Jersey [Sagalyn and Sternlieb 1973] indicate that zoning tends to restrict the supply of new housing in metropolitan areas, particularly in the suburbs. The most damaging evidence against zoning, however, is found in two studies by Peterson

*The author is Assistant Professor of Economics, Dartmouth College. Helpful comments from individuals too numerous to name were received when this paper was presented at seminars of the Dartmouth College Economics Department and the Committee on Urban Public Economics. The advice of two anonymous referees was especially useful. Research was supported in part by a grant from the Lewis H. Haney Fund at Dartmouth College. The Urban Institute generously supplied research facilities during a leave in which an earlier draft was rewritten.

[1974, 1977]. In the first, a Boston suburban sample showed that the gains from zoning by residents did not outweigh the losses to owners of property which might be developed or converted to forbidden uses. The second showed that the net effect of certain zoning restrictions in a Washington, D.C., suburban area is to lower the average value of land. If zoning were efficient, the losses from zoning restrictions would be equal to the gains from whatever benefits accrue to these restrictions. Average land values should not be affected. Peterson's studies and the others suggest strongly that there are gains from trade remaining from zoning.

Explanations for these defects fall into two categories. One is that zoning's shortcomings are endemic to all local government decisions. The collectiveness of zoning is the problem [Ellickson 1973; Siegan 1972]. If this were true, however, we might observe that some suburbs err by allowing too little development, while others allow too much. But the empirical consensus is that zoning allows too little development. Furthermore, collective decisions by municipalities in other endeavors have been shown to reflect more rationality and sensitivity to economic conditions than zoning does [Bergstrom and Goodman 1973].

The other explanation is that zoning is an exercise in monopoly power for the benefit of local homeowners [Ellickson 1977; Hamilton 1977; White 1975]. While this seems closer to the mark, it does not explain how this monopoly power can be effective in metropolitan areas with many communities. For example, the Boston SMSA contains 78 independent municipal and township governments, a modest number compared to many other SMSAs outside the South. If one community attempts monopoly gains, developers can select sites in others nearby. What needs to be explained is why all communities acting independently seem to restrict development so much.

A secondary issue concerns the apparent choice of zoning over other means of land use controls. If zoning is so inefficient, why does it persist? Private covenants, public acquisition of land or development rights, and nuisance law are all substitutes for zoning which have largely fallen into disuse or remain untried. It is insufficient to argue that these institutions have administrative problems which inhibit their use, for zoning clearly has such problems also. Nor is it valid to evaluate the problems of other institutions as they now exist. Had there been a demand to use them, adjustments could have been made by the legislatures and the courts to implement them, just as they did for zoning.

The plan of the remaining sections is to develop a more satisfactory theory to explain both the inefficiency of zoning and its continued popularity. In the next section, the distribution of property rights implied by zoning is reviewed. Zoning is found to be defective in that rights are not fully assigned. Section 3 develops a fiscal motivation for zoning which, when coupled with the defects described in section 2, shows why zoning results in excessive restriction of development and why it is preferred to more efficient methods of land use controls. In section 4 we examine the extra-legal means by which zoning can be leased or sold to make it more efficient, and we conclude that they are inadequate. Section 5 extends the municipal services motivation to show the effects of zoning on land values and size of a suburban community.

Throughout this paper we shall focus on suburbs in politically fragmented metropolitan areas. A substantial proportion of suburban land is undeveloped and owned by a relatively small group of people. Although succession of land use in central cities is important, the development of vacant land in suburbs has been the greatest source of controversy over zoning.[2]

The Assignment of Property Rights Under Zoning

An important branch of the modern economics of property rights stems from an article by Coase [1960]. In it, he demonstrated that the party to whom exclusive property rights are assigned in problems of external cost does not necessarily affect the resulting output equilibrium. The theory assumes that rights are fully assigned, trade may be conducted costlessly, the resulting contracts are easily enforceable, and the initial distribution does not affect demand. In the context of zoning, the Coase theorem implies that it does not matter whether land use rights are vested in the community or in the nominal property owners. In the former case, landowners could purchase exceptions from restrictions for any land use whose value exceeded the (negative) value of the external effects to the community. In the latter assignment, the community could purchase from the landowners any use whose offense to them was greater than the value of that particular land use to its owner. Under the Coase theorem's assumptions, the use of land in either case would be identical in equilibrium.

The assumptions of the Coase theorem are extreme, but the theorem provides a fundamental insight which is useful in examining zoning. As we shall see, zoning offers a generous distribution of rights to the community. If these are excessive, the landowners ought to be able to buy their way out of them. The aforementioned empirical evidence suggests that this does not always happen. The property rights approach then leads us to inquire about the barriers to trade which may be inherent in the institution of zoning itself.[3]

The assignment of property rights involves at least three aspects: (1) the right to exclude others from resources (control), (2) the right to enjoy the income from the use of the resources (leasing), and (3) the right to transfer these resources (selling). Zoning withdraws part of the right to use property as a private owner sees fit and gives this control to the political authorities of the municipality. We shall summarize the nature and limitations of this control.[4]

Despite some variations among states, the basic operation of zoning is fairly similar in most urban areas. Zoning authority has been granted to local governments by similar legislative acts in nearly every state. Communities are not usually compelled to adopt zoning regulations. When they do, a comprehensive plan stating the objectives to be achieved is often urged upon them, but few enforceable constraints are put on these plans. The primary constraints upon community zoning have come from the courts. The economically important precedents are described below.

Compensation need not be paid to a landowner whose property value is lowered by a zoning restriction. However, the community may not compel the owner to develop the land for a particular use, nor may it force the owner to allow public access. Either of these would require purchase of the land, perhaps by eminent domain.

Zoning may not prohibit *all* uses of a class of property. This would normally constitute a "taking" and be invalid under the Constitution. Some of the rent must be left to the nominal owner, but it is clear that it need not be the return from the land's most profitable use.

Zoning must show some "reasonable relation" to the preservation of "public health, safety, morals and general welfare" of the community. It is not clear what the standards for reasonableness are, but it apparently does *not* mean benefit-cost analysis, even in the most casual sense. The magnitude of loss by the landowner need not be weighed by benefits to the community. In some extreme cases the loss has been invoked by judges to invalidate some actions, but for the most part the rule of reasonableness can be characterized as "benefit—" analysis.

The disadvantage of the landowner is further compounded by the presumption of constitutionality of zoning. This means that the landowner who challenges what he believes to be an unreasonable zoning decision must bear the burden of proof of showing that the community is at fault. This sharply reduces the cost of zoning to the community, since it need not build an elaborate case to exonerate itself. Beyond this, the practical burden of acting as a zoning review board has usually caused higher courts to decline to review zoning cases except in areas of the most flagrant abuse.

The "general welfare" of the community which zoning is supposed to promote refers exclusively to existing residents, not to potential residents or people in nearby communities. Some state courts have recently shown some sympathy to arguments for "regional needs" to be covered by zoning, but most courts still presume that zoning is for community members only.

The characterization of zoning so far suggests a proprietary club. As such, it would be efficient except as the diversity of opinions in the club made decisionmaking difficult. The club could establish as many restrictions as the courts would uphold. It would then sell or lease them to the highest bidder, reserving those whose value to themselves exceeded the highest bid. As the Coase theorem notes, the initial distribution of rights might affect demand for land, but the result would otherwise be the same as ownership of the rights by any other type of proprietor.

The advantage of this distribution of rights over others is presumably that it makes the consequences of interdependencies (externalities) of land use more easily controlled by the decisionmakers. However, by justifying zoning as part of the community's police powers, the courts have placed strong inhibitions on the proprietary use of zoning. The police power may not be sold, nor may its normal functions be made conditional on receipt of some payment. Straightforward sales or leases of zoning as described above would undermine the whole rationale of the police power, which assumes that the market does not work for the particular activities. To sell zoning would be analogous to selling elevator safety certificates or restaurant health inspections Thus, communities may not ordinarily lease their rights to produce income, nor may they capitalize on them by selling them to some party who can. Courts in some states uneasily accede to bartering arrangements, whereby a developer can submit to some conditions or in-kind payments imposed by the community in return for favorable rezoning of his land. Communities may also impose "subdivision exactions" on a developer to help the community pay for the cost of *some* municipal services, but these are usually restricted to services that accrue directly to the subdivision. No court in the United States, as far as I know, has recognized existing community residents as full legal proprietors of the rights assigned to them by zoning.[5]

Thus, zoning may be characterized as an incomplete assignment of property rights. The first of the three basic aspects—control—is generously assigned to the community, but leasing is permitted only in certain limited ways (discussed in section 4), and selling is almost totally prohibited. Consequently, the allocation of resources controlled by zoning will be different from that obtained under alternative, fully assigned property rights.

Behavioral Motivation and Institutional Choice

In order to understand the consequences of the misassignment of property rights under zoning, it is necessary to have some model of what zoning is used for. Zoning legislation itself and most economic studies of zoning have emphasized the relationship between zoning and the local public sector [Mills and Oates 1975]. To simplify the present analysis, we will assume that local municipal services are financed by a fixed-share per capita tax which may vary among communities. We will neglect school expenditures for reasons discussed in section 4.

Because zoning is most important as a constraint on partially developed suburban communities, we must describe local political behavior in urban expansion. Assume that preferences for land use can be ranked from least restrictive to most restrictive (greatest development to least development), and that the preferences of some median voter will rule. There are two groups in any community who are of interest here. First there are "proprietors" who own undeveloped land or who may otherwise gain from community development. The other group will be referred to as "lodgers," residents who view their community solely as a place of residence. They may own the lots they live on, but they do not own any undeveloped land, and, as commuters to other places for work, they have no other financial interest in the community.[6]

The rural communities on the fringes of growing metropolitan areas are likely to be politically dominated by people who stand to gain from community expansion: farmers, other landowners, store owners, or real estate dealers. As the urban area expands, resident lodgers arrive to live in new homes. Eventually, but well before the community is fully developed, the lodgers take over the political apparatus controlling the zoning board.[7]

We now examine the factors which the lodgers' fictional representative, the median voter, considers in deciding about the remaining open land. Having chosen his community and residence, the lodger is assumed to maximize utility over two goods, neighborhood quality, Q, and other goods. Neighborhood quality includes such pleasures as peace and quiet, personal safety and property protection. It also includes aesthetic qualities derived from improved open spaces such as large lawns and gardens and unimproved woods, fields and meadows which still exist in most suburban areas.[8]

Production of Q is traditionally associated with municipal services, M, such as police and fire protection, waste disposal, traffic management, and public parks. Some of these might actually be provided privately, either voluntarily or by edict, but they still should be counted in M for our present purposes. For a given population, more municipal services produce more or better Q. However, none of these services qualifies as a pure public good. The size of the group consuming Q makes a difference. In general, more residents require more aggregate municipal services to produce the same level of neighborhood quality. The relationship between M (aggregate municipal services) and N (total population) for various levels of Q is shown in Figure 1.

Figure 1 attempts to show simultaneously the relation among total municipal services, population, and open land. To do this, we assume that the community has a fixed total amount of land. Each housing unit takes up a uniform amount of open land and adds a fixed number of persons per acre. Thus there is some maximum population, N^*, at which all open land is used up.

The production isoquants for Q are quadratic functions in N. This is to describe a stylized story of municipal development over time which seems to fit the experience of many suburban communities. Initially, the growth of municipal services is relatively slow. More people require more services, but the size of the tax-sharing group increases fast enough to allow lower average costs per capita. As population increases, the greater density eventually produces more congestion of the services, and per capita costs begin to rise.[9] The average and marginal costs per capita for one level of Q are shown in Figure 2, which is derived directly from Figure 1 assuming constant factor prices.

As costs begin to rise, most suburban communities are apparently aware of a realistic substitute for municipal expenditures: development limitation. This accomplishes two things. First, it provides an indirect control on population so that the number

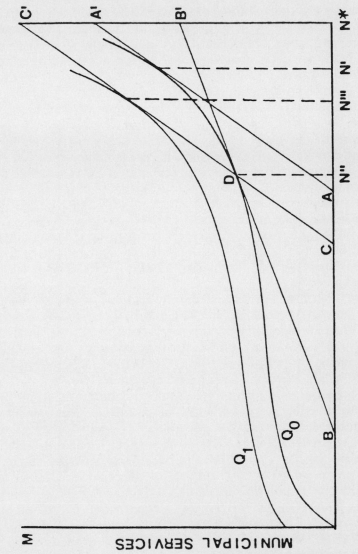

FIGURE 1

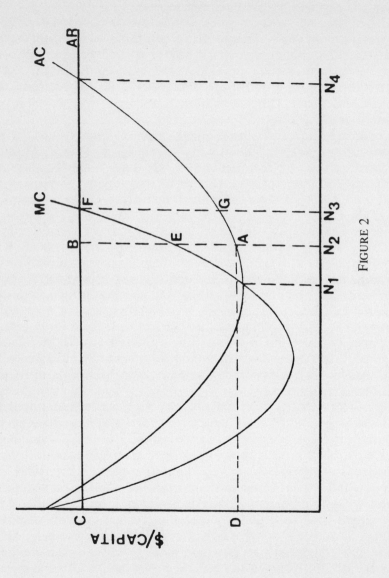

FIGURE 2

(and type) of people consuming any direct municipal service is limited. Second, it preserves the open spaces (or at least lowers the density of housing) which are becoming increasingly scarce and may directly add to neighborhood quality. The question now is how the community can limit development.

There are many ways besides zoning by which open land could be preserved or density reduced. For example, land could be purchased by the community as a whole and used as a park or a preserve. It could also be purchased by individuals within certain neighborhoods. As a substitute for either type of purchase, less-than-fee interests might be acquired to allow only certain types of development.

Under any purchase arrangement, a market price must be paid for the land or for the value of the use which is forgone. This price is illustrated by line AA' in Figure 1. Its slope is equal to the ratio of the market price of land and municipal services.[10] (Recall that open land is read from right to left; hence the reverse slope of the price lines.) Equilibrium population and open land (or density) would be at N'.

Under zoning, however, the land need not be purchased. Regulatory authority is available free of charge. Since suburban owners of vacant land are a minority, the political cost is minimal. However, there are some costs associated with zoning. The ordinance must be properly designed and enforced. Furthermore, zoning may not be so restrictive that it eliminates *all* possible uses for a given piece of property. Thus, the appropriate price for zoning is BB' in Figure 1. Its slope is lower because there is little opportunity cost to restrictions which inhibit population growth and the use of open land. Landowners are prevented by the rules of zoning from "buying back" the restrictions on their land. The equilibrium population in this case will be N'' less than N', and there will be more open land or lower residential density than there would have been had a market price been paid. Zoning thus causes lower population density or too little development conpared with market-tempered restrictions.

It is important to note the advantage of zoning to existing residents. With it, municipal service expenditures are much lower than they would have been under some other system, so more disposable income is available to preexisting residents. (Alternatively, zoning allows the community to purchase more Q with the same expenditure. We do not examine the general choice here.) Other systems of land use controls—private covenants, nuisance laws, and municipal acquisition of open land or development easements—all would require that land be purchased or owners otherwise compensated. Although zoning is inefficient in that it does not require residents to perceive the correct opportunity costs of the land, it does give the community a set of property rights which are more valuable than these alternatives. This helps explain its continued popularity and the historical decline of other forms of control.

This conclusion is important in discussions of zoning reform. It is often assumed that all parties are interested in improving the efficiency of land use. However, if increased efficiency means a redistribution of valuable property rights, the people who are adversely affected will resist the reforms, regardless of the efficiency improvements. For example, we may agree with Siegan [1972] that land use would be improved by abolition of zoning, replacing it with voluntary covenants. But the people who currently benefit from zoning—the resident lodgers in our model—would surely resist this redistribution of rights unless they were compensated for their loss. Lacking some compensation scheme, current resident lodgers are better off with the rights which zoning offers, even though they are not fully fungible.

One may suggest, in defense of zoning, that some lack of fungibility *should* be incorporated into zoning because of spillover effects. Groups outside a community may be affected by its developments, and it may not be practicable to include all those affected in the bargaining. Legally limiting the fungibility of zoning may be a desirable "second-best" way to represent these interests.

Such an approach might be justified if each zoning case involved large numbers of people or if zoning regulated activities whose undesirable effects were distributed over a wide area or were difficult to identify by source. Water or air pollution most likely fall into these categories, but surely most of the problems dealt with in the typical suburban zoning ordinance do not. Noise, congestion, unsightliness, air circulation, and access to sunlight are usually neighborhood effects, in the popular sense of the word. To deal with them, voluntary exchanges among small numbers of people seem possible. The only question is what set of rules best facilitate such exchanges. The foregoing analysis suggests that zoning, with its incomplete assignment of property rights, actually prevents many transactions between the parties who are affected, and so causes land to be used less efficiently. For most of the activities regulated by zoning, then, lack of fungibility does not yield a desirable second-best solution because a "first-best" solution seems possible in so many situations.

It is not clear what the result would be if resident proprietors controlled zoning. Although they can exercise controls over vacant land, it may not be in their interest to do so. Some proprietors would gain and others would lose. The possibilities for logrolling could result in a compromise which called for very little zoning, which would allow vacant land to be perceived as having a market price. These considerations, rather than political backwardness, may account for the lack of strong controls in rural areas. The reality of suburban politics, however, seems to be that a great deal of power does rest in the hands of resident lodgers.

Leasing and Selling Zoning in Reality

Another distribution of property rights might be considered in the problem of the previous section. Suppose that communities were allowed to lease their existing zoning restrictions, but were prohibited from establishing any more restrictions than they originally had.[11] Under this system, zoning would be efficient in the sense that it would not distort relative prices of vacant land. This would be represented in Figure 1 by line CC', drawn through point D to illustrate that existing open land *could* be chosen, since leasing zoning is not mandatory. But because of the new opportunity cost of zoning resulting from its fungibility, less vacant land will remain undeveloped.

Resident lodgers are converted into proprietors by full assignment of leasing rights. They could, if they so desired, select higher levels of Q, financing the increased municipal expenditures with the leasing of zoning rights, as suggested in Figure 1.[12] We might go even further and also allow the community to sell zoning outright. Then, depending on the demand for land in their original community, they might sell their rights altogether and select another community, taking the gains from the sale with them. This would allow land use in their original community to be more intensive with the same or even a lower level of Q to suit the demands of newcomers. Thus, saleable zoning would not only allow more intensive use of vacant land, it would also allow existing land use to change. In effect, being able to sell zoning also implies being able to sell neighborhood quality.

The restrictions on selling or leasing zoning are actually not so complete as to eliminate all trade. An important form of income from the lease of zoning is referred to as fiscal zoning. This is the practice of attempting to zone for land uses which will impose

relatively few municipal costs and generate relatively large local
tax revenues. The difference is referred to as the "fiscal surplus"
of the activity. The largest single local expenditure in most communities is education. Thus, the activities with the largest fiscal
surpluses are often those which have few school-age children
associated with them, for a given level of taxable property (or
other tax base).

In a seminal paper on the topic, Hamilton [1975] demonstrated
that the local property tax can become a head tax when new entrants
to a community are required by zoning to consume exactly the same
value of housing as existing residents. The result depends on a
sufficiently large number of communities to satisfy all levels of
demand, and an elastic supply of sites for all activities. Fiscal zoning
is regarded solely as a device to ensure that new households pay for
the local services which they consume.

Hamilton's paper is an important contribution to understanding
zoning motivation and the consequences of its use. Without denying
its importance, however, we wish to point out some of the limitations on the process which make fiscal zoning a less than complete
lease of zoning by the community.[13]

The first limitation is judicial hostility to the practice. Many state
courts have held such a motivation is beyond the scope of the zoning
enabling act. Nonetheless, it is clear that communities are capable
of masking their fiscal concerns with a master plan which refers
only to environmental concerns, with which the courts seem quite
sympathetic. However, this subterfuge turns fiscal zoning into a
blunt weapon, excluding more uses than necessary. For example,
it may be necessary to exclude all apartment houses on an environmental basis, rather than just those with many school-age children.

The second problem is that the process tends to inhibit change
in the income level of people in the community. If the earliest residents in a zoned community are rather wealthy, they will tend to
want additional residents who are both wealthy and willing to pay
for the same set of local services. Lower-income residents, who may
want less housing and fewer local services, will have to find another
community. Since the supply of communities in a metropolitan
area in reality seems to be fairly inelastic, if not fixed, this process
generates too few locations for lower-income people, and adds to
their housing costs (or their commuting costs, if they must find a
community farther from the urban fringe).

The most important problem with the process is that certain local
services may be subject to congestion and use a fixed input. Hamilton's

local service paradigm is education, which probably exhibits constant costs per pupil for a large range. In terms of the production function in Figure 1, school services isoquants would be a set of straight lines of various slopes extending from the origin. This would cause the corresponding marginal and average cost curves in Figure 2 to be horizontal lines. If these were the only services of any importance to current residents, they would be indifferent to how many people lived in their community as long as their housing consumption (and hence property tax payments) were equal to theirs. (This assumes new residents have the same number of school-age children per family, on average, as existing residents.)

This relationship does seem reasonable for school expenditures, but, as argued earlier, it does not seem valid for other municipal services whose object is production of neighborhood quality. As public education is increasingly financed at the state and national level, neighborhood quality services become more important. The latter are more subject to congestion and involve a nonreproducible input, land. Under these conditions, the average cost pricing implied by most local tax systems cannot be efficient.

There may be informal devices to secure marginal cost pricing in such instances. One device might be for the developer of new housing to agree to higher than average property tax assessments. This would not work well for two reasons. First, most states have uniform property tax laws, so such agreement could not be enforced even if they were entered into. Second, the new residents become members of the community themselves. They can vote in community elections, and, if they gain enough power, they can see to it that the stream of benefits is diverted to serve them. An exclusive long-term lease of zoning is made much more difficult because new residents become part of the group which makes decisions about the use of the benefits.[14]

Despite the judicial inhibition on *community* sales of zoning, there is no formal barrier to *private* arrangements between developers and neighbors. Developers could offer some payment to nearby neighbors to persuade them not to protest at the hearing of the zoning authority reviewing their application for a variance or a rezoning. Although this may happen occasionally, it does not seem to be widespread. The explanation, I believe, lies in the absence of legal sanction (as opposed to outright prohibition) of the bargaining process. Bribing potential voters does not seem to be illegal, but the agreements are not contracts.

One problem of such judicial laissez-faire is that negotiations do not have the force of a formal contract, so that side payments by developers to residents are a necessary but not sufficient condition to get approval. Courts have held that local laws may make neighborhood review a necessary part of any rezoning, but final power must rest with community authorities. This creates additional uncertainty for both parties, since there is no guarantee that any agreements they arrive at will be enforced. Furthermore, because zoning is vested in the municipality rather than in the affected neighborhood, it is possible for unaffected or hypersensitive third parties to seek gains by obstructing some project, thus adding to negotiation costs.

The second difficulty is that the informal agreements between developers and their neighbors do not "run with the land." That is, the contracts are not binding on successive owners of the property. A developer who applies for a zoning variance may persuade neighbors not to object to his proposal by paying them some amount. If, in the time of negotiation, one of the neighbors so persuaded sells his home to someone else, the new resident must also be reckoned with. The newcomer may demand a payment, even if he was aware of the agreement between the developer and the former owner. If the courts recognized that the original owner and the developer had made a legitimate contract, and that this contract "ran with the land," the new owner could be excluded from any proposed benefits. But the law of zoning falls under the police power, and no limitation of this power can be written into a deed or otherwise transferred legally. The new neighbor must be recognized, and this must discourage some negotiations. Given the lengthy start-up times for most developers and the rapid turnover of suburban housing, this may be a significant barrier.

Perhaps as a result of these difficulties, few rezonings are obtained on the basis of a legal cash payment. Instead, arrangements such as gifts to local charities or financing of new public works are often used. While these are not always sufficient to guarantee appropriate zoning, they at least avoid some of the difficulties of individual negotiation. Even if they are effective in obtaining rezoning, these tactics have costs as well, since the value of such gifts to residents is typically lower than the cost to the donor. Furthermore, these tactics have the same problems as fiscal zoning. New residents become beneficiaries of the gifts and they also change the political makeup of the community. Fiscal zoning and informal private arrangements are thus imperfect substitutes for legally valid leases or sales of zoning. Full opportunity costs will not be perceived by community decisionmakers.

Community Size and Land Values

We return now to the efficiency issues introduced in section 3. Using the same municipal services production function, we shall modify the argument to account for differences in land rents within the suburban communities. This modification will also enable us to examine one of the issues common in the urban public finance literature, that of optimal community size. Tiebout [1956] argued that the optimal population for a residential community was that at which municipal service costs per capita are at a minimum. We shall show that this is generally not true for suburban communities under our conception of local services, but that zoning will tend to prevent true optimal size from being achieved.[15]

Assume a metropolitan area in which all activities but residential services are conducted at some point in a central city. Surrounding the city are a large number of suburbs of discrete size. The only physical difference among them is distance from the central point. At any given distance there are a number of communities which have a scarce resource, land, used in the production of residential services, including neighborhood quality. Cost curves for neighborhood quality are identical for every community, but they are discrete within the community. (That is, a community cannot be divided into two communities with identical cost curves.) For convenience, we assume that each potential resident of any community demands residential services identical to those consumed by present residents, so that community homogeneity is enforced by market conditions. We assume, as before, that the addition of a new household to the community subtracts one unit of vacant land from it, adding to the density and eventually to the congestion of neighborhood quality.

The initial or "pioneer" residents of a given community choose some level of neighborhood quality, Q_0. This level of Q is maintained throughout by increasing expenditures on municipal services. The "average cost" curve (municipal cost per capita to maintain Q_0) at different levels of population is shown in Figure 2, along with the corresponding marginal curve.

Tiebout's proposition was that optimal community size is achieved when the number of residents corresponds to minimum average costs. This would be N_1 in Figure 2. He argued that communities could use various devices, including zoning, to achieve that population. However, his result holds only in a world in which land rent is not important. Tiebout recognized this difficulty in his beach

example, where there are not enough communities with beaches to satisfy all consumers, but he did not analyze the situation in any detail. In a world where differential rents can arise, we will show that N_1 is not optimal.

At a community within the outer edge of the metropolitan area, land will command positive rent for urban housing. In Figure 2, we represent the demand for location on a uniform plot of land in the community by a horizontal line, AR (average revenue). The demand is elastic because the community is one of many at the same distance from the central city. AR shifts up at communities closer to the central city because of reduced commuting costs, but it does not vary within a given community. Housing is the only rent-producing activity, and it is produced under constant costs over the range we are considering.

Neighborhood quality is tied to location, so the average costs of producing it must be subtracted from the demand for sites to obtain rent per unit of land devoted to housing. (Thus we are talking about rent net of congestion costs.) For example, at point N_2 in Figure 2, average rent equals AB. Total rent for housing equals ABCD, or, equivalently, the area bounded by the MC curve, the AR line, and line segment BE.

In a system in which all property rights are held by landowner-developers (as in a privately owned planned community) the optimal community size will be N_3, at which point MC = AR. Beyond this point, additional housing will yield no rent to the developer, not because his capital costs are rising, but because additional municipal service costs to maintain Q_0 will cause residents to choose some other community.

N_3 is optimal in the sense that total land rent for housing (the only land use) is maximized. It is not at the minimum average cost per person for producing Q_0 because sufficient rent is generated by new development to be able to compensate those who suffer the increased costs of municipal services. For example, at N_2 a developer could rent an additional lot for amount AB (AR minus AC of services for that lot). This would impose on earlier residents costs equal to EA, the difference between marginal and average costs per capita. The owner could compensate them for their higher costs and still keep amount BE for himself. BE is the "marginal rent" at N_2, if compensation must be paid.[16]

If control of development rests with the existing resident lodgers rather than with the owners of vacant land, the range of possible community sizes is between N_1 and N_3. If owners of vacant land

can directly compensate existing residents for their higher cost of maintaining Q_0, then the optimal size will be achieved. For each lot developed, landowners would pay existing resident lodgers the difference between the MC curve and the AC curve. With this minimum side payment, there is still positive rent (the vertical distance between MC and AR) to be had by a landowner up to N_3.

However, as we have seen, zoning law tends to discourage such transactions. Present residents are likely to continue to perceive the opportunity cost of the land use rights they control at a lower-than-market cost, and optimal community size is not likely to be achieved. If such transactions were completely forbidden, community size would remain at N_1.

The analysis can account for some of the empirical evidence about zoning referred to in section 1. At N less than N_3, average land rent for the entire community (i.e., rent for housing divided by both developed and undeveloped land) is lower than at N_3. In this sense, zoning lowers land rents. But land rent per *existing* housing unit is higher at populations less than N_3. This will tend to make housing costs in the suburbs higher than they would be under other systems of land use controls. This is not because only one small suburb has excessively restricted land for housing, nor is it caused by a conspiracy among the suburbs. It is because every suburb in the metropolitan area faces similar circumstances that the total, uncoordinated effect will shift the supply of suburban housing sites to the left, with all of its consequences for metropolitan housing prices and economic structure.[17]

The last result is probably what makes economists tend to think of the motivation for zoning as a monopolistic conspiracy to increase existing residents' land values. However, a downward sloping demand curve plays no part in this analysis. Even if there were inelastic demand, zoning would tend to discourage residents from appropriating the gains. In this sense, zoning is worse than monopoly, since production of housing is even further restricted. For example, if AR were downward sloping and the marginal revenue curve cut the marginal cost curve at point E in Figure 2, a monopoly developer would allow N_2 units. However, with zoning, lodgers have no more incentive to expand beyond N_1 than they did in the competitive situation, since the rents may not be appropriated by them.

Figure 2 can also be used to present another rationale for present zoning law. This argument holds that though zoning may cause underdevelopment, it is necessary to prevent the evil of overdevelopment. If there were substantial barriers to communication and exchange between landowner-developers and resident-lodgers in the community, and if the former had the right to develop without the latter's consent, too much development would indeed take place. Resident lodgers would not be able to pay the landowners to limit development to any maximum intensity. Developers in this case perceive the land rent on each lot as the difference between the AC curve and the AR line. In other words, they take the community's average rent for housing as their marginal rent. This would cause communities to expand to N_4, where $AC = AR$. New residents impose additional costs on older residents which are greater than the marginal benefits of locating there.

This argument might provide a basis for assigning control over development to community residents (as is already the case) rather than to landowner-developers. It would seem to depend on whether one regards overdevelopment as a greater problem than under-development, and on the distributional consequences of the assign-ment. But this is surely not an argument for inhibiting the sale of development rights as is the case under present zoning law. If it is impossible to sell these rights (by the assumptions of the argument), then it is redundant to prohibit sales. If it *is* possible to sell them, the argument is wrong.

I find from innumerable reports of illegal private sales that it really would be possible to sell the rights publicly if the law allowed it. Development is not so mysterious that local officials cannot deter-mine their constituents' best economic interests, especially when there is an open and obvious opportunity cost. These sales would tend to lead communities in Figure 2 from N_1 to N_3 (but not beyond) under our earlier assumptions about suburban governments. Other transactions costs might retard this process somewhat, but it could only improve the allocative efficiency of the present situation.

Conclusion

Our analysis has suggested that zoning represents an incomplete assignment of property rights. Communities enjoy generous controls over land use, but they cannot fully lease or sell these rights. This causes land subject to zoning to be perceived as having a lower opportunity cost than under fully assigned rights. This in turn causes too little development in zoned communities, higher prices for new housing in the metropolitan area, and lower average values of subur-ban land. It is not necessary to assume monopolistic control over land use by communities or to resort to public choice failures to obtain this result, though both may be additional factors.

Despite its inefficiency, zoning does offer a bundle of property rights to suburban residents which are more advantageous than most alternatives. Limited but low-cost control over other people's property is more advantageous than having to pay for it. Reforms such as those proposed by Ellickson [1973, 1977] and Siegan [1972] would limit this control or abolish public rights altogether. These will surely be resisted by the apparently powerful political interests of suburban homeowners.

A more likely direction for reform is to increase zoning's fungibility. Some steps in this direction are transferable development rights, which allow the community to barter zoning restrictions for a limited set of public goods [James and Gale 1977]. For example, an owner of a historical building may be persuaded to preserve it in return for additional development rights elsewhere. If these programs became generally fungible and if they were accepted by the courts, they would approximate the fungible system described in section 3. Though these tendencies will make zoning more efficient, they raise problems of vertical and horizontal equity. Some discussion has begun on what the just distribution of property rights should be in this situation [Ellickson 1977; Nelson 1977], but more research on the ultimate incidence of zoning restrictions should be done before fungible zoning is formally approved by legislators or jurists.

NOTES

[1] Crecine, Davis and Jackson [1967], Rueter [1973], Mieszkowski [1973]. But contrast Stull [1975].

[2] We shall be concerned with overall restrictions on housing supply rather than on particular types of housing or of other land uses, though the analysis in this paper may be applied to these other motivations. For a description of recent court cases involving the types of limitations we are concerned with, see Zumbrun and Hookano [1977].

[3] It would lead us more generally to inquire about all transactions costs which might inhibit such exchange. We concentrate here on those transactions costs imposed by the legislative and judicial systems because they may be more amenable to reform than others and because they seem to have been overlooked in most other studies. Exceptions to the last point are Ellickson [1977], Nelson [1977], and Tarlock [1972].

[4] The following summary of the legal and institutional arrangements was derived from several secondary sources, the most important of which was Williams [1975].

[5] Ellickson [1977] regards zoning as in fact fungible. This is despite the general judicial hostility to "contract zoning" and other devices to formalize the arrangements. While it is clear that some leasing of zoning authority is widespread,

there are real barriers to even this process, which we shall take up in the next section. The issue is really one of degree: should we emphasize zoning's fungible aspects or its deficiencies in this regard? For our present purposes, it seems useful to emphasize the deficiencies, since most other aspects of real property are fully fungible, and since empirical evidence suggests that there are important barriers to trade.

[6] The distinction between motivations of owners of undeveloped land and other residents in zoning issues was first developed by Davis [1963].

[7] For a discussion of the various participants in suburban land controversies, see Linowes and Allensworth [1973]. They make it clear that suburban zoning is not dominated by landowners and developers.

[8] Stull's [1975] regressions for a Boston SMSA sample suggest, however, that undeveloped land has a *negative* influence on the value of single-family homes. This runs counter to survey results by Knight and Menchik [1974] and my casual impressions from newspaper articles and conversations with local officials. The difference might be accounted for by Stull's including *all* undeveloped land as a residual category. It also seems possible that proportion of undeveloped land might be a proxy for distance from the Boston CBD, which was, surprisingly, not significant in his regressions.

[9] Whether congestion actually exists in provision of local services is an unresolved empirical issue. Studies of municipal service costs and group size are not very enlightening because they tend to measure expenditure on inputs (e.g., police services) rather than the desired outputs (e.g., public safety), and because they overlook private provision of such services. If desired output measures could be established, the case for congestion might be stronger. In any case, it is clear that community officials *believe* there is potential congestion of neighborhood quality.

[10] Of course the actual price line may differ slightly depending on the arrangements adopted. Eminent domain acquisitions might cost less than purely voluntary exchanges. The important point is that some approximation of the market is demanded in any of these devices.

[11] For this hypothetical case, we assume that the legislature passes an enabling law which allows all communities to lease existing restrictions, but not to establish any new ones without compensation to the landowners.

[12] The new equilibrium population, N''', is not identical to that obtained where all rights were retained by landowners (N'). This is because fungible zoning makes preexisting residents wealthier than before, so they will demand better neighborhood quality. Since they can in this example only *lease* their rights, not sell them, they must stay in their own communities to enjoy the income this provides them. They may sell their housing to someone else, capitalizing the value of the lease that way, but the income and consumption of Q from the lease continues to accrue to the buyer. *Selling* zoning implies foregoing any future control or income. When existing households sell zoning and move, buyers of their housing would purchase it at a lower price which reflected their limited rights (lack of zoning authority). Thus, new residents of the community are treated equally in both situations. Under a lease, they are compensated with the income; under a sale, they are compensated by lower housing prices.

[13] For other criticisms of fiscal zoning, see Hirsch [1977].

[14] These qualifications are probably much less important for zoning of commercial and industrial property. They generally do not alter the voting

makeup, and they consume different types of local services. As I have suggested in a previous essay [Fischel 1975], this enables communities to extract compensation from firms for their neighborhood effects by requiring them to pay some fraction of the total tax levy in excess of direct costs they generate.

[15] This issue relates only indirectly to the optimal size of a metropolitan area, with which most of the recent literature has been concerned. Our communities are strictly clubs for the consumption of residential services. Moreover, we are not "disproving" Tiebout's hypothesis that a system of communities can provide an efficient level of local public goods by allowing migration. Our amendment is just that optimal size for such communities may not be at minimum average costs per capita when location and congestion are introduced.

[16] In a completely built or planned community, the developer would typically charge each buyer FG, the average rent at full development. In actual planned communities, developers take pains to restrict initial residents' control over subsequent development to assure that maximum rent need not be shared and all planned development can be completed [Reichman 1976, p. 288]. In publicly zoned municipalities, however, the community might extract more than the minimum compensation from the developer unless it were inhibited by other authorities such as the courts [Ellickson 1977].

[17] For an examination of these consequences of zoning restrictions in terms of the standard urban economics model, see White [1975].

REFERENCES

Bergstrom, Theodore C., and Goodman, Robert P. 1973. "Private Demands for Public Goods." *American Economic Review* 63 (June): 280-96.

Coase, Ronald H. 1960. "The Problem of Social Cost." *Journal of Law and Economics* 3 (Oct.): 1-44.

Crecine, John P.; Davis, Otto A.; and Jackson, John E. 1967. "Urban Property Markets: Some Empirical Results and Their Implications for Municipal Zoning." *Journal of Law and Economics* 10 (Oct.): 79-100.

Davis, Otto A. 1963. "Economic Elements in Municipal Zoning Decisions." *Land Economics* 39 (Nov.): 375-86.

Ellickson, Robert C. 1973. "Alternatives to Zoning: Covenants, Nuisance Rules, and Fines as Land Use Controls." *University of Chicago Law Review* 40 (Summer): 681-782.

——————. 1977. "Suburban Growth Controls: An Economic and Legal Analysis." *Yale Law Journal* 86 (Jan.): 385-511.

Fischel, William A. 1975. "Fiscal and Environmental Considerations in the Location of Firms in Suburban Communities." In *Fiscal Zoning and Land Use Controls,* eds. E.S. Mills and W.E. Oates. Lexington, Mass.: Lexington Books.

Hamilton, Bruce W. 1975. "Zoning and Property Taxation in a System of Local Government." *Urban Studies* 12 (June): 205-11.

——————. 1977. "Zoning and the Exercise of Monopoly Power." *Journal of Urban Economics* (forthcoming).

Hirsch, Werner Z. 1977. "The Efficiency of Restrictive Land Use Instruments." *Land Economics* 53 (May): 145-56.

238   W. A. FISCHEL

James, Franklin, and Gale, Dennis. 1977. *Zoning for Sale: Transferable Development Rights.* Washington, D.C.: The Urban Institute.
Knight, Robert I., and Menchik, Mark D. 1974. *Residential Environmental Attitudes and Preferences: Report of a Questionnaire Survey.* Madison: University of Wisconsin Institute for Environmental Studies.
Linowes, R. Robert, and Allensworth, Don T. 1973. *The Politics of Land Use: Planning, Zoning, and the Private Developer.* New York: Praeger.
Mieszkowski, Peter M. 1973. "Notes on the Econimic Effects of Land-Use Regulation." In *Issues in Urban Public Finance.* Saarbrücken: Institute International de Finance Publiques.
Mills, Edwin S., and Oates, Wallace E., eds. 1975. *Fiscal Zoning and Land Use Controls.* Lexington, Mass.: Lexington Books.
Nelson, Robert H. 1977. *Zoning and Property Rights.* Cambridge: MIT Press.
Orr, Larry L. 1975. *Income, Employment and Urban Residential Location.* New York: Academic Press.
Peterson, George E. 1974. *The Influence of Zoning Regulations on Land and Housing Prices.* Working Paper no. 1207-24. Washington, D.C.: The Urban Institute.
————. 1977. "Land Prices and Factor Substitution in the Metropolitan Housing Market." *American Economic Review* (forthcoming).
Reichman, Uriel. 1976. "Residential Private Governments: An Introductory Survey." *University of Chicago Law Review* 43 (Winter): 253-306.
Rueter, Frederick H. 1973. "Externalities in Urban Property Markets: An Empirical Test of the Zoning Ordinance of Pittsburgh." *Journal of Law and Economics* 16 (Oct.): 313-50.
Sagalyn, Lynne B., and Sternlieb, George. 1973. *Zoning and Housing Costs.* New Brunswick: Rutgers University Center for Urban Policy Research.
Siegan, Bernard H. 1972. *Land Use Without Zoning.* Lexington, Mass.: Lexington Books.
Stull, William J. 1975. "Community Environment, Zoning, and the Market Value of Single-Family Homes." *Journal of Law and Economics* 18 (Oct.): 535-57.
Tarlock, A. Dan. 1972. "Toward a Revised Theory of Zoning." In *Land Use Controls Annual,* ed. F.S. Bangs. Chicago: American Society of Planning Officials.
Tiebout, Charles M. 1956. "A Pure Theory of Local Expenditures." *Journal of Political Economy* 64 (Oct.): 416-24.
White, Michelle J. 1975. "The Effect of Zoning on the Size of Metropolitan Areas." *Journal of Urban Economics* 2 (Oct.): 279-90.
Williams, Norman. 1975. *American Planning Law: Land Use and the Police Power.* 5 vols. Chicago: Callaghan and Co.
Zumbrun, Ronald A., and Hookano, Thomas E. 1977. "No Growth and Related Land-Use Legal Problems: An Overview." *The Urban Lawyer* 9 (Winter): 122-56.

13

The Efficiency of Restrictive
Land Use Instruments

I N 1926, in the landmark case of *Euclid v. Ambler Realty
Company*, the United States Supreme Court held that local
zoning ordinances were clothed with a presumption of legal
validity, unless demonstrated to be "clearly arbitrary and unreasonable."[1] At that time, Justice Sutherland indicated that the possibility should not be ruled out that in the future cases might occur
where ". . . the general public interest would so far outweigh the
interest of the municipality that the municipality would not be
allowed to stand in the way."[2] Since then, lower costs of transportation have brought about decentralization of both residences
and employment. Increased production specialization has made
interregional migration fairly common. Thus, today it might seem
that the day foreseen by Justice Sutherland has arrived, and that at
present the general public interest does not necessarily correspond
with that of the municipality. Yet, the U.S. Supreme Court has
retained its 1926 position. The Court has refused, as recently as 1974
in the Bel Terre case, to reexamine its scope of review of zoning
cases.[3] When a district court in *Construction Industry Association
of Sonoma County v. City of Petaluma*[4] held that the desire of
present residents to retain the "small town character" of Petaluma
was not compelling and thus invalidated the Petaluma plan, it was
overturned on appeal.[5]

Some state supreme courts have taken different positions. The
New Jersey Supreme Court in *Southern County of Burlington*

The author wishes to acknowledge the assistance of Stephen E. Margolis,
research assistant, on economic aspects, and of Mary Downey, Joel G. Hirsch
and David Shilton, on legal aspects. Two anonymous reviewers offered valuable
comments. This research was partly supported by a grant from the Committee
on Research of the Academic Senate of the University of California.

*Professor of Economics, University of California, Los Angeles.

Copyright © 1977 University of Wisconsin Press and the Board of Regents
of the University of Wisconsin System. *Land Economics* **53** (2): 145-156,
1977. Reprinted by permission.

NAACP V. Township of Mount Laurel held that zoning must promote the general welfare. A municipality cannot only look to "its own selfish and parochial interest and in effect build a wall around itself...," but must consider the needs of the region as a whole and offer an "appropriate variety and choice of housing."[6] A similar position was taken by the Pennsylvania Supreme Court in *National Land Investment Company v. Kohn*[7] and the New York Court of Appeals in *Berenson v. Town of New Castle.*[8]

Lawyers have been struggling with exclusionary land use problems in terms of the rights and obligations of the parties involved, while economists have been concerned with the nature of efficient communities.

Our objective is to identify the reasons why newcomers might impose uncompensated costs on a jurisdiction, as well as the consequences of various arrangements to deal with these costs. Specifically, we will seek to show that while, for example, large-lot zoning may increase efficiency in the presence of local property taxes, it is not the most efficient exclusionary instrument. Our analysis will be restricted to those cases in which the goods and services which crowd are augmentable. Schools, roads, libraries, etc., can all be expanded if sufficient revenues are available. These involve resources which are ubiquitous, though not abundant. This, we feel, is the typical suburban case. The contrasting case is that of unique resources, where the crucial crowding involves an item of unusual historic, scenic, or environmental interest.[9] Here, the usual congestion discussion applies, and the problem is best treated as an externality.

We will begin by considering the effects on land use of the local property tax, first in the absence and second in the presence of exclusionary schemes. Thereafter we will examine effects of three major exclusionary instruments, and finally offer some concluding considerations.

Local Property Taxes and their Effects on Land Use

Restrictions on growth may appear to the casual observer to represent interferences with an otherwise well-functioning market, and as such they may be presumed inefficient. For example, the trial court in *Construction Industry Association of Sonoma County v. City of Petaluma* ruled that the city could not "deny the future" or "avoid the increased responsibilities and economic burdens which time and natural growth would invariably bring," implying that the future is necessarily efficient and equitable.[10] Neither is necessarily correct. Local excluding measures are not imposed on a free and unencumbered market; they can be as much a correction of existing distortions of a free market outcome as a new distortion.

Tiebout models seek to identify the conditions under which jurisdictional choice creates an effective market for local public services. Revenue is raised by lump-sum taxes and user charges, and there are very many communities, a high degree of mobility, and complete information. As a consequence, citizens' choices result in an efficient combination of public goods. Under Tiebout's assumptions, a U-shaped average cost curve with respect to the number of persons served allows communities to cover costs of operation, while charging residents the marginal cost of their presence in the community. This in turn assumes that communities will operate at optimum scale; where increasing population would decrease average cost, marginal cost must be low compared to other communities, so that the community should attract new residents. Where average cost is reduced by decreasing population, population will fall, or at least no new entrants will be attracted, since marginal cost is high compared to communities operating at optimum scale.

Crucial to Tiebout models is reliance on lump-sum taxes that force the decision maker to consider the true cost of his presence in this community or one with differing levels of public service. Departing from lump-sum financing negates the efficiency results.[11] Tiebout models also assume absence of locational constraints due to employment, nongovernmental services, or amenities. Where location is constrained, many communities are needed with equivalent access to, say, employment centers, or complementarity of housing and public goods. This latter approach suits traditional urban location models producing an orderly income gradient: quality public services for the rich and inferior services for the poor. No one chooses an inefficient location with respect to commuting cost, since centralized employment sorts out individuals by income, and therefore by demand for local public services. This effect requires merely that housing and local services be normal goods rather than complements. With decentralized employment, efficient location involves no such sorting out of houses by income. The choice of community may therefore involve optimized public goods packages only with increased commuting cost. However, the market for land and voting by eventual residents should assign jurisdictions to locations in an efficient way. Where there are industries with many low-skill/low-wage people, adjacent communities should cater to the demands of low-income households for public goods. Where skills and incomes of residents are high, local governments should accommodate their preferences.

In contrast to the assumption in the Tiebout model, property taxes produce most local funds. While we will assume that the local property tax is the sole revenue source, an income tax gives similar results. Models of fiscally induced migration are long run, since incentives for migration do not create immediate wholesale relocation. In our long-run model, locational decisions are viewed as if a group of prospective residents approached an undeveloped plain with jurisdictional boundaries already established. We assume: (1) no dominant central business district, and for now all firms located in uniformly dispersed commercial jurisdictions; (2) within residential jurisdictions all land is put to residential use, nonconforming uses are dealt with efficiently and units of different densities are sufficiently separated from one another that higher-density developments will impose no significant direct externalities on lower-density developments; and (3) no racism or snobism, i.e., presence of one race or income class will not, in itself, affect persons of another race or income class. Thus, we confine our analysis to fiscal motives. Other motives for exclusion will, we believe, tend to reinforce our results.

With some fairly normal restrictions, we can demonstrate incentives to zone out new land uses. Following the usual Tiebout assumptions, we have a cost function $C = C(Q,n)$, with Q the quantity of public service which any household can consume and n the number of households in the jurisdiction. $C_{qq}(Q, n)$ and $C_{nn}(Q, n)$ are both assumed to be positive. The latter assumption is somewhat different from the usual assumption for public goods, although in line with Tiebout who assumed the average cost curve to be U-shaped with respect to population. (Some empirical literature supports this assumption, though it suggests that certain locally provided goods are not public goods.)

The property tax rate t for a jurisdiction with no outside funding will be $t = C(Q, n)/V$, where V is the total value of property in it. For the tax rate to be unchanged in the presence of a new entrant, we require that $t(\partial V/\partial n) = C_n(Q, n)$. Where the community is of optimum size and tax revenues are just sufficient to cover $C(Q, n)$, then $t\ V/n = C_n(Q, n)$. The average tax revenue is equal to the average cost of government which equals marginal cost at the optimum jurisdiction size. Construction of houses with values below (above) the average house value will raise (lower) the tax rate.

Jurisdictions thus have an incentive to encourage high-value properties. For any given level of services, the tax rate will be lowest where per capita property values are highest. Low tax rates attract households, causing high growth rates in jurisdictions with high property values. However, as will be demonstrated below, the highest-density developers tend to be the highest bidders per unit of land in fiscally favorable locations. Bradford and Kelejian [1973] have shown that fiscal advantages are significant in explaining interjurisdictional mobility. Aronson and Schwartz [1973] found that 69% of migration in the fifties and 89% in the sixties brought fiscal advantages to the mover. A household planning a given housing consumption can reduce tax payments or increase public goods consumption by locating in a jurisdiction with high property values. Those choosing small houses impose on others some of the costs of providing them with public goods.

The first effect of local property taxation is that builders will sacrifice locational efficiency in order to effect wealth transfers. Since a parcel of land will go to the user placing the highest value on the combined productivity and tax characteristics of the land, the normal assurance that the market allocates to the highest-value use is impaired. For example, consider the locational tendencies of two categories of development: category 1—high-density housing (apartments—APTs), and category 2—low-density housing (single-family dwellings—SFDs). We also designate S_i to denote the structure value of a dwelling unit per household in category i, and d_i to be the density development in category i in terms of households per acre.

Consider communities a and b which are close to an employment center, with a being closer than b. Equal numbers of trips, m, are made by all households, with the cost of trips from communities a and b denoted by C_a and C_b, respectively, and with $C_b > C_a$. In the absence of a property tax, builders of each category prefer a to b and offer bids accordingly. However, apartment builders will pay $d_1 mC_b - d_1 mC_a$ more for an acre in a than for an acre in b. For SFDs the difference between values of land in the two jurisdictions is $d_2 mC_b - d_2 mC_a$. Since

$$d_1 mC_b - d_1 mC_a = d_1 m(C_b - C_a)$$

and

$$d_2 mC_b - d_2 mC_a = d_2 m(C_b - C_a)$$

apartment builders will be the high bidders in equilibrium for land in community a_1 because $d_1 > d_2$ by assumption. Apartments will tend to be located in a and single-family dwellings in b. Let us institute a local property tax that covers costs and consider the bid price per acre, assuming constant density for each type of development.

Assume an initial allocation of structures which conforms with the efficient pattern described above. Consider first the basis of assessment to be the total value of lots plus structures' assessed value per acre for communities a and b. (L is the value of an acre of land.)

	Community a	Community b
APTs	$d_1 S_1 + L_a$	$d_1 S_1 + L_b$
SFDs	$d_2 S_2 + L_a$	$d_2 S_2 + L_b$

Initially, $L_a > L_b$, although no magnitude can be assigned to $L_b - L_a$, and in fact these values will be changing, with L_a falling and L_b increasing as locations change from the initial position where there is no property tax. (It will be shown that whether $L_a \gtrless L_b$ will not affect locational tendencies introduced by the property tax.) Now introduce property taxes on residential property sufficient to cover costs. Assuming constant returns to scale with respect to population size, and communities a and b providing equal services (or at least having equal per capita expenditures),

$$t_a = C/[(d_1 S_1 + L_a)/d_1] = C/(S_1 + L_a/d_1)$$

$$t_b = C/[(d_2 S_2 + L_b)/d_2] = C/(S_2 + L_b/d_2)$$

where C equals per capita local public service cost.

Note that $t_a \gtrless t_b$ according to whether $(S_1 + L_a/d_1) \gtrless (S_2 + L_b/d_2)$. While it cannot be determined which inequality holds, the overwhelming empirical evidence is that property value per household within metropolitan areas is greater in low-density settlements away from employment centers.

Builders of apartments tend to pay a premium for an acre in b, based on the difference in tax rates equal to

$$1/r[(d_1 S_1 + L_a)t_a - (d_1 S_1 + L_b)t_b]$$

Similarly, builders of single-family dwellings tend to pay a premium

$$1/r[(d_2 S_2 + L_a)t_a - (d_2 S_2 + L_b)t_b]$$

where r is the appropriate discount rate. Rearranging terms, we have for each category:

$$\text{APTs: } [(d_1 S_1 + L_a)t_a - (d_1 S_1 + L_b)t_b]/r$$

$$= [d_1 S_1 (t_a - t_b) + (L_a t_a - L_b t_b 0]/r$$

$$\text{SFDs: } [(d_2 S_2 + L_a)t_a - (d_2 S_2 + L_b)t_b]/r$$

$$= [(d_2 S_2 (t_a - t_b) + (L_a t_a - L_b t_b)]/r$$

The premium induced by the property tax favors a reversal of the initial distribution of homes if

$$d_1 S_1 (t_a - t_b) + (L_a t_a - L_b t_b) >$$

$$d_2 S_2 (t_a - t_b) + (L_a t_a - L_b t_b)$$

or equivalently

$$d_1 S_1 (t_a - t_b) > d_2 S_2 (t_a - t_b)$$

Thus, so long as the property value per household is lower in a than in b, and the structure value per acre is greater for APTs than for SFDs, we are assured that the locational tendency induced by the property tax is the reverse of that induced by locational advantages. Whether the effect of the tax advantage overcomes that of the locational advantage depends on the relative magnitudes of $d_1 S_1$ and $d_2 S_2$. In particular, location will be reversed if

$$d_1 S_1 (t_a - t_b) - d_2 S_2 (t_a - t_b) >$$
$$d_1 m(C_b - C_a) - d_2 m(C_b - C_a)$$

While this condition will not hold in all cases, it is likely that for some buildings, particularly those at the margin with respect to location or those of extremely high value per acre, an inefficient location is chosen.

A second inefficiency introduced by the property tax without zoning is instability of aging communities. Unlike Henry Aaron

[1974], we do not regard the property tax as a general tax on all capital since, aside from exemptions, each jurisdiction establishes its own tax rate. The property tax introduces instability because of substitutability of capital in one location for that in another.

Consider a local government which derives all its revenue from a tax on residential property, receives no grants, and whose services "crowd" with respect to population. The local government cost function is $C = C(Q, n)$ with $C_n(Q, n)$, $C_{nn}(Q, n)$, $C_q(Q, n)$ and $C_{qq}(Q, n) > 0$. Property tax payments for the jth household are $T_j = tV_j$, where t is the effective community tax rate and V_j is the market value of the dwelling owned by the jth household. (We ignore renters; however, if the property tax is shifted completely, the results hold for renters.)

Total tax payments will be:

$$T = \sum_{j=1}^{n} tV_j = t \sum_{j=1}^{n} V_j = tV$$

where V is the total value of property in the jurisdiction, i.e.,

$$V = \sum_{j=1}^{n} V_j$$

Since local tax revenues must cover the total cost of local government, $C = T = tV$; so $t = C/V$, or simply, the tax rate must equal the total cost of local government divided by the total value of property in the jurisdiction. The usual maximization for the consumer, treating Q as fixed (the consumer will not always be in equilibrium with respect to Q), gives:

$$\text{Max } U_j(X_j, V_j, \overline{Q}) \text{ st. } P_x X + \frac{C(\overline{Q}, n)}{V} V_j + rV_j = Yx, v_j$$

$$L = U(X_j, V_j, \overline{Q}) - \lambda(P_x X_j + \frac{C(\overline{Q}, n)}{V} V_j + rV_j - Y)$$

where $\overline{Q}$ is the exogenously determined level of public output, r is the rate of interest, P_x is the price of non-housing consumption X, and Y is household income defined to include the imputed rent from equity in the home. We differentiate to obtain the first-order conditions

$$\frac{\partial L}{\partial X} = \frac{\partial U}{\partial X} - \lambda P_x = 0$$

$$\frac{\partial L}{\partial U_i} = \frac{\partial U}{\partial X} - \lambda \left[\frac{C(\overline{Q}, n)}{V} + r \right] = 0$$

and the constraint

$$P_x X_j + \frac{C(\overline{Q}, n)}{V} V_j + r V_j = Y = 0$$

From the first two conditions we have the usual result that

$$\frac{\frac{\partial U}{\partial X_j}(X_i^*, V_j^* \, \overline{Q})}{P_x} = \frac{\frac{\partial U}{\partial V_j}(X_j^*, V_j^*, \overline{Q})}{\frac{C(\overline{Q}, n)}{V} + r}$$

which has the conventional interpretation that the marginal utilities per dollar of additional expenditure are equated in all areas of consumption. Thus, $[C(\overline{Q}, n)/V] + r$ is recognized as the unit price of housing consumption.

Thus, the quantity of housing chosen by j will fall with decreases in V, ceteris paribus. Further, increasing n and thus increasing $C(\overline{Q}, n)$ will decrease V_j^* unless V is increased in proportion to the increase in $C(\overline{Q}, n)$. Thus, V_j^* will fall if $(\partial C/\partial n)(\partial V/\partial n) > C/V$. Therefore, if C is increased and V is not increased proportionately, the equilibrium value of V_j will fall. Thus, $\partial C/\partial n > t(\partial V/\partial n)$, so consumers will want to adjust downward their consumption of housing. With no constraint on the V_i of newcomers, it is likely that the above inequality is satisfied. With household i entering the community, $\partial V/\partial n = V_j$, so the above inequality becomes $\partial C/\partial n > t V_i$, i.e., household i's marginal effect on government expenditure is greater than its tax payment.

In the light of higher housing prices, households will consume less housing services by reducing maintenance, and new entrants will build less expensive houses. Thus, even if the jurisdiction were to attract families with the same income and tastes as the original residents, the initial disturbance will cause C/V to keep rising. Some residents will leave because of these conditions. Adjustments of the quality of housing services will tend to reinforce the initial disturbance. The process can be stopped if we have revenue from outside sources, R, and commercial property with value V_c; then $t = (C - R)/(V + V_c)$. If V_c and R are large and independent of the tax rate and local expenditures, the initial reduction of V may have a negligible effect on property tax. Further, if there are land-intensive industries, and increasing t reduces the value of land for residential users, V_c might be increased, exerting a further stabilizing influence.

In addition to the effect of local property taxes on locational efficiency and instability of aging communities, a third inefficiency relates to reduction in the variety of available communities. Martin McGuire [1974] has shown that segregation of individuals into groups according to their tastes for public goods is efficient. Where all members of a given community pay the same amount toward support of local government, segregation into relatively homogenous jurisdictions will occur as a voluntary response, with similar incentives for segregation resulting for all groups. McGuire shows that forced integration is an inferior redistributing device, since an equivalent wealth transfer by lump-sum taxes and grants would leave both parties better off. After the transfer occurs, each group is free to choose the combination of public and private consumption most preferred by its members, given their tastes and incomes. The property tax does not force integration in any direct sense, but it makes it necessary for low-income households to move into higher-income jurisdictions to benefit from the redistribution mechanism.

Where groups are perfectly segregated according to tastes, the choices that the community makes will represent the interests of each member of the community. Where tastes are mixed, individual preferences must be compromised. Aronson and Schwartz [1973] have demonstrated that with redistributive tax schemes, no equilibrium exists in the allocation of persons to jurisdictions until all communities have the same average incomes and per capita public expenditures. Satisfaction of this condition will certainly reduce the range of choice of local public services available to consumers, and therefore their well-being.

Where all individuals are confronted by the full cost that they impose on the local government, "voting with one's feet" can lead to homogeneity within communities, and local decisions can be reached without encountering major conflicts with individual preferences. The local property tax alone, without exclusionary zoning, will create heterogeneity in communities. The potential for re-distribution will cause wealthy communities to attract high-density development with smaller individual dwellings, until per capita property values are equalized across communities. Thus, as a redistributive device, the property tax succeeds only where efficiency is sacrificed.

The property tax, in the absence of exclusion, probably redistributes from rich to poor. But the redistribution is partial and inaccurate. The poor, unable to move, remain in poor jurisdictions; the rich remain in wealthy, "built-up" jurisdictions, where they avoid redistribution. Property-tax-related fiscal advantages in suburbs have attracted expensive properties; the resulting migration has contributed to the fiscal crisis of cities. Since each generation of affluent Americans tends to locate in new jurisdictions, tomorrow's old suburbs will face similar crises. The result is costly movement of households and unnecessarily rapid depreciation of housing capital. Thus, redistribution is limited by successive rounds of, at least in part, fiscally induced mobility; what redistribution does occur, occurs only at great cost.

A further consideration is property tax incidence. Normally it is assumed that the tax is entirely shifted to eventual occupants, since the supply of housing is, in the extreme long run, quite competitive. However, a supplier of housing would not "pass on" the benefits of any unusual tax advantages that his unit possessed. Even if "balanced" communities could be assured, redistribution is not assured. Rental and sale prices of structures are determined in competitive markets. Therefore, tax benefits applying to relatively few properties would not be passed on to consumers so long as their next best alternative is to buy or rent downtown, where tax rates are high and services are poor. Where a community's favorable tax base allows greater per capita expenditures for public services, rent would be bid up by tenants to reflect these advantages. In short, in a competitive market where marginal units remain in areas offering an unfavorable tax-benefit package, the occupant would receive little or no benefit. Consumers get what they pay for and little more; the tax advantages accure to the initial owners, i.e., builders who manage to acquire the rights to "balance" a community by their action. (Note: builders are usually the plaintiffs in exclusionary zoning cases.)

Exclusionary Instruments and their Effects

We turn next to three classes of excluding devices: large-lot zoning, population ceilings and quotas, and construction permits.

Large-Lot Zoning

In keeping with our long-run setting, we assume that laws are imposed on undeveloped land, or land to be eventually redeveloped. Communities are not differentiated by their present land uses. Thus, every community can establish a minimum lot size requirement. To attract households which build expensive structures, communities seek to make land (per acre) relatively inexpensive by requiring large lots. Thus, large-lot builders need not compete with higher-density builders to might value land very highly.

While this strategy may work for a single community acting alone, it must fail when all communities take similar action to attract the rich, and there is a fixed number of rich households. Amenity-rich communities would have the highest prices for fixed-sized lots. If these locational amenities are normal goods, the rich will seek them. The poor will get the least desirable locations, since large-lot zoning precludes high-density developments near places of employment. As long as incentives exist to segregate households by income, the emerging patterns will reinforce whatever motives caused the rich to locate in one jurisdiction and the poor in others. Since jurisdictions with expensive structures can support government services at a relatively low ad valorem tax rate, every household seeks to locate in the richer communities. But builders of expensive structures derive the greatest tax advantages and will bid highest for lots in communities with high per capita assessed valuation. Households will sort into communities according to housing values. Accordingly, every community seeks the largest legal minimum lot size with expensive structures.

Under large-lot zoning, the property tax approximates a lump-sum tax, with all households paying the same amount for any given level of services. As in the Hamilton model [1975], in order to achieve a given number of choice levels for public goods, more communities are required than in the Tiebout case [1956]. This first inefficiency is unimportant if the population is large relative to the efficient community size. Residents might also consider themselves better off under a smaller lot size constraint since at the high per acre land prices, which capitalize tax savings, smaller lots would be chosen. However, this "cost" to the household is an illusion, since the purchase price of a lot reflects the price of the right to construct a residence in the community. If smaller lots were specified, the market clearing price for lots would fall by only the marginal evaluation of space itself, and the price per acre would increase. By adopting large-lot zoning, the community actually accomplishes a transfer of wealth from the previous nonresidential owners to prospective residents. (With a large minimum lot size, the owner of undeveloped property must transfer a large amount of land in order to capture the prospective residents' evaluation of the right to locate in a community.)

There is a second inefficiency compared to the Tiebout case. Arbitrary lot size constraints match the marginal evaluation of land with its opportunity cost (recreational uses, agricultural uses, etc.) for only a few residents. For most communities the largest allowable minimum lot size poses an inefficiency which could, however, be eliminated if they were to determine the optimum lot size for the residents that they would ultimately attract. Any jurisdiction acting alone in adopting a minimum lot size below the legal limit would attract smaller dwellings. Thus, where courts do not discriminate, but allow all communities to set the same lot requirement, some loss must occur.

A third loss is that efficient community size with respect to public goods consumption is no longer assured. Given fixed jurisdictional boundaries, population size is determined by the lot size. Incentives for adjusting lot size requirements may result in a more efficient scale for local governments, but not necessarily for private consumption.

Population Ceilings and Quotas

Population ceilings and periodic construction quotas have the political appeal of appearing not to exclude any particular income group but only to control population size or growth. Still, they affect composition and size of the jurisdiction. An absolute population ceiling has effects similar to the minimum lot size requirement. Temporary constraints or moderate population restrictions may merely promote orderly growth. Where a community acting alone restricts the rate of growth, distortion toward more expensive structures results. In the long run, minor growth restrictions produce results similar to the no-exclusion case.

Small absolute population limits or new construction quotas allowing merely replacement of absolete structures have effects similar to those of lot size requirements—a sorting out of individuals into communities accordint to the values of their residences. The process is similar to the minimum lot size case.

Compared to the Tiebout model, a population ceiling imposes costs by requiring more communities than there are different packages of public output, since purchasers of a given level of service may prefer several different qualities of housing. Again, complementarity in consumption will limit the inefficiency. The ceiling does not misallocate land between residential and nonresidential uses, since the builder is free to choose an efficient lot size once the right to build has been acquired. There does exist the possibility of inefficient scale, since no automatic forces produce a community size which minimizes average cost. However, public officials attempting to minimize average cost could do so by adjusting the population ceiling.

The property tax without excluding devices will produce a distortion as decision makers reduce consumption to avoid the tax. Under large-lot zoning, the initial entry fees paid in the form of higher lot prices will be larger the greater the value of structures in the community. Thus, there is an excess burden generated by this scheme since the price for additional units of housing services is equal to the cost of producing this service plus the increased entry fee that would be paid. The population ceiling scheme has similar effects, which governments could alleviate by auctioning off building rights and generating revenue for the community. Revenue could be used to reduce the annual property taxes by an amount equal to the annual earnings on the entry fee, so the fee itself would create no distortion of the housing decision. The sorting out of structures by value is preserved, since anyone building a smaller house than those common in the jurisdiction derives a smaller tax benefit and therefore would not be willing to pay the entry fee. Thus, the population ceiling could provide opportunities for the distribution of building rights in such a way as to eliminate the tax distortion of the housing decision. However, the inefficiency associated with the need for "extra" communities in order to match housing and public goods preferences remains.

Construction Permits

Different construction permit fees, i.e., payments in cash or kind for the right to build, could be charged for different land uses in the same community. Mieskowski [1973] has pointed out that if local governments can charge permit fees which are equal to the capitalized value of the difference between costs imposed by a land use and revenues generated by it, no incentive exists to zone out any particular land use. Thus, we could transform all ad valorem taxes into a lump-sum tax. A "fair" fee for a given structure is the capitalized value of the difference between actual tax payments and cost imposed on the community servicing an additional household. The latter could be approximated by the average tax payment in the community. Using the community's tax rate, the assessment of the new unit of the average assessment in the jurisdiction, computation of permit fee would be mechanical.[12]

Construction permit fees pose problems where there is inflation, where costs of existing government services increase, or where local government expands services. When total revenue must be increased, those with low-value properties would pay less than a proportionate share of the increase. New services create a problem if financed by property taxes but not if by user fees. Special breaks could accrue to housing with limited service requirements, e.g., housing for bachelors or the elderly.[13]

Why, then, don't we replace the property tax by a lump-sum tax? First, in jurisdictions with fiscal advantages, current residents probably have paid prices which reflect the capitalized value of these advantages; changing to lump-sum taxes can result in decreased capital values and wealth transfers. Construction permit fees have the advantage of countering incentives and justification for exclusion; they promote efficient choices for local government expenditures. Furthermore, if higher levels of government want to provide low-income groups with particular goods, e.g., education, they can readily subsidize these fees. In this way, distributional and allocative objectives can be planned specifically rather than determined by accident.

In summary, large-lot zoning can produce the following losses: (1) an increase in the number of communities required to provide a given number of public goods choices; (2) inappropriate lot sizes for some communities; and (3) inefficient scale of local government operation. Two of these distortions are absent under population ceilings and all under construction permits.

Some Final Thoughts

In the absence of evidence to the contrary we have assumed that heterogeneity per se is not beneficial; however, it does offer distributional advantages. Where a jurisdiction seeks to protect ubiquitous resources, it is necessary to compare the social costs and benefits of a whole system of constraints applied to a large number of jurisdictions. Property taxes cause inefficiencies which can be modified by various exclusionary measures. Lot size requirements,

population ceilings and priced construction permits are successively
more effective at approximating the efficiency results of the Tiebout
model. However, each of these succeeds only to the extent that the
property tax is converted to a lump-sum tax. If the property tax is
unassailable politically, the construction permit fee appears to be
the least of the evils. If higher levels of government have compassion-
ate concern for the location and public goods consumption of the
poor, such fees could easily be subsidized. We should never forget
that the sole economic and legal justification for all land use control,
including exclusionary zoning, is circumvention of resource mis-
allocation by private markets, whether it results from monopoly
power or externalities.

NOTES

[1] Euclid v. Ambler Realty Co. 272 U.S. 395 (1926).
[2] Ibid., p. 390.
[3] Village of Bel Terre v. Boraas 94 S. Ct. 1536 (1974).
[4] 375 F. Supp. 574(N.D. Cal. 1974).
[5] 522 F. 2b. 897 (1975).
[6] 67 N.J. 151, 363 A. 2d 713 (1975).
[7] 419 Pa. 504, 532, 215 A 2d 597, 612 (1965).
[8] No. 430, December 2, 1975.
[9] The Santa Barbara Mission and Lake Tahoe are examples of unique resources, one historical, the other scenic. A new entrant increases the crowding
experienced by all persons in the jurisdiction, and there is no way to augment
the resource to avert crowding. In the ubiquitous resource case, the facilities
which crowd are the schools, the roads, the parks, all of which can be aug-
mented if sufficient revenues are available.
[10] 375 F. Supp. 574 (N.D. Cal. 1974).
[11] To restore the Tiebout results, even in the presence of a property tax,
Hamilton [1975] uses a minimum property value requirement to transform the
property tax into a fixed charge. For an equilibrium, a large number of communities, each with a different property value, is required. Negishi [1974]
and Rufolo [1976] have assumed complementarity of housing and public
goods consumption to restore the Tiebout results.
[12] With assessed value per household, A, assessment of ith property, B,
and community tax rate, t, the annual "fiscal transfer" to the ith property
is $t(A - B_i)$. Where ℓ is life of the structure and r is the interest rate, the present value of the fiscal transfer over the life of the structure is

$$F = \sum_{j=1}^{\ell} \frac{t(A - B_i)}{(1+r)_j}$$

r could be chosen to correspond to the local government's bond rate since this
rate represents the opportunity cost for funds for the jurisdiction. The structure's life could be set uniformly or declared by builder, with additional payment required if life exceeds the original declaration.

[13] Reduced fees should accrue to all builders of units within the specified class, rather than special "deals."

REFERENCES

Aaron, Henry, 1974. "A New View of Property Tax Incidence." *American Economic Review* 64 (May): 212-27.

Advisory Commission on Intergovernmental Relations. 1972. *State-Local Finances: Significant Features and Suggested Legislation.* Washington, D.C.: U.S. Government Printing Office.

Aronson, J. Richard, and Schwartz, Eli. 1973. "Financing Public Goods and the Distribution of Population in a System of Local Governments." *National Tax Journal* 26 (June): 137-60.

Bradford, David, and Kelejian, Harry. 1973. "An Econometric Model of Flight to the Suburbs." *Journal of Political Economy* 81 (May/June): 566-89.

Edel, Matthew, and Sclar, Elliott. 1974. "Taxes, Spending, and Property Values: Supply Adjustment in a Tiebout-Oates Model." *Journal of Political Economy* 82 (Sept./Oct.): 941-54.

Hamilton, Bruce W. 1975. "Zoning and Property Taxation in a System of Local Government." *Urban Studies* 12 (June): 205-11.

Hirsch, Werner Z. 1970. *The Economics of State and Local Governments.* New York: McGraw-Hill.

McGuire, Martin. 1974. "Group Segregation and Optimal Jurisdictions." *Journal of Political Economy* 82 (Jan./Feb.): 112-32.

Mieskowski, Peter. 1973, "Notes on the Economic Effects of Land Use Regulation." In *Issues in Urban Public Finance.* Saarbrücken, West Germany: Institut International De Finances Publiques.

Negishi, Takashi. 1974. "Public Expenditure Determined by Voting with One's Feet and Fiscal Profitability." *Swedish Journal of Economics* 74 (Dec.): 452-58.

Oates, Wallace E. 1969. "The Effects of Property Taxes and Local Public Spending on Property Values: An Empirical Study of Tax Capitalization and the Tiebout Hypothesis." *Journal of Political Economy* 77 (Nov./Dec.): 957-71.

Rufolo, Anthony M. 1976. "Tie-Inn Sales and Local Public Goods." Ph.D. dissertation. University of California, Los Angeles.

Tiebout, Charles. 1956. "A Pure Theory of Local Governments." *Journal of Political Economy* 64 (Oct.): 416-24.